"James Brassett offers an indispensable analysis in Affective Politics of the Global Event that pushes beyond paradigmatic and institutional debates. Brassett shows how traumatic events do not so much disrupt rarefied structures as they demonstrate the everyday resilience (and politics) of market interactions – in the process challenging the rationalist premises that united realist, liberal and constructivist perspectives alike."

– Wesley W. Widmaier, Associate Professor, School of Government and International Relations, Griffith University, Australia

"This book offers a broad-ranging engagement with the affective dimensions of global events. Examining phenomena as diverse as terrorism and financial crises, Brassett shows how our collective emotional perception of traumatic events also shapes how they unfold and generate practices of resilience."

– Roland Bleiker, Professor of International Relations, University of Queensland

Affective Politics of the Global Event

Market life is increasingly conducted in the shadow of global events such as 9/11, the sub-prime crisis and Brexit. Within International Political Economy (IPE) two broad positions can be discerned: either the event is 'just an event', a superficial spectacle in an otherwise straightforward story of power and hierarchy, or the event is large enough to be considered a 'crisis'.

While sympathetic to such arguments, this book develops a more performative politics of the global event, arguing that the very idea of the event must be placed in question. How is the event constructed? How are market subjects performed in relation to the event? This book argues that emotional and psychological discourses of 'trauma' and 'resilience' provide an important affective register for understanding how the global event is 'known', how it is governed and how the affective dimensions of market life might be lived. By identifying the contingent rise of these discourses, the author de-stabilises and re-politicises the apparent existential veracity of the global event. The critical possibilities and limits of the affective turn in market life can then be rendered according to classic questions of IPE: who wins, who loses and how might it be changed?

An important work for advanced scholars and students of International Political Economy, 'everyday and cultural political economy', crisis and resilience and broader debates on globalisation.

Dr James Brassett is Reader in International Political Economy at the University of Warwick. He was previously RCUK Research Fellow in the ESRC Centre for the Study of Globalisation and Regionalisation. Brassett works on the politics of globalisation with a focus on questions of ethics, governance, crisis and resistance. His first book is entitled *Cosmopolitanism and Global Financial Reform: A Pragmatic Approach to the Tobin Tax* (Routledge, 2010; Paperback, 2013), and he is Co-editor of the International Political Economy of Everyday Life (i-peel.org). His work has been published in leading journals such as *European Journal of International Relations*, *International Political Sociology*, *International Studies Quarterly*, *New Political Economy*, *Review of International Studies* and *Review of International Political Economy*. He is currently working on a book entitled *British Comedy, Global Politics: The Everyday Practice of Resistance* that engages the role of everyday resistance in the global political economy.

Ripe Series in Global Political Economy

The RIPE Series published by Routledge is an essential forum for cutting-edge scholarship in International Political Economy. The series brings together new and established scholars working in critical, cultural and constructivist political economy. Books in the RIPE Series typically combine an innovative contribution to theoretical debates with rigorous empirical analysis.
The RIPE Series seeks to cultivate:

- Field-defining theoretical advances in International Political Economy
- Novel treatments of key issue areas, both historical and contemporary, such as global finance, trade, and production
- Analyses that explore the political economic dimensions of relatively neglected topics, such as the environment, gender relations, and migration
- Accessible work that will inspire advanced undergraduates and graduate students in International Political Economy.

The *RIPE Series in Global Political Economy* aims to address the needs of students and teachers.

A Global Political Economy of Democratisation
Beyond the Internal-External Divide
Alison J. Ayers

Securing Finance, Mobilizing Risk
Money Cultures at the Bank of England
John Hogan Morris

Affective Politics of the Global Event
Trauma and the Resilient Market Subject
James Brassett

For more information about this series, please visit: www.routledge.com/RIPE-Series-in-Global-Political-Economy/book-series/RIPE

Affective Politics of the Global Event

Trauma and the Resilient Market Subject

James Brassett

Routledge
Taylor & Francis Group
LONDON AND NEW YORK

First published 2018
by Routledge
2 Park Square, Milton Park, Abingdon, Oxon OX14 4RN

and by Routledge
711 Third Avenue, New York, NY 10017

Routledge is an imprint of the Taylor & Francis Group, an informa business

British Library Cataloguing-in-Publication Data
A catalogue record for this book is available from the British Library

Library of Congress Cataloging-in-Publication Data
A catalog record for this book has been requested

ISBN: 978-0-815-39973-5 (hbk)
ISBN: 978-1-351-17140-3 (ebk)

Typeset in Times New Roman
by Apex CoVantage, LLC

Contents

Acknowledgements

As in many books, it is hard to fully reflect the help, support, input and engagement that friends, colleagues and family have provided over the course of researching and writing this one. Because of the nature of the subject, especially in relation to trauma, I have been able to learn of personal stories from people I know, or some that I have just met. While I can't pretend that the argument does justice to the manifold experiences that are had in the name of affect, I would like to say a special thanks to those people who spoke on those (their) subjects. It all went into the mix. In academic terms, I have been blessed with some of the most interesting, thoughtful and engaging IPE colleagues. The book has benefitted greatly from conversations with Marco Andreu, Andre Broome, Chris Clarke (who generously read the first draft), Ben Clift, Juanita Elias, Chris Holmes, Ruben Kremers, Lena Rethel, Shirin Rai, Ben Richardson, Chris Rogers, Tim Sinclair and Mat Watson. As I trespassed into other fields, such as security, I am grateful to Chris Browning and Nick Vaughan-Williams for pointing me in the right direction on more than one occasion. Beyond Warwick, I have benefitted from input and encouragement by Claudia Aradau, Roland Bleiker, Dan Bulley, David Chandler, John Hogan Morris, Emma Hutchison, Matt McDonald, Cian O'Driscoll, Chris Rossdale, Amin Samman, Len Seabrooke, Brent Steele and Wes Widmaier. Susanne Soederberg and three anonymous reviewers provided incisive and generous feedback on the first draft. Finally, several years of teaching the MA in IPE at Warwick has challenged my thinking on the politics of globalisation. The rich discussions that developed over seminars, film club and (occasional) socials have been both enjoyable and ageing. Which brings me to the most important points. In the course of writing this book, I have watched my daughter grow up into a sophisticated teenager, who, despite being just ten years old, is able to fill up my affective life far better than any words on a page. My wife has enjoyed and endured the fact that I can only really articulate my thoughts to her, usually after a coffee and with quite an intense look on my face. Somewhere along the line, we got a cat, who sat next to me while I wrote the final draft. But the book is dedicated to my dad. Before I knew it, he taught me about the power of affect and the value of resilience.

Preface

How does a global market come to life? By life, I mean exciting, visceral, mundane and emotional. Maybe it's a peculiar question. Surely, the global market just 'is'; it's just a space where buyers and sellers meet and exchange. Yet for writers in International Political Economy (IPE), a critical reflex has often worked to undermine this straightforward – *naturalised* – image. For scholars of IPE, a number of cuts can be made at this idea of markets.

A first cut is to 'peer beneath the veil of appearances'. Here we find the global market is actually a 'contested arena', where powerful actors (states, corporations, media, etc.) engage with – *and rival* – each other. On this view, the idea of the global market must be placed in historical context (the ascendance of a particular market form) and understood in terms of emerging issue areas, be it (international) trade, finance or development. A second cut might go deeper to theorise the 'critical' role of social structures such as class, race, gender or rationality per se. We could even bring these lines together to posit that such social structures are *productive of* the issues and actors in the contested arena. Thus IPE might begin to re-describe the very concept of the 'global market' as an ideological artefact, or a discursive construction, an imaginary born of the modernising, liberalising, westernising, rationalising tendencies that make – *and remake* – us good market subjects?

This book operates somewhere within the analytical and theoretical schema of IPE. But my question seeks something different to the existing and important work on structures, issues and actors. Put crudely, I am interested in the stuff of the 'global'. For all that, I am persuaded by a set of critical moves made in the name of debunking, or contextualizing, the very idea of a global market, I am still interested in how we think and practice global market life. In this sense, I am struck by how intimacy is created: *How do everyday market subjects find the global in any way compelling?* This is less a question of conceptual veracity than of how we bring coherence to market life. *What made me get up one day and think about the impact of the Tunisian attacks on global tourism? Why do I have a nagging doubt that I should pay more attention to the tens of thousands of people who die from poverty-related causes every day?* Or – to borrow from Charlie Brooker – *what do any of those numbers at the end of the news items on growth and inflation actually mean?!*

Of course, in isolation, any one of these questions could be pulled apart, dissected, explained or belittled as the flotsam and jetsam of mediatised society: "It was discussed on the news in that way", "There was an advert which affected me", "Bono put it on my iPhone", etc. But taken together, they usher at the everyday experience(s) of the global market, how it is performed, dramatised and inhabited by – and for – a set of market subjects: the consumer, the worker, the young, the human, the individual.

So how does a global market come to life? Because we do it every day. We do it when we purchase food from a supermarket. We do it when we turn on the TV (or turn it off). We do it when we put on our clothes and take a journey somewhere, either by car or by train or by foot. Many do it through social behaviour: Often, our houses and parties are elements in a wider political economy of debt and aspiration. In some cases, we don't care. Very often we do. The rise of alternative economies in the global market is a sign that individuals and groups care about their subject positions in the global market. Fair trade, slow food, peer lending, Bitcoin, co-operative squatting, co-operative windmills, Local Exchange Trading Systems, charity, Project RED, Live AID, Comic Relief, downshifting, urban gardening, car share, park and ride, Michael Moore, the Campaign Against the Arms Trade, swap shops, etc. These all suggest that something about the global market animates people beyond interests, structures or discursive performance.

Such ventures are held up as the epitome of a *new ethics*, where fairness and responsibility might be enacted through small adjustments to market logic. Often, this is juxtaposed with the 'non-ethics' of neo-liberalism, whereby self-interest maximisation can be supplanted by sympathy, solidarity, creativity and faith. But this ethical/non-ethical binary is both misleading and important. It is *misleading* because the subjects of markets are in a continual process of emergence. The construction of free markets is always already about the invention of new rationalities and subjectivities. This relies on an ethics, 'good' market subjects and 'bad' – a dividing practice. It is *important* because it speaks to how the global market is constituted through (and against) ethics. We imagine a form of decency. We think that progress is possible. We know – and debate about – when something is wrong. The idea of 'global ethics' is not simply an abstraction for cosmopolitan theorists. It is an everyday imaginary of the global market, as central to alternative economies as it is to debt crises, protest marches and fiscal rectitude. For all that certain theories might attempt a separation between positive and normative logic when speaking about 'the global economy', market life entails ethics, emotion, resistance, boredom, etc., etc., etc. Simply put, my question is, how does a global market come to life? How is it lived as ethical, emotional, boring? A central argument developed in this book is that these 'affective dimensions' of market life are increasingly rendered through a moral economy of the global event.

Event-trauma-resilience

Global events are an increasingly prominent part of everyday market life. If a bomb goes off in Egypt, we wonder about its implications for tourism and development. If Greece re-negotiates its bailout with the European Union (EU), the whole world stands waiting in anticipation of a 'Lehman-style' event. This is not only a symptom of the news media cycle but also a constitutive element of our political context. From disasters to crises, from terrorist attacks to 'progressive' events such as the Olympics, market life is increasingly punctuated by, and responsive to, global events.

While such events appear as unambiguously disruptive or catastrophic in nature even, a number of scholars have pointed to their fundamentally political nature that, while hard to reconcile with previous narratives of politics, forces us to reflect on how we come together in global context:

> [W]hen one thinks of the major risk events of recent decades – Chernobyl, 9/11, climate change, the financial crisis, Fukushima, the euro crisis . . . [t]hree features are common to them all. (1) Because they give rise to a dramatic radicalization of social inequality both inter-nationally and intra-nationally, they *cannot* continue to be conceptualized in terms of the established empirical-analytical conceptual instrumentarium of class analysis as 'class conflicts in the class society'. By contrast, they indeed vary the narrative of discontinuity as contained in the theory of the world risk society. (2) Before they actually occurred, they were *inconceivable.* (3) They are *global* in character and in their consequences and render the progressive networking of spaces of action and environments tangible.
>
> (Beck, 2013)

Previous discussions of the global event in IPE have focused on impact. Here we might think about the end of the Cold War and the debates over globalisation, or else how an economic or financial crisis is constructed (Kirshner, 1998; Strange, 1994; Widmaier et al., 2007). A basic question – across perspectives – is to ask how the event 'impacts upon' the politics of market life. Does it produce growth or unemployment, continuity or change? While sympathetic to, and critically engaged with, such literature (especially in Chapter 1), my research problem emphasises a slightly different line of analysis: that the *very idea* of the global event must itself be placed in question. How do we think of the event? Who is the 'we' of the event? What possibilities and limits are entailed in this set of assumptions? Thus while it might be tempting to write off global events as part of the random, unpredictable nature of market life – the inevitable consequences of living side by side – that ignores how 'a concept' of the global event has been narrated in relation to everyday life, indeed, *through* a distinctive and emerging idea of the market subject. This infers a cultural political economy of the global event whereby imperatives are established, relations performed and rationalities developed (Best and Paterson, 2010).

Rather than begin from an analytical definition of global market life – in spatial, temporal, instrumental or sovereign terms – my aim is to think through the performative politics of the global event as constitutive of that life. By stepping away from a traditional understanding of events as random occurrences that punctuate an otherwise linear progress of history, the empirical focus of the book necessarily turns to the politics of naming and performing the event, how the event is naturalised and how it relates to questions of market subjectivity (Brassett and Clarke, 2012). In particular, the book will focus on two increasingly important discourses of the global event: trauma and resilience. These discourses work to produce and legitimate an intimate relation between market subjects and the global event that foregrounds a certain set of affective logics. Far from a random puncture in an otherwise straightforward timeline, knowledge about trauma and resilience require that the global event is both represented by, and experienced through, emotive tones of shock, devastation and loss, as well as the need – *indeed the human will* – to 'come together' and recover. On these terms, the related (and unrelated) discourses of trauma and resilience are read as part of an everyday register that both produces and contains the affective politics of the global event.

Trauma tells a story of universal human vulnerability in the context of vital existence, where pain, loss, sympathy and progress are woven to the event: we all might be faced with trauma one day; we all – so the logic goes – can understand and empathise with this existential condition (Fassin and Rechtman, 2009). Resilience, conversely, tells a story about adaptability and strength. While we might face challenging events in life, with the right planning and common sets of practices, we have the ability to 'bounce back' (Chandler and Coaffee, 2017). Both rationalities interpret and locate the idea of the event in discourse, and they also provide a set of co-ordinates for subjects to live through and engage with market life before, during and after the event. Yet their rise to prominence presents an ambiguity for critical thought and politics. On the one hand, trauma and resilience are used and deployed to justify rapid mobilisations of sympathy and solidarity in the face of the worst vagaries of global market life. The 'trauma' of financial crisis, poverty or indebtedness can serve as a rallying cry for critique and engagement by non-governmental organisations (NGOs), the media, individuals, etc. Equally, the need for a resilient banking sector, or resilient market subjects who develop their financial literacy over time, can promote forms of community, self-understanding and 'preparedness' before the event. Each rationality can therefore serve as a contingently useful set of discourses for intervening in, and generating governance auspices for, particular causes. On the other hand, however, they each carry a potentially disciplinary dimension: individuals are performed in relation to an event; there is a 'before and after', a narrative of good and bad responses. For all that, this ethics of the individual/event can provide sites of intervention, indeed an impetus for humanitarian responses, the logics of trauma and resilience can also be generalised in a way that limits the political possibilities entailed. For example, emotionality – i.e. that we might sympathise with trauma victims – can easily segue into a form of emotional governance: *that we must* sympathise in a particular way, through an ordered set of practices.

Discourses of the global event are productive. Pixar movies produce a friendly narrative of good liberal subjects who learn how to respond to traumatic events in a 'healthy way'. But when such ideas are elaborated and developed through emerging discourses of 'resilience', that increasingly manifest in self-help guides and prevailing forms of 'talk therapy', critics have argued, we can see a re-phrasing of neo-liberalism in terms of emotional discipline; the event itself is stripped of discursive content, such that politics becomes a technique: preparing for and adapting to a succession of events that 'just happen' in market life (O'Malley, 2010). Adaptability is thus performed as a 'healthy' social norm – a move which blunts our capacity to critique the global event in question by foregrounding an ethics of response.

While such ambiguities are deeply problematic, this book argues that a performative approach is capable of identifying and engaging both how discourses of the global event work, but also how they can break down or fail (Butler, 2010). Indeed, by engaging such limits – of generalisation and government – the book avowedly builds to a discussion of *resistance* within market life. Performativity is not simply a story of government through discursive reiteration; it also provides "the resources from which resistance, subversion, displacement are to be forged" (Butler, 2012: 23). In subsequent chapters (especially 4, 7 and the conclusion), I argue that practices of resistance might be democratic, radical or subversive, yet across the spectrum, they reflect on the contingency of trauma and resilience, inviting – or inciting – subjects to think and do market life differently.

How does the global market come to life? Through the performance of logics and emotions that highlight our common vulnerability, our need for (and the vital role of) sympathy and the importance of 'growth' for market subjects. Beyond the issues and actors, or the critical interests and ideologies of globalisation, I seek to license the lived experiences, embodied desires and resistant possibilities of everyday market subjects. In this way, the everyday and cultural political economy of the global event is invested with emotion, ethics and a politics of empathy that strikes at interesting new possibilities and problems for IPE: *How is the market subject made and re-made? How is market life invented and re-invented? What are the possibilities and limits of this affective politics?*

Introduction
Austerity, affect, event

An interesting facet of the austerity period in Western politics has been the rise to prominence of a certain kind of emotional sensitivity in both mainstream and critical coverage of the economy. Economic affairs, crises and issues such as unemployment, skills, savings, borrowing and so on are increasingly communicated in terms of first-person narratives, feelings, hopes and dreams, but also pain, depression and sadness. For example, Russel Brand illustrates the power of this affective turn:

> Most of the people who criticized me have a vested interest in the maintenance of the system. They say the system works. What they mean is "the system works for me". The less privileged among us are already living in the apocalypse, the thousands of street sleepers in our country, the refugees and the exploited underclass across our planet daily confront what we would regard as the end of the world. No money, no home, no friends, no support, no hand of friendship reaching out, just acculturated and inculcated condemnation.
>
> (Russell Brand, 2013)

Part of this trend is driven by the relatability dynamic of modern news reporting: any story – *every story* – must be set in terms that individual viewers can relate to. Therefore, if a news item seems complicated, as the global economy often does, then it's better to interview individual savers, consumers or borrowers about their *personal opinions* so that viewers can better 'understand'. Think of the vox-pops with *Northern Rock* savers during the sub-prime crisis, or Greek citizens discussing the effects of public-sector cuts. Indeed, these individuating moves are now commonly made by politicians seeking to couch their interpretation of the economy in some straight emotional honesty. David Cameron's infamous 'we're all in it together' speech recounted several such individual stories about 'ordinary people':

> I got an email from a guy called Viv Williams. He lost his job last year and was desperate to get back into work. But he had a mortgage to pay so he went to register for Job Seeker's Allowance. He'd twisted his ankle and walked in with

> a limp, so you know what they said? They told him he couldn't register for Job Seeker's Allowance because he wasn't fit to work so he'd have to go on incapacity benefit. He told them there was nothing wrong with him, that he wanted to work. But no – he wasn't allowed to. This is a man who wanted to take responsibility for himself and his family and the system said no, you've got to depend on the state. As he says: "I told them, you're having a laugh." But it's not funny. The welfare system today sends out completely crazy signals.
>
> (Cameron, 2009)

This emotive and individuating dynamic in public discourse on market life is important and, as yet, barely articulated within the study of IPE. As the tone of modern politics has become more emotional and more focused on personal experience, so it is also beginning to blur a once cherished separation between the economy and everyday life. While the 'stuff' of markets was once represented in terms of rationality assumptions – cold calculations, instrumentalities of demand and supply – a new common sense appears to be emerging in the popular imagination that questions the very possibility of such a separation. The emergence of groups such as Occupy, *Los Idignados* and the Post-Crash Economics Society all suggest that the economy, and especially finance, is intimately bound up with everyday life in a way that is both visceral and politicising.

On this view, the media relay is an increasingly important element in market life. Through the relentless grind of 24-hour news and social media, aspects of everyday life now cross seamlessly with apparently 'large' issues such as global finance. In the wake of the sub-prime crisis and resulting credit crunch, for instance, individual bankers were widely represented as exhibiting risky, irresponsible and, often excessively masculine traits (Griffin, 2013; Prügl, 2012). Likewise, individual borrowers were commonly and critically regarded as being driven by a fantasy: a dream of current enjoyment that could not face up to the practicalities of paying off debts (Montgomerie, 2009; Watson, 2009). As austerity began to bite, it was widely conveyed that the unemployed would not simply adjust or re-skill; instead, they would suffer personal anxiety and loss of confidence as they came to depend on 'precarious' work (Standing, 2016). In short, the lived experience of markets is increasingly represented through an affective register, which means that people such as Russell Brand and David Cameron are able to speak the same language while disagreeing profoundly.

An affective dimension in the cultural portrayal of markets is not unprecedented, of course. Hollywood movies such as *Cinderella Man* (2005) or *The Pursuit of Happyness* (2006), for example, avowedly sentimentalise the individual struggle for economic viability – understood as self-respect – in the harsh uncaring world of economic depression, class and racial hierarchy. While historical in dimension, these films seek to tell a story for the audience of today: you can survive, you can succeed. Equally, the gritty world of UK cinema has long encouraged a focus on the human experience of economic life. Think of the class-oriented realism of Ken Loach with films such as *Kes* (1969) or *My Name Is Joe* (1998). In more light-hearted tones, albeit with a similar, almost anthropological, sensitivity to the lived experiences of economic restructuring, mainstream films such as *The Full Monty* (1997) and *Billy Elliot* (2000) situate individual, family and community experiences within a powerful emotional story of struggle, decline, intense responses and hope.

To recall, part of the feat of *Billy Elliot* was to place the 1980s miners' strike in the context of a young boy growing up in a close-knit family where the mother dies: thus a divisive period in the history of British political economy is recast as a story about basic human emotion. The resulting narrative discussion of anger is suffused with multiple layers: anger at change, anger at loss, anger at weakness. Both the father and the older brother are angry with Thatcher for closing the mine, yet they are also angry because of the early death of their wife and mother. This critical torment, concentrated in a small home, in a small town, becomes the catalyst for Billy to develop *and build* his own emotional journey against and beyond his situation – a journey that results in artistic and (we might suppose) economic success when he becomes a ballet dancer. Writ large, the unexpected outcomes of market life can sometimes confound the bleakness of emotional and structural contingency.

In such films, the cultural production of market life has sought to foreground human experience, pain and ambiguity, albeit with the possibility for wonderful outcomes. At the end of the emotional journey, characters can reach a kind of resolution. On these terms, this emotive narrative may seem like an obvious and ready trope for media commentators to draw upon. It is relatable, dramatic and offers a potential arc from a bleak 'here' to a potentially more promising 'there'. Importantly, though, this does not necessarily imply a penchant for 'saccharine' stories with happy endings.

In recent decades, media coverage of the economy has proved itself entirely capable of dealing in the darker side of emotion (Brassett and Vaughan-Williams, 2012b). For example, in news coverage of the protracted negotiations over an EU bailout for Greece, emotion and suffering have been high on the agenda. While the EU and specifically the Germans could be portrayed in cold, rational, almost 'unemotional' terms, mainstream news stories were replete with references to 'the anger on the streets' of Athens and the humanitarian crisis in Greece (Foy, 2017). Economic journalists such as Paul Mason experienced an impressive rise to prominence through a narrative coverage of the Greek bailout as an affective concern. Key for such commentators is the idea that the economy and economic crisis is an important issue, not only because companies or countries might gain or lose money but also because of the lasting emotional effect on people and communities (Mason, 2015). Thus Mason regularly cited anarchist graffiti, emotive slogans such as Syriza's 'hope begins here' and even produced a film whose title referenced the highly evocative slogan #thisisacoup. At least in broad terms, therefore, it's entirely plausible to conceive of emotion as a way of understanding, inhabiting and engaging the politics of global markets in more critical or emancipatory terms.

Questioning the critical potential of affect

So what is wrong with emotion? By invoking widely accessible ideas of personal emotion – hopes, fears, sadness, shock, etc. – the media is able to hail a certain, if limited, idea of everyday market life. While it would be easy to caricature emotion as a cliché, saccharine or tranquilizing affair, I would argue that this emergent affective register belies a more critical potential. Broadly, emotions are an integral part of human experience that should be recognised within a social scientific agenda which has sometimes privileged rationality or power in its quest for knowledge (Hutchison and Bleiker, 2008). More strategically, the quality of relatability in emotion – i.e. that it can draw together wider social issues through stories of personal experience stories – implies an important communicative potential (Brassett and Smith, 2010). Beyond the packaged narratives of media portrayal, a broad cultural turn to focus on the affective dimensions of crisis and austerity can usher in new possibilities. From the point of view of critical IPE, this speaks to a long tradition of questioning the apparent instrumentalities of market logics – self-interest, demand/supply, profit and scale – because they ignore, or better subsume, the political, cultural and ethical dimensions of market life (Gill, 1991; Higgott, 2000). Indeed, the separation of emotion from markets, or, more precisely, the separation of 'certain emotions' from the dominant imaginary of markets, has long been regarded as a key problematic within the analysis of capitalism (Hirschman, 1981). The rise – or return – of emotion in everyday market life could thus be understood as a small part of a wider project to undermine the naturalised instrumental logics of globalisation.

Simply put, emotion animates people; it can involve them in issues and debates that might otherwise seem dry, technical or 'just economic'. On this view, emotion might be articulated as one element in a form of praxis "to escape from the reifications of capitalist ideology, imagine alternative forms of living, and embrace alternative, people-centred values" (Jones, 2008: 212). Likewise, for advocates of a more radical vision of global democracy, the move to portray the economy in affective terms could support a more fundamental critique of globalisation, as politically contested *and contestable* (Scholte, 2012). Thus the affective mediation of market life could form part of an emerging critical vocabulary of global politics, carrying the potential for – if not the certitude of – more involving and challenging conversations about the global economy (Dryzek, 2000).

There is a practical- and policy-oriented potential in this growing embrace of the affective dimensions of markets. For a range of anti-globalisation activists and critical NGOs, an expressed goal of their efforts has been to 'sensitise' publics to the emotional and psychological consequences of global trends such as post-Fordism, industrial agriculture and the effects of financial crisis (Brassett, 2009b). Indeed, the current resurgence of resistance politics – through Occupy, *Los Indignados*, *Syriza* or Momentum – can be read as only the latest manifestation of a long-felt need to critique the over-riding economism of globalisation (Della Porta, 2015; Gill, 2000). Polanyian double movements might help to explain this current social reflex to argue that markets do matter, that they do affect people's lives (Yarrow, 2017). Against the 'hegemonic' logic of neo-liberal austerity, a certain reading of affect could portray it as the 'culmination' of a popular form of critical politics that seeks to de-mystify, educate and agitate.

However, what lacks in this turn to engage the critical possibilities of emotion is any deeper reflection on the historical and political dimension(s) of 'affect'. Emotions such as sympathy or empathy are often portrayed as an unproblematic improvement upon the prevailing instrumental or power political form of analysis (e.g. Ariffin et al., 2016). In the humanitarian logic of global politics, for example, it is considered straightforwardly good that we can feel sympathy for distant suffering; it is progressive that we can feel empathy with global others (Chouliaraki, 2013; Fassin, 2012). On this view, *feeling itself* is rendered as a goal of critique. Lost in this movement is any reflection upon the contingency of emotion: How did it emerge to play the role that it does in global market life? What are the possibilities and limits presented by this emergence? Who is equipped to speak the language of affect?

We therefore need to foreground a *politics of emotion*. Indeed, this has been one of the key arguments of the sociological literature on emotion and affect (Ahmed, 2013; Pedwell, 2014). In broad terms, this literature looks at the contingency of emotion – in both its public and private forms – and analyses how emotional language can supplement, or even drive, hegemonic or exclusionary projects. On this view, emotionality can be a problematic way of 'knowing' market life since it works *within* existing structures of power. For instance, as Carolyn Pedwell (2012: 175) argues, a "critical approach to thinking through the transnational politics of empathy needs . . . to take into account empathy's uneven nature and effects – how 'empathetic' self-transformation can (re)constitute unequal affective subjects and relations of power". Much like sympathy before it, empathy may say rather more about the privileged position of the person who experiences it than its capacity to change that situation. In an analogous critique of humanitarian discourses of pain and suffering portrayed within NGO campaign materials, Sara Ahmed (2013: 22) identifies the potential ambivalence of emotion in the global context:

> The over-representation of the pain of others is significant in that it fixes the other as the one who "has" pain, and who can overcome that pain only when the Western subject feels moved enough to give. . . . [G]enerosity becomes a form of individual and possibly even national character; something "I" or "we" have, which is shown in how we are moved by others. The transformation of generosity into a character trait involves fetishism: it forgets the gifts made by others, as well as prior relations of debt accrued over time . . . . the West gives to others only insofar as it is forgotten what the West has already taken in its very capacity to give in the first place . . . feelings of pain and suffering, which are in part effects of socio-economic relations of violence and poverty, are assumed to be alleviated by the very generosity that is enabled by such socio-economic relations. So the West takes, then gives, *and in the moment of giving repeats as well as conceals the taking.*

On this view, any potential strategic value in the affective turn must be understood as performative of new (hierarchical) relations of self and other. Much like the traditional Marxist critique of charity, emotional tropes of sympathy or empathy can easily segue into a legitimation device (Žižek, 2009). This is not just an ideological smokescreen; rather, it plays on a particular genealogy of emotion that first divides it from reason, then raises certain emotions as attractive, and then – at least in the current period – brings it to bear upon market subjects living in a global context. Think of the portrayal of the Greek bailout with its delineation of Germans as rational and unemotional, while the Greeks are portrayed as both suffering from humanitarian crisis and angry at austerity. The narrative works within a genealogy of power and reason as separate from and – ultimately – superior to emotion (read: natural, feminine, in need of control, etc.) (Christou, 2016). In short, there is a complex politics of knowing and performing emotion that needs to be unpicked.

Sara Ahmed (2013: 4) suggests that instead of asking the question, "What are emotions?" critical scholars should instead ask, "What do emotions do?" From this point of view, the contingency of emotion and emotionality carries a set of unacknowledged hierarchies and silences that 'do' certain things to market subjectivities. When managers and policymakers value 'emotional intelligence', for instance, and seek to weave it into education, development training or even military technique as a straightforwardly progressive supplement, we should question the critical value of affect (Pedwell, 2014). Affect might be seen, in authoritative terms, as something which works to order and arrange market subjects according to a roster of acceptable moral agency.

One strand of literature on the politics of emotion has sought to foreground the 'governmental' nature of affect (Davies, 2015; O'Malley, 2010). Far from being a critical counterpoint to neo-liberalism, authors within this literature regard emotion as entirely complicit in a set of disciplinary logics that simultaneously individualise and responsibilise market subjects. Titles such as 'Smile or Die' (Ehrenreich, 2010) and 'The Happiness Industry' (Davies, 2015) point to a pernicious tendency to generalise and depoliticise emotion through markets. From this more governmental perspective, emotionality can play an important role in the (re)invention of market subjects. In positive thinking, for example, individuals are implored to see a world of possibility where a continual nurturing of their own talents can lead to positive outcomes in the market (Seligman, 2002). Positive thinking can lead to a better job, better salary and better work life balance; *whatever you put your mind to really*. Advocates of this cognitive mastering of emotion suggest the market subject is actually empowered to change and manage his or her situation. However, critics argue that a flip side of such 'empowerment' is the wider de-politicisation of any negative market outcomes. This is because a negative market situation – be it poverty, unemployment, lack of promotion, etc. – is rendered as simply a challenge to think positively. The elision of objective outcomes with emotional make-up leads to a position whereby market subjects are encouraged to read market life in affective terms: happiness instead of wealth, depression instead of unemployment, stress instead of overwork. As Will Davies (2011: 68) quips, "Unhappiness has become the critical negative externality of contemporary capitalism." In short, emotionality becomes, at best, an artificial proxy for understanding individual behaviours; at worst, it provides a framework for judging individuals as personally responsible for any 'negative' experiences of market life. Affective discipline.

Emotion, therefore, presents a dilemma for critical thought and politics. While the language of emotion does important work to animate the everyday life of global markets as a 'lived experience', which echoes wider debates about de-mystifying and politicising globalisation, the language of emotion must be understood as contingent and political. This is because emotion emerges within and reproduces market life in the context of certain power relations. Cutting to the chase: the affective turn in market life can support both critical and hegemonic forms of politics; there is thus an ongoing politics of emotion in market life. How did emotion come to play a prominent role in a cultural understanding(s) of market life? What are the possibilities and limits of this affective turn in everyday IPE? And how might such possibilities and limits be engaged?

The global event of affect

On 14 June 2017, a fire spread through the Grenfell tower block in Kensington, London. News footage rolled (and repeated) for several days showing how the fire spread quickly up the tower as people either ran out or sheltered in their rooms, calling out the windows for help. While tower blocks are generally designed to prevent the spread of fire, early reports suggested that the recent refurbishment of the tower had involved the use of 'cheap' external cladding that was potentially more flammable than safety regulations advised. On the day after the fire, Channel Four News interviewed the rapper Akala:

> The people who died and lost their homes, this happened to them because they were poor. We are in one of the richest spaces, not just in London, but in the world. Repeated requests were ignored. There is no way rich people would be living in a building without adequate fire safety. [. . .] It was an eyesore for the rich people who lived opposite. So they put panels, pretty panels on the outside, so the rich people who lived opposite wouldn't have to look at a horrendous block.

Akala's powerful intervention speaks to what I will argue is a crucial element in the genealogy of the politics of affect: the rise of the global event. Events can shock, amaze and *involve* disparate people in the affective mediation of global politics, whether it be the class relations of social housing in Grenfell, or, in the case of 9/11, the vulnerability of an apparently secure West. The global event seems to carry an intuitively appealing affective dimension. From humanitarian disasters such as the Ethiopian famine or the Indian Ocean Tsunami, to terrorist attacks such as 9/11 or Charlie Hebdo, the performance of the global event has been productively tied to ethical concerns for human suffering and vulnerability (Chouliaraki, 2013; Jones, 2017).

How should we think about the relationship between emotion and the global event? On one level, we might focus on the changing repertoires of vulnerability and sympathy that have emerged from the regular and public display of emotion in response to global events. For instance, the rise of memorials such as Anzac Day in Australia and 9/11 in the US have played an important role in normalising the idea of public mourning (McDonald, 2010). In the wake of almost any disaster, there is now a common reflex amongst (seemingly remote) politicians and publics to express sympathy and empathy with the people affected, whether it be through public statements – e.g. "we are all Americans today" – or even by changing a Facebook status to the national flag of the affected country (Browning, 2017). While we might instinctively question whether such public displays of emotion are 'genuine', or whether the grief is experienced in similar terms by 'everyone', the repertoire of response is established (Furedi, 2004). Such popular expressions of grief normalise a logic that global events require some form of affective response, that everyday market life is now responsive to the 'interruption' caused by global events in emotional and individual terms.

On another level, however, the very logic of this response – which appears so ordinary, so intuitive – underpins a performative orchestration of emotions *around* global events. In the overlap between austerity and affect in everyday market life, for example, it is not just that we are encouraged to feel sympathy for 'the unemployed', but specifically those *who have been made unemployed* by a particular event – i.e. the global financial crisis. There is a narrative link between the subjects/objects of affect and the discursive narration of particular global events. For example, as Chapter 3 will discuss, the recently popular critique of individual bankers for excessive risk taking has been explicitly tied to a widespread performance of the sub-prime crisis as a traumatic event (Brassett and Clarke, 2012). The intensity of emotion involved in the performance of this global event produced a wide – and wild – uptake of critical positions against the apparent perpetrators. These associations are not 'merely' representations, but continue to perform in popular critiques of austerity, which juxtapose the excessive risk taking of bankers with the mundane lives of working-class families whose taxes underpinned the bailout of the banks and who now suffer from the effects of social welfare retrenchment (Hozic and True, 2016). The orchestration of emotion around particular global events can be the basis for thinking about the future politics of market life as people return to, and re-perform, the 'idea' of the event. Thus the way we 'know' the event is performative of the kinds of politics – transformative, disciplinary, resistant – that can emerge. A fundamental contention of this book is that a logic of event-response is neither accidental nor arbitrary, but develops through an intimate performance of specific forms of emotional knowledge about the event – namely, trauma and resilience.

Discourses of trauma and resilience provide a ready and supportive language for governing the affective politics of global events, by – essentially – 'ordering' and 'managing' (knowledge about) emotion. Against the happy image of positive thinking, the affective politics of the global event is not only represented in positive terms but also performed and narrated in darker, more exceptional terms:

shock in relation to crisis, fear in relation to terror, along with associated public grieving through memorials, and even crowdfunding to support victims. These are existential questions that might once have been left in the background of politics, indeed everyday life, that are now regularly and commonly deployed in the daily news cycle of events (Browning, 2017). This is not just background noise. Humanitarian organisations, moral theorists, security experts and even celebrities all grapple to interpret such events in political and ethical terms. Band Aid was presented an image of Ethiopian 'famine' as an embodiment of global poverty and humanitarian suffering (Jones, 2017); 9/11 was narrated as an icon of vulnerability; nearly all post-event landscapes are presented as scenes of both devastation *and* recovery, reciprocity and (increasingly) resilience. On these terms, I argue, we must remain sensitive to how *a concept* of the global event has developed so as to draw together, and *give meaning to*, our coverage of, and responses to, these apparently disparate 'happenings' (Brassett and Vaughan-Williams, 2012a).

The basic proposition that I want to develop and engage in this book is that the manner in which global events are 'known' has perpetuated a set of affective rationalities that work to underpin how market life is lived – as 'global', as 'individual', as 'emotional'. It is not simply that the affective dimensions of austerity have been realised in an unproblematic manner, updating the sentimental component of an already pre-existing market reality. Rather, particular forms of emotion have been licensed and mobilised in highly mediated terms: emotion 'does' things (Ahmed, 2013). For example, news media have drawn on images of natural disaster when describing the economy; the global financial crisis has been described as a 'traumatic event' akin to a 'tsunami'; European bond markets have been portrayed as entering a tragic death spiral; Lehman brothers was an earthquake, etc. A widespread portrayal of these traumatic elements of market life has gone hand in glove with a human centred concern for the 'pain' and existential uncertainty that market subjects experience. A traumatic narrative is established: the global event 'happens' and emotional responses of individual market subjects follow. A politics of response emerges that might be humanitarian, seeking to support debtor subjects, or governmental, using the humanitarian emergency to bail out the banks and impose austerity, yet, I argue, either way, it is knowledge about trauma that foregrounds the global event and its relation to market subjects. (Brassett and Clarke, 2012). It is not that emotion is 'added onto' market life, but rather how discourses of the global event, like trauma and resilience, perform (within) contingent hierarchies. What do affective discourses of the global event do? What 'ethics' and 'politics' do they produce? What understandings of the subject do they perform?

My central argument is that emotional discourses of 'trauma' and 'resilience' have come to play an important role in how the global event is 'known', how it is governed and how the affective dimensions of market life are lived/permitted. This argument has two central implications for the way in which we think about and engage the political economy of the global event. First, it provides a route into understanding and interpreting the possibilities and limits of the affective turn in market life. The idea that particular forms of emotion are known and licensed in certain ways, publicised via the spectacle of the global event, mediatised through the prism of trauma or operationalised through the logics of resilience holds implications for the classic questions of IPE: *who wins, who loses and how might it be changed?* In short, differential capacities to speak through trauma and resilience suggest a politics of agency within market life. Secondly, by identifying the contingent rise of these emotional discourses of trauma and resilience, my argument seeks to de-stabilise and politicise the apparent existential veracity of the global event. Whereas discourses of trauma and resilience comprehend the possibility of the global event as a fundamental category of our (uncertain) market life, a performative approach understands this manoeuvre as itself contingent and malleable.

Drawing these points together, I seek to contingently engage and develop a political dimension to these rationalities of the global event – namely, the performative agency of market subjects. As will be discussed, a common idea within trauma and resilience is that subjects can comprehend, feel, respond to and *adapt through* the emotional experiences of events. While elements of this discourse are clearly problematic, licensing a form of knowledge that could become hegemonic or governmental, I seek to engage a set of productive lines of thought. Rejecting some of the stronger disciplinary or governmental diagnoses of trauma and resilience, which posit them as part of a continued and ongoing victory of neo-liberalism, I seek to anticipate the possibility of a *resistant market subject*. By engaging a set of themes and issues in the genealogy of trauma and resilience – event-response, cognitive-emotional, private-public – I argue that a market subject may be thought of as aware of the contingency of their global market life, yet able to perform it differently, in less violent and more imaginative ways. In this sense, the cultural political economy of global events is contingent and ambiguous, yet productive of new possibilities for living market lives.

Outline and argument

The book is divided into seven chapters and a conclusion. The first chapter sets the research problem within the theoretical range of IPE and makes the case for developing a performative approach to the affective politics of the global event. This performative approach underpins the subsequent six chapters, which are spread over two sections. The first section develops a critical engagement with the discourse of trauma, and the second section addresses the emergence of a discourse of resilience. A concluding chapter seeks to anticipate a theory of the resistant market subject. I will now briefly outline the argument of each chapter and suggest how they build towards the conclusion.

Chapter 1 is entitled ‘Political Economy of the Global Event: Crisis and Performance’. It introduces the rise of the global event in discourses of market life. From the sub-prime crisis, to the Eurozone debt crisis, from the Chilean mine disaster, to Hurricane Katrina, the politics of market life is increasingly portrayed and relayed in terms of particular events. This ‘event-alisation’ of politics has important implications for how we conceive of time, space and community. Questions arise as to who is affected? Who should respond? What is the overarching moral frame for evaluating such events? Chapter 2 is entitled 'Everyday Politics of the Global Event: Discourse, Performance, Subject'. It seeks to situate and define the theoretical framework of the book by introducing and engaging the literature on media events and their symbiotic position with consumer culture (Chouliaraki, 2013: Jones, 2017; see also Richey and Ponte, 2011). It is argued that the question of how to understand such cultural discourses of the global event – the media spectator, the 'concern' for 'distant others' – can be productively engaged through everyday and cultural IPE. An emergent politics of the global event relies on certain contingencies of media and communications connectivity that mediate between the subjects who experience events and those who don't, but it also requires an affective register, the performance of culturally resonant discourses that can draw these disparate subjects together. In terms of method, I, therefore, outline a schematic division of the politics of the global event that can isolate and explore in turn: 1) *The discourse of the event* (trauma or resilience): how has a certain discourse of the global event emerged; what are its logics; what are its ethics? 2) *A performance of the event* (sub-prime or resilient finance): how does it perform market life? What idea of the subject does it entail? Is the performance successful or does it break down in some way? 3) *The subject of the discourse* (traumatic or resilient): how is the market subject performed? How does this connect to or confirm existing patterns of market life? How do certain performances resist and/or subvert these patterns? And this combination of theory and method underpins the structure of the next two sections of the book.

Having rendered the political economy of the global event as a question about the contingent performance of political possibility, the rest of the book is divided into two sections that each address one affective discourse of the global event: trauma and resilience. The first section, Trauma and the Global Event, seeks to draw out and engage how a modern discourse of trauma has worked to narrate the global event in terms of an ethics of vulnerability and empathy. Chapter 3, entitled 'Trauma and the Global Ethics', articulates the growing importance of trauma as a discourse of the event towards the end of the twentieth century and in the early stages of the twenty-first century. It argues that 9/11 is a seminal event in the emergence of this affective politics, which saw numerous commentators and academics begin to engage in terms derived from psychological knowledge about trauma (Brassett, 2011). In particular, a number of critical theorists narrated 9/11 in terms of trauma as an ethical move to make us more sensitive to the politics of vulnerability entailed. This association between ethics and trauma, and between trauma and the global event ushered in a complex set of affective relations. Understood as a discourse on vulnerability, trauma has gradually emerged as an important ethico-political language of the event (Fassin and Rechtman, 2009).

In political terms, this implied an ambiguity. While narrating events in terms of trauma might serve to mobilise interest in and sympathy for the victims of trauma, it entails a certain hierarchy. Whose wounds count? Who is excluded by the language of trauma? Indeed, critical approaches to trauma highlight the problematic governmentalities of the subject entailed by assuming 'normal' forms of emotional response, arguing that this process of knowing the subject is better conceived as a form of 'therapeutic governance' (Pupavac, 2001). There is thus a 'politics of vulnerability' that foregrounds a difficulty with 'feeling' in relation to a global event. Binaries between the individual and the community suggest an order to traumatic events, whereby personal emotions are drawn on to overlay sovereign politics (Edkins, 2003; Furedi, 2004). On this view, the ethical possibilities of the traumatic global event – of recognising vulnerability and fostering more empathic relations – must be understood as a contingent and unstable achievement. The humanitarian and governmental dimensions of trauma seem to play out in unpredictable ways.

With trauma having emerged as a language of the global event, it is possible to explore the popularity and discursive adaptability of 'trauma ethics'; from a relatively discrete psychological definition to the more popular sense in which trauma acts as a metaphor of pain, the traumatic narrative is able to orchestrate and manage the emotional dimensions of the global event in certain ways. Indeed, Chapter 4, entitled 'Trauma and the Sub-prime Crisis', sets out to explore how the politics of vulnerability associated with trauma was mobilised to understand and render the global financial crisis in humanitarian terms of suffering and vulnerability (Brassett and Clarke, 2012). A range of traumatic imagery was deployed to narrate the sub-prime crisis of 2008; references to a financial tsunami were widespread, encapsulating media rhetoric of shock, devastation and disaster. A number of event-response logics kicked in as the sub-prime crisis was compared to the trauma of 9/11 and the Wall Street Crash (Samman, 2016). There was a mobilisation of humanitarian responses: savers and homeowners were portrayed as 'victims' of this financial devastation, and a form of everyday empathy was mobilised (Watson, 2009). More critically, the chapter discusses how the invocation of trauma permitted a number of exceptional moves within sovereign power: bailing out the banks, defining perpetrators, foregrounding surveillance as the appropriate regulatory response (Best, 2017; Brassett and Vaughan-Williams, 2012b). However, despite the governmental and disciplinary overtones of the traumatic discourse of the sub-prime crisis, the chapter identifies a number of resistances, ranging from comic subversions of the 'media hype' to instances where campaign groups actively inhabited the trauma discourse and turned it to critical ends.

This possibility of resistance is developed further in Chapter 5, entitled 'Trauma and the Market Subject', which seeks to develop a theoretical and strategic account of how trauma can be used for different ends: critical, emancipatory or subversive. Against the more disciplinary interpretations of trauma as an element in a wider set of practices of 'therapeutic governance', I return to the idea of the market subject as *a political* subject. While the language of trauma might carry a sterile 'recovery or fail' possibility, this is by no means the only experience or argument that can be had in its name (Fassin, 2008). Thus the chapter draws together elements of a critical performativity in trauma and highlights particular strategies for critiquing market life that emerge. In particular, I examine the use of trauma in critical documentaries about disaster – e.g. *When the Levees Broke* (2016) – which self-consciously promote the abject subjects of violence and neo-liberalism, as a critique of state power. Here trauma is occupied as a strategic emancipatory move. More problematically, perhaps, I then engage with the turn to 'trauma comedy' in films such as *The Big Lebowski* (1998) and *Team America* (2004) in order to explore joking about traumatic events, PTSD and death as mechanisms of resisting the assumed coherence of trauma itself. On this view, I argue that trauma can be occupied to sensitise, politicise and subvert the disciplinary politics of the global event in terms that recover the political dimensions of market life in imaginative terms.

The next section is made up of three chapters which address a second important discourse of the global event that has arguably superseded trauma in the imaginary of the global event – namely, resilience (Chandler and Coaffee, 2017). If trauma carries certain proclivities to judge the individual, to 'impose' governance, it is partly in response to this that trends towards resilience thinking have taken place in psychological counselling circles (Bisson, 2007). Indeed, this book takes resilience as a discursive counterpart to trauma, a reverse positive geared towards anticipating rather than responding to the event, a point which is discussed in Chapter 6, 'Resilience and Neo-liberalism'. From the high point of trauma, a number of trends have ushered towards the emergence and proliferation of a discourse of resilience (Howell, 2015a). While trauma foregrounded the potential for an event to 'wound' the psyche or emotions of an individual, resilience has an altogether more positive etymology. Here the capacity to 'bounce back', 'adapt to' and thrive after an event is highlighted (Comfort et al., 2010). Resilience to the extreme event is taken as an emergent quality of individuals or systems; adaptability in relation to extreme events is performed as an 'ethical good' to be fostered (Walker et al., 2004).

However, precisely because of this focus on the adaptability of individuals in relation to uncertainty, critical theorists have tended to regard resilience as a suitably fitting discourse of neo-liberalism (Lentzos and Rose, 2009). Whereas trauma performs the event as something to respond to, resilience anticipates it as something to prepare for proactively. This is an interesting shift in emphasis because the event moves from being a conditional possibility in trauma theory, to an existential (un)certainty in resilience: the response is foregrounded if you like. While a focus on the positive adaptive qualities of individuals is an interesting and well-meaning development, critics inveigh that the discourse has begun to work as a supplement to neo-liberalism (Joseph, 2013a; Walker and Cooper, 2011). Here the emphasis is on the capacity of resilient individuals to adapt to and thrive through the apparently natural uncertainties of neo-liberal market life. From self-help manuals that train market subjects how to live with free markets, to education programs which foster resilient learning in Key Stage 1 disaster scenarios, there is clearly much of significance to market life in resilience (Bulley, 2013; O'Malley, 2010). However, while this neo-liberal diagnosis of resilience appears to mark a certain completion – a generalisation of the logic of the event as the governing uncertainty of market life – I will develop a performative critique of this view. There is a curious tautology in critical accounts whereby the apparent completeness of resilience seems to be assumed almost before its emergence. Not only does this risk handing an easy victory to a problematic form of neo-liberal governance but also it underplays the capacity of everyday market subjects to perform resilience differently (Brassett and Vaughan-Williams, 2015). By foregrounding the performative instability of resilience as a discourse of the event in everyday market life, it is possible to explore a more contingent set of interactions between rationalities and market subjects of resilience.

Thus Chapter 7 – 'Resilience and (Everyday) Finance' – sets out to engage some of the larger claims of governmental approaches to resilience. While resilience has spread through the corridors of global financial governance in a manner that governmentality theorists take as synonymous with a new stage of neo-liberal governance, I argue that it is possible to think about financial resilience in more open, contested and, ultimately, local terms (Brassett and Holmes, 2016). Everyday and cultural IPE highlights the lived experiences and agency of market subjects for thinking about the uptake and generalisation of wider discourses of market governance (Best and Paterson, 2010). Against the prevailing focus on 'big actors' within a wider system of political-economic relations, such approaches focus on small, everyday actors: their choices and inclinations (Hobson and Seabrooke, 2007). Building on this literature, I argue that a tendency within governmental approaches is to assume a straight acceptance of resilience discourse by market subjects. By developing on accounts of the financial market subject as contingent, ambiguous and – in Paul Langley's (2007) terms – 'uncertain', I develop the performative agency of financial subjects in relation to resilience. On this view, the capacity to resist neo-liberal discourses of finance appears both widespread and highly productive for new forms of alternative finance such as debt resistance and alternative banking systems (Scholte, 2013). In the wake of the sub-prime crisis, credit crunch and European debt crises, we have seen an impressive mobilisation of movements that resist austerity, debt and quantitative easing, as well as, the pervading logic of financial governance: 'too big to fail'. Against the generalised conception of the event in resiliency discourse, I will argue that it is often the popular, everyday and vernacular discourses on the global financial crisis, *qua event*, that provide the inspiration for alternative finance. Far from an empty signifier, the event is lived, experienced, interpreted, hated and subverted. The capacity for critique, resistance and innovation by and through everyday market subjects seems far greater than is conceived in either the mainstream or critical literature on the subject.

Resilience, like trauma, is a discourse of politics like any other; it is open to critique, challenge and re-invention. In Chapter 8, 'Resilience and the Market Subject', these themes are brought to fruition in a discussion of the cultural production – and subversion – of resilient market life. Films such as *Toy Story*, *Shrek* and *Finding Nemo* tell an important emotional story about life that is charged by serious and traumatic events, yet geared towards learning, adapting and growing. On these terms, I argue that the cultural political economy of the global event is ongoing and unstable; it requires the production and acceptance of widespread repertoires of emotional literacy, preparedness and market community. Following the work of Jack Halberstam (2011), I argue that such films contemplate new forms of intimacy and emotional becoming that work beyond established heterosexual norms of self and family. In this way, they open up new modes of market life that can be resilient in unexpected ways. On the one hand, this (newly) celebrated emotional literacy is commensurate with the more disciplinary or governmental diagnoses of resilience – as both pervasive and de-politicised (O'Malley, 2010). Consumer culture again comes to the fore to legitimate the production of ever more complicit market subjects. On the other hand, I will argue that emotional competence is actually quite useful for the critique and resistance of market life, especially insofar as such movies foster new possibilities for the market community. Indeed, emotional competence can be parodied and/or otherwise resisted in a manner that produces new forms of resilience.

Affective economies of the global event, like trauma and resilience, mark out a new terrain in the politics of market life. What is interesting is how each discourse emplaces the event as a fundamental category of individual and social experience. The global event is set in emotive relation with the individual such that we might evaluate appropriate and inappropriate responses. In this sense, trauma and resilience provide rationalities for knowing and governing the global event that *both follow* and – through resilience planning – *precede* the event: responsiveness is performed as an ongoing quality of market subjectivity. While critical IPE might seek to cut through the event-alisation of politics, regarding it as either a distraction or an emotive smokescreen for updating neo-liberalism, my argument engages the particularities and nuances of this emerging milieu. This is done so as to re-politicise the global event as a performative element in market life and to re-conceive of the agency of market subjects as resistant and creative.

1 Political economy of the global event

Crisis and performance

Introduction: how should we think about the global event?

Recent decades have seen an intensification of media attention paid to, and political interest in, global events. The 24-hour news and social media now run through a seemingly endless stream of natural disasters, terrorist attacks, industrial accidents, mass shootings, extreme weather and, of course, economic crises (Dayan and Katz, 1992; Katz and Liebes, 2007). The rise of the global event can be understood as a symptom of the media age (Hepp and Couldry, 2010). For example, the so-called CNN effect has long suggested that global politics is increasingly entwined with the practices of international news reporting, which can sway domestic public opinion to the plight of distant strangers (Robinson, 2002). Moreover, the nature of global events can fit a very neat news story cycle of (more-or-less) nine days, simple narratives of shock, sympathy, moral judgement and requirements to 'do something' or 'learn lessons'. While perceived as disruptive or shocking, event-driven news can actually reproduce a fairly straightforward politics, whereby policymakers are called upon to respond (Livingston and Bennett, 2003). What ethical and political dilemmas do these global 'media spectacles' (Kellner, 2002) give rise to? Does the rise of the global event challenge the state-centric ontology of politics? Should global mechanisms of response and governance be established? Given the reactions to certain events – e.g. 9/11 and the Indian Ocean Tsunami – can the global event open a path to new forms of community (Hutchison, 2016)?

One important line of reasoning is that the global event is *simply that*: an event which is global in scale. For example, Baylis and Smith (1997: 7) define globalisation as the "process of interconnectedness between societies such that events in one part of the world more and more have effects on peoples and societies far away". In more nuanced terms, Anthony Giddens (1990: 64) suggested, "Globalization can . . . be defined as the intensification of worldwide social relations which link distant localities in such a way that local happenings are shaped by events occurring many miles away and vice versa." For his part, Ulrich Beck went further to situate global events as part of a new world risk society (1999). Indeed, he argued for a form of reflexive learning where the fact of globalisation would – through the gravity of certain 'cosmopolitan events' – promote ethical growth (2013). While sceptical of the stronger claims of globalisation theory, this chapter will argue that the politics of the global event is not something peripheral in market life, an interruption to its normal workings, but rather a constitutive element in its emergence. The section on **The event of globalisation?** will argue that the basic idea of globalisation – interconnectivity, mobility, networks, etc. – can indeed provide a useful context to understand and engage the politics of the global event. However, rather than proceeding with an analytical definition of 'the global' in scalar terms – in order to ask questions such as is it a universal event; does it affect everyone in the same way? – I will argue that the political dimensions of the event should be foregrounded, asking how and why particular events are narrated 'as' global. The section on **The contingency of the global event**, therefore, addresses the examples of the Chilean mine disaster and the *Charlie Hebdo* attacks in Paris. In basic terms, it is not at all obvious that either event should have become narrated as 'global'. The narrative work which underpins this emergence carries a number of loaded qualities: heroism, freedom, civilisation, etc., which might be placed in question. This is a politics of the global. While both events are important, per se, and certainly affected people in grave ways, there is an interesting contingency to how these particular events were narrated as being of wider 'global' significance.

This politics of the global event reflects a process of social construction; identifying a story, a set of key protagonists, and a moral arc (Hay, 1996). Importantly, both events reveal a narrative of good and bad subjects that bear upon wider issues of market life; how to achieve development, when to defend civilisation (Browning, 2017). In this way, we begin to see the link between the social construction of the global event and the details of whether and how it resonates with, or affects, market life. The section on **The global event as crisis?** therefore analyses the work of constructivist and critical scholars for whom the significant question in any crisis is: how is it understood, and how does this understanding perpetuate a transition back to 'normal' circumstances? On this view, the way events are constructed as crises is a mechanism for restructuring market life, whether via the exclusion of scapegoats – e.g. corruption and trade unions – or the legitimation of market life by appeals for better transparency, information, or competition. However, while this literature helps to understand how global events might be narrated as political crises, I argue that the nature of market life can be overdetermined. Despite a focus on 'social construction', it is assumed that a 'normal' set of circumstances, however hierarchal and exploitative, can be returned to. This assumption both naturalises a particular form of market life – liberal capitalism – and reduces the role of the global event to a distraction or smokescreen. On some readings, the event becomes an 'opportunity' for budding entrepreneurs to exploit the crisis and secure market advantages (Johnson, 2011; Klein, 2008).

In response, I outline a case for the development of a performative approach to the politics of the global event. The section on **The global event as contingent performance** draws on the IPE literature on performativity and work of Judith Butler (2010) in particular, to argue that we need to take each event in terms of its context, particularities, *and contests*. The global event is not a universal concept – pace Beck – but neither is it a mere social construction that is amenable to some primordial market rationality. It does not 'happen' in a manner that is straightforwardly 'global' or an 'event'; rather, the very process of filling out these concepts is the political question. It is in the manner and the mode of the performance of the global event that its politics can be ascertained. From a performative perspective, the way discourses of the global event are narrated, and how subjects take them on (or not), is the central question. Beyond a vision of emotion as a catalyst for the reconstruction of liberal capitalism, we can question how affective discourses of the global event are performative of new modes of market life.

The event of globalisation?

One way to situate the politics of the global event is to focus on the scalar and sociological dimension in order to provide a definitional take. Indeed, the literature on globalisation provides an important set of co-ordinates for thinking about the basic tenets of the global event: scale, interconnectivity, supra-territorial qualities (Scholte, 2005). Although theories of globalisation have received substantial criticism in IPE for – amongst other things – downplaying the agency of states, and overplaying the political importance of supra-territorial relations (Hirst and Thompson, 2009), it is fair to say that the 'global context' of political economy has become an important framework (O'Brien and Williams, 2010; Broome, 2014). Globalisation studies anticipated much of our current conjuncture by focusing on a set of sociological changes associated with technological innovation, geographical mobility, and network forms of organisation (Castells, 2009). With the expansion of technologies like Facebook and iPhones into everyday life, a once controversial social science debate now seems like a rather banal statement of the obvious: we live in a (more-or-less) globally interconnected world.

The political implications of globalisation are more contested, however. A changing geography was held to loosen the hold of sovereign or state-centric accounts of politics, allowing for new forms of political community and supra-territorial governance (Linklater, 1998; Scholte, 2005). A number of scholars took up these empirical trends to develop ethical critiques of sovereignty, methodological nationalism, and related conceptions of modernity (Beck, 2000; Giddens, 1990). It was not simply that globalisation allowed for the growth of supra-territorial communities, but that through such complex entwinements, new forms of knowledge could play a prominent and reflexive role in social change (Beck, Giddens and Lash, 1994). On this view, the global event can work as both an exemplar of our new global context and a signal point for our emerging global consciousness. What happens when people can 'see' events on the other side of the world like the Ethiopian famine or 9/11? For cosmopolitan scholars, and authors associated with the rise of 'globalisation theory', a growing consciousness of the interconnectivity of our global lives demonstrated by such events could highlight our emerging 'communities of fate'; and would necessitate a re-thinking and a re-articulation of rationalities and practices of governance at the global level (Held, 2010; Linklater, 1998).

While elements of the cosmopolitan-globalisation thesis might help to situate and interpret the rise of global events, there is a sense in which the 'theory' can over-determine the political content of each event. Indeed, as critics have argued, there is an interesting tautology in globalisation theory, whereby the thing to be explained – i.e. globality – begins to work as the explanation itself (Rosenberg, 2000). By extension, the global event can be rendered as a confirmation of the necessity to think about politics in global terms – i.e. a global crisis necessitates global governance, a global disaster requires global solidarity, etc. Or as Ulrich Beck (2009: 11–12) described the *cosmopolitan event* of 9/11:

> The mass media produce the spontaneous concurrence of the catastrophic event (or its anticipation) in real time in a global scale with active presence and participation of the whole of humanity. It is the traumatic shock experience, this real-life thriller in everyone's living room that tears down the walls of national indifference, overcomes the greatest geographical distances and creates a kind of cosmopolitan solidarity.

In short, the elision of an empirical claim with a normative vision can make for some grand theory, which may require unpacking in terms of common IPE questions of who benefits, why, and how might it be changed?

By foregrounding the significance of the global event for cosmopolitan ethics, there is a danger that we lose sight of a critical standpoint (Brassett, 2008). Indeed, this can be viewed as symptomatic of wider issues in globalisation theory, which can sometimes downplay question of power and hierarchy. For some globalisation represents a normalizing discourse of power that merely updates capitalist logics of expansion and accumulation (Hay and Marsh, 2000; Weber, 2002). A number of empirically driven critiques identified the material concentrations of trade and financial flows in predominantly Western states (Hirst and Thompson, 2009), raising theoretical questions about the euro-centrism of globalisation studies (Phillips, 2005). More critical scholars have argued that hierarchies in world politics persist *because of*, not despite, globalisation, and that attempts to sanitise the concept through 'reform' distract from its complicity in capitalism, imperialism, and patriarchy (Bello, 2005). On this view, the global event may be seen as far more politically contested and problematic than merely recognising our common humanity.

It is not simply that market instrumentalities are intensifying forms of interaction, but that the forms of network organisation are *actively shaping* modes of market subjectivity. For example, the logic of the social network carries important implications for how we live, think, and present ourselves to others. In a global context, the event is experienced differently; it is more intimately produced, through media images, communicated and discussed through social media. Indeed, it is now common for a good proportion of early footage from disasters or terrorist attacks to be made up of smartphone shots uploaded via social media (Allan and Thorsen, 2009). Events do not simply happen but are produced and mediated. The nature and form of this production is an important element in the politics of the global event that will be discussed in the next section.

Critics rightly question the hyperbole of globalisation theory – as ideology, as analytical inflation, as a sociological front for cosmopolitanism (Rosenberg, 2000). But this should not distract from a wider research problematic to understand the lived experiences of market life *as global*. Indeed, it is precisely because globalisation is a contested and contestable concept that the politics of what counts as a global event is so important. While one individual in one country might be tapped into global circuits of consumption, borrowing, and media, this does not mean that their experience of globalisation is the same as another person in another place. For example, consuming a global event like the World Cup – on a sofa with a sponsor beer – is a far cry from the experience of migrant workers who produce the event, building the stadiums and infrastructure (Nauright, 2004). On these terms, the differential experience of global mobility highlighted by certain events; between a skilled Western elite and an unskilled, non-Western, marginalised population of migrant workers, is precisely an important and critical concern (Bulley and Lisle, 2012).

Events animate the politics of globalisation. Their production, consumption, and contest illustrate (and produce) the differential levels of inclusion and autonomy that underpin globalisation. Our ability to turn on a TV, or access the Internet; that we very likely already have a market relationship with the people involved in global events (e.g. by consuming their product), point to a range of ethico-political dilemmas. The politics of the global event is therefore an important prism for understanding the emergence of market life as globalised, not its confirmation. We therefore need to begin to unpick the contingency of how events become narrated as global.

The contingency of the global event

While global events are deeply embedded within empirical trends associated with globalisation – interconnectivity, integration, mobility, networks, etc. – the cosmopolitan move to emplace the global event as a signal point of globalisation theory is problematic. Attempts to ascribe a generative power to global events must first engage with *the politics of globality*: who is included/excluded, on what terms, and how might such hierarchies be contested? On this view, the politics of the global event is better thought of as a fulcrum for engaging the wider dilemmas of globalisation (Brassett, 2008).

This section will introduce and discuss two global events on these terms: the Chilean mine disaster and the *Charlie Hebdo* attacks. While neither of these events is straightforwardly 'global' in significance, I argue that the way they are narrated as global – indeed as events – can raise important dilemmas (Fassin, 2015). In this way, the political construction of each event can illustrate how global market life is portrayed: as brave, as liberal, as rule following, etc. The associations and attachments, solidarities and exclusions that arise are, no doubt ephemeral, even contested. But, to a certain extent, *that is precisely the point*. There is a productive politics of the global event that can both enchant and perform (new) market subjects (Weidner, 2016). In what follows, I introduce elements of each event and recount how they were narrated as globally significant. The aim is not to provide a definitive statement on their content or meaning, but rather to draw out commonalities and particularities to their representation as *global*.

The Chilean mine disaster, 2010

How does an event become global? The Chilean mine disaster that began with a mine collapse trapping 33 miners underground could have been a story about poor safety standards, or, indeed, the failure of private mining companies to adhere to such standards. Years of under investment and poor safety regulation had meant that collapses in Chilean mines were relatively common (Pilger, 2010). Indeed, the San Esteban mining company had received numerous warnings and fines regarding safety in the run up to the collapse (Bonnefoy, 2010). However, this was not the narrative that prevailed in the global media.

A stark practicality was that 33 men were trapped around 700 metres down and out of contact. It was a fair expectation that the miners had either been killed in the collapse or that they would likely starve or suffocate in the near term. Initial coverage suggested a straightforward disaster.[1] However, the story quickly changed as widespread public expressions of concern provoked a political intervention: President Pinera rejected advice from his officials and made an impassioned call for their rescue (Carroll, 2010). Somewhat unusually, the government took over control of the faltering search, and very quickly, national media began to show interest in the story. Indeed, cars across Chile began to carry banners that read "fuerza mineros" (be strong miners) (Allen, 2010). With state backing, a number of boreholes were drilled and listening devices deployed. Seventeen days after the accident, on August 22, a note written in bold red letters appeared taped to a drill bit, it read, "*Estamos bien en el refugio, los 33*" ("*We are well in the shelter, the 33 of us*") (Carroll, 2010). Once the rescuers, and the world, knew that the men were alive, Chile implemented a comprehensive plan to both care for the workers during their entrapment and to rescue them. Indeed, the human experience of the miners became a key narrative of news coverage, with their physical and mental survival a source of regular commentary (Franklin, 2010). A media city quickly grew outside the entrance to the mine, and resources started to roll in from state, private donations and international organisations. There was even a school set up for the children of the miners.[2] After 69 days underground, a TV and Internet audience of around 1 billion people watched the 33 brought safely to the surface on 13 October 2010 by a winching operation that lasted nearly 24 hours.

This remarkable reversal in fortune of the miners was coupled with a rapid mediatisation of the story. From a simple accident, with little hope, the government was able to support and drive a story of emotional intrigue, bravery, hope and fortitude (Jimenez-Martinez, 2014). Numerous national tropes were woven to this story: it came in relatively quick succession to the Chilean earthquake and Tsunami, both of which had united the country in the face of extreme devastation;

it involved very simple and appealing human stories of individuals trapped in adverse conditions, just trying to survive. As a collaborative rescue, it seemed to embody the spirit of a brave Latin American nation embracing global networks of expertise to succeed (Weidner, 2016). Such was the global impact of this good news story that Oakley's move to donate sunglasses to each of the miners is estimated to have resulted in over 40 million dollars' worth of brand exposure.[3]

This is a curious politics. While neo-liberal privatisation and lax safety standards *arguably caused* the accident in the first place, the event that emerged was a uniting and globalising force. Long after the disaster, the president of Chile would carry mementos from the mine, rocks and photos, to give to foreign dignitaries while signing trade deals. Absent from the media portrayal, for instance, was any discussion of the Mapuche Indians who had been systematically excluded from the union rights afforded to 'genuine' Chilean miners. Instead, the market, the nation and, indeed, the marketing potential of this (now) global event was subsumed within a story about heroic development (Weidner, 2016). The hope of a nation was read through the bravery of the miners. A story that might have been a critique of a particular form of market life – i.e. privatisation, emerged to become a spectacle of co-operative global development, even serving to advertise Oakley sunglasses and the trade benefits of Chile in the process (Jimenez-Martinez, 2013).

Charlie Hebdo, 2015

How should we think about ostensibly 'non-economic' events? What narratives of community and value(s) emerge? The (first) Paris terrorist attacks of 2015 were a far shorter and more intense event than the Chilean mine disaster. Initially, two gunmen attacked the headquarters of the satirical newspaper *Charlie Hebdo*, killing 12 people and injuring several others.[4] The assailants escaped and began a running gun battle through the streets of Paris, which resulted in further deaths. National news media managed to circulate images of street fighting and shooting from around mid-day, and it very quickly gained coverage around the world. But an important dimension of these attacks was the sense of an unfolding operation. Part terror attack, part manhunt, images and news circulated on news and social media which emphasised that the assailants were highly trained and effective fighters, seemingly able to outmanoeuvre authorities with multiple points of attack. What appeared to be a straightforward revenge attack on *Charlie Hebdo* staff for publishing images of the prophet quickly transformed. In a separate incident, a further gunman shot at a police officer and took hostages the next day at a kosher supermarket near the Port de Vincennes. By January 9, police had tracked the original assailants to an industrial estate, where it appeared they had taken multiple hostages in an industrial estate. French armed forces moved quickly on both sites. Three terrorists were killed, along with four hostages, who died in the Vincennes supermarket before the intervention.

Again, one interpretation of the attacks might be that they were an indictment of French security arrangements. Instead, though, a number of more positive images began to emerge. There were reports of a hero in the industrial estate who hid in some cardboard and managed to help police by communicating over his mobile phone. In the siege at the kosher supermarket, 15 hostages were rescued and the gunmen killed. A positive narrative emerged surrounding Lassana Bathily, a Muslim shop assistant born in Mali, who was hailed as a hero in the crisis for risking his life to hide people in a downstairs refrigerator room.[5] Indeed, there was a new dimension to the construction of these events. While mainstream news images did much to convey the sense of emergency, the Internet and social media also worked to magnify the narrative of the event (Sreberny, 2016). A crucial point was the circulation of actual footage of a police officer being killed. While the mainstream news media was clear to play looping images of the terrorists shooting into the streets, they (like most Western media outlets) refused to show unedited footage of a policeman being shot while he pleaded for his life. Circulating this footage on the Internet arguably charged the emotional response to the attacks and elevated a sense that the attackers were bringing 'unethical' combat to the streets of Paris.

Dider Fassin (2015) talks about how the event was portrayed as an attack on the Republic, an attack on civilisation. A popular hashtag – #jesuischarlie – emerged to typify the public and international mood. The form followed previous instances of public engagement with major events in the US such as #Iamtrevonmartin – an expression of solidarity that expressed a rejection of violence and a sympathy for the victims (sreberny, 2016). Just as the Chilean mine disaster was narrated to legitimate a brave and virtuous nation, so too was the Paris attacks developed in a manner that exalted the French nation. Indeed, it became a global touchstone for leaders around the world who attended a national day of mourning. *Charlie Hebdo* became a monument to free speech. Leaders from across the world gathered in Paris to express solidarity. But again, the politics of this narration was widely debated. On the one hand, it was clear that certain leaders – e.g. Viktor Orban, Ali Bongo and Benjamin Netanyahu – were an awkward fit with the script of free speech and democracy (Fassin, 2015: 3). On the other hand, there were legitimate questions to be asked about the orchestration of this national and global event around *Charlie Hebdo* specifically. The French state had previously tried to shut down and censor Charlie Hebdo, yet now it moved to underwrite the print run of the magazine. In the UK, Will Self (2015) openly criticised a form of satire that caricatured the prophet, suggesting that it targeted the weakest in European society. Indeed, the weaving of *Charlie Hebdo* to the myth of the Republic meant that people who did not identify with the *Charlie Hebdo* were questioned; schoolchildren were punished for questioning the magazine (Fassin, 2015). A critique of double standards emerged in light of an outpouring of Islamophobia across the country. Wider questions about, for instance, the global context of mass migration to Europe, or the colonial legacies of France, were left out of the discussion or legitimated via the inclusion of Lassana Bathily, the brave shop assistant who was given French citizenship. Liberal freedoms, on particular sovereign terms, were thus portrayed as the central meaning of this global event.

The global event as crisis?

The global event carries an important politics of meaning. It is not simply that the growing interest in global events is a demonstration of our emerging global interconnectedness *pace* cosmopolitan-globalisation theory. Instead, the ways in which such events are narrated *as global* can rather serve to highlight the contested politics of globalisation. By this is meant the growth and spread of interconnectivity, mobility and technological innovation, and the rise of network forms of organisation is neither universal nor equally experienced. Instead, the contingency of how the event is mediated and produced *as global* rather serves to animate the contested politics of globalisation: hierarchy, exclusion, violence.

In the previous section, the Chilean mine disaster and the *Charlie Hebdo* attacks were analysed in terms of how they were narrated as global. Importantly, each event portrayed an ethics – be it the brave miners or the liberal/tolerant nation – and thus each event was elevated to the level of global concern through a focus on the individual dimension – e.g. the brave Muslim shop assistant. Equally, the more negative elements of each story were downplayed or woven to a process of legitimation. The events became a way of forgetting: lax safety standards, racial dimensions of citizenship, ongoing curtailments of freedom, double standards on the use of violence, etc. On this view, the politics of the global event is an energising, legitimating, visceral moment in market life. The Chilean mine disaster presents an ethical story about heroic global development, shorn of the awkward dilemmas over inclusion and regulation that might be seen by many as a primary concern (Jimenez-Martinez, 2014; Weidner, 2016). The French terrorist attacks present a story about tolerant liberalism and free expression without recourse to the subtext of European privilege and the double standard of violence against Muslims inside and out (Fassin, 2015). From this insight, two questions arise: How should we theorise the global event? What is common to the politics of these events, and how does it speak to or affect the content of market life? This section will introduce an important mode of crisis analysis in IPE – namely, critical constructivism – in order to begin to draw out this contingent politics of the global event.

A crisis theory of the global event?

The idea of crisis has a long lineage in IPE. Crisis is often taken as an important moment in market life – a rupture or instability that can provide insight on how the global economy is changing, power imbalances, etc. (Kindleberger, 2001; Strange, 1996). Broadly, while previous theories of economic crisis saw the moment of crisis as an important moment for revealing how material forces of a market economy were imbalanced in some way – by positing blockages or insufficiencies in some aspect of market-as-mechanism – the discipline of IPE has emphasised a deeper politics of crisis. On this view, a tendency has been to focus on how crisis is governed, whether via powerful states or institutions, or via particular ideas about how markets should operate (Broome et al., 2012). Here the role of ideas, interpretations and intersubjective interventions, as well as the agency of speech actors and discourse generators has been highlighted (Blyth, 2013; Hay, 1996; Seabrooke, 2010; Widmaier, 2010). From a critical constructivist perspective, it is the way a crisis is narrated that serves to govern whether or how we should expect to see continuity of change in market life. On this view, crisis theory in IPE can provide important theoretical insight on how, why and with what effects certain events are narrated as crisis (Broome et al., 2012: 11–12).

Amin Samman (2015) argues that within the debates on IPE crisis theory, we can see the uncomfortable drawing together of two traditions of thought on market life. On the one hand, there is a rational or economistic idea of crisis, which refers to a period of market instability produced by certain imbalances or exogenous shocks. Such imbalances might be caused by ongoing differences between prices and wages, or between wages and personal debt, for instance. Within IPE, for instance, a historical orientation can focus attention on how crisis can be understood as a working through of alternative accommodations to different versions of growth. As Widmaier (2010: 130) argues,

> In terms of explaining change, what matters most [. . .] are the shifts in production possibilities – which may build slowly, but ultimately manifest themselves in punctuated crises. Such "major" events in turn facilitate efforts by self-interested agents to realign societal coalitions in ways that support new policy departures.

On this view, crisis is an essentially technical affair that punctuates the development of the market mechanism as political and societal interests reconcile themselves to – *inter alia* – free competition, transparency, changing demographics, etc. The crisis moment happens in terms of a major rupture and period of accommodation to a new mode of growth, thus producing a 'major event' in political-economic history – e.g. the Great Depression.

On the other hand, there is a more critical idea drawn from Marxism that thinks of crisis as working through of dialectics in the social relations of productive capitalism. This more structural lineage suggests that crisis highlights an immanent or potential shift in the regime of accumulation. On this view, a crisis is something more than just market instability produced by exogenous shocks; instead, it represents a more deeply political moment – a conceptual opening: to become conscious of ourselves as a class, or perhaps to build a new regime of accumulation like communism, which might resolve such structural tensions.

Against these opposing visions of crisis, Samman (2016) argues that critical constructivist work attempts to plough a middle furrow. Neither the mechanistic image of markets nor the potential teleology of structural Marxism are quite taken up. Instead, constructivist IPE develops based on the notions of contingency to produce a socially situated, reflexive ontology of crisis, whereby the interpretations of particular events as crisis becomes the appropriate intersubjective politics for engagement. As Widmaier surmises

> [C]onstructivists have argued that agents cannot directly interpret material shifts, and are instead constrained by a deep or intersubjective "uncertainty".

> Put differently, agents cannot make efficient use of information, and so must interpret events in terms of some socially constructed conventions before they react to them. Constructivists accordingly cast crises less as "exogenous shocks" that compel adaptation than as events that agents must themselves give meaning to, a view which highlights a wider scope for deliberative and persuasive practices.
>
> (2010: 130–131)

Recalling Paris, the failure of the system to secure the safety of the citizens was rapidly narrated through blame of the perpetrators as *their failure* to accept the (positive, tolerant) values of the system. Not only is structural change averted but also the very structures of exclusion and violence which might be challenged by the event are re-legitimated: marches for international solidarity, Islamophobia, etc. A similar diagnosis can be applied to Chile. The system failure – poor investment, lax regulation – which arguably caused the crisis was replaced by appeal to the fortitude and bravery of the victims. A narrative emerges of 'heroic development': a tiny embattled country bravely engages with global networks of donors and rescue agencies to re-legitimate their version of market life. Thus we return to the question of how one or another discourse of the event 'succeeds'?

From a more critical perspective, Bob Jessop has sought to develop a theory of crisis by placing such 'competing discourses' for consideration alongside a more structural account (Jessop, 1993, 2013). This argument foregrounds the extant regimes of accumulation that do exist and asks how they develop and legitimate themselves; here the construction of different events *as a crisis* can be an important political dynamic, per se, as it allows alternative regimes to promote themselves (Jessop, 1993). On this view, crisis moves from being a deliberative politics of meaning to a form of power struggle:

> Asymmetries of power are especially significant in the selection of crisis-interpretations and their translation into crisis-responses and imagined recovery scenarios. This helps to explain the re-assertion of key elements in the neoliberal project despite the initial shock to that project from the form, timing, location and incidence of . . . crisis.
>
> (Jessop, 2013: 241–242)

On this view, events do not take place in a vacuum, and the meaning of crisis is not 'purely constructed' through a competition between discourses; rather, the social contingency of a regime of accumulation (and discourses about that regime of accumulation) matters. Ideas about the role of France as an icon of civilisation, or of Chile as a 'brave developing nation' in the world economy, can serve as an important context for the negotiation of a particular narrative of the global event.

The global event as contingent performance

Despite the insightful analysis of the role of narrative, and a recognition of the strategic interactions between agents and elites over defining the narrative of events as crisis, IPE crisis theory can remain limited to a 'rational' competition between discourses. A deeper questioning of market life, the lives led by market subjects, the ethics that draws them together or pulls them apart is left beyond the analysis. Instead, the event is understood in terms of the relative agency to deliberate over discursive forms of accommodation with one or another structure of accumulation. Certain limitations follow.

Crisis theory is only really engaged in the analysis of events that are narrated as a crisis. This might appear as too obvious to mention, but it bears reflection. A basic proposition of crisis theory in IPE is that an event is worthy of study insofar as it amounts to a crisis, whether it be in terms of crisis within market life or a more fundamental crisis of accumulation – i.e. capitalism (Broome et al., 2012: 11–13). On the one hand, it is not clear how, if at all, natural disasters or terrorist attacks would fit within this form of analysis, except insofar as they might highlight or produce a wider crisis of, say, emergency planning or civil society. On the other hand, any event that did not achieve the status of crisis would be left out of the analysis, thus defining in advance what could or could not be considered an important global event. This highlights a limit on the nature of the political within crisis theory, which arguably curtails what an event *can be* or *do*. An event is either seen to disrupt the 'normal' workings of market life or not. Such an approach effectively assumes a knowable stable 'reality' and then permits social construction in terms of the ideas and beliefs that agents might have during a crisis of that 'reality'. In short, from a post-structural perspective, a hierarchy of meaningful constructions is established before discussion even begins (Zehfuss, 2002). Thus we might equally question what is 'not constructed' in these crisis events? One might equally posit the state, the market, the market subject, ethics, etc., as social facts to be explained. Overall, these appear to be unproblematic background concepts – a context within which rational deliberation over their next most viable accommodation can be carried out. Market life is straightforward, just contested.

Events happen. If an event is deemed to highlight certain instabilities or disjuncture in market life, then it becomes a crisis. During a crisis, there might be intensified instability, narrative construction and competition of the correct discursive interpretation of the crisis. And this narrative crisis may well reflect different theories, paradigms or ideologies of market life (Widmaier et al., 2007). But the question of what counts as political, indeed, the political itself, is taken as a relatively unproblematic battle between discourses. Power is held by people dependent on their position within structures that they might discursively critique. This might lead to a continuation of hierarchical forms of liberal capitalism or a new accommodation/class compromise via one or another rationality of the regime of accumulation. While this may be a useful analytical cut at the global political economy that moves discussion beyond technical or economic pragmatism, I will argue that it may prove a limited and limiting approach to the politics of the global event.

Approaches to crisis theory in IPE are clearly an important way of diagnosing the politics of a global event. By highlighting the crisis narrative and the deliberative politics of the event, we can identify how the interpretation of events as crisis foregrounds a politics of meaning in market life. However, despite the attractiveness of this rationalisation of crisis for thinking about how an event is negotiated in strategic terms; this section will articulate a performative critique. While sympathetic to crisis theory, I argue that it can work to limit our understanding of 'the political' in relation to global events. The generative power of the event can be downplayed through a conception of politics as a rational, public debate between agents who can reason. Even in the more critical orientation, the substance of crisis is reduced to the negotiation of different versions of an accumulation regime – i.e. the event merely presents an 'opportunity' for this negotiation to occur. Across these differing versions of crisis theory, either rationality, or a particular regime of market 'reality' or some combination of both is left intact as the fundamental arbiter for resolution.

Building from this sympathetic critique of crisis theory, I will develop a performative approach based on the work of Judith Butler (2010). On this view, the idea of an 'event' is problematised as a discursive achievement per se. What is done in the name of the event, how a politics of competitive persuasion is established, and how a rationality of future events is constructed, opens up questions of 'the political' in relation to the global event itself. From a performative perspective, discourses of the global event constitute the event and the global as a 'say-able' element of the political. This entails a wider performance of market subjects capable of 'hearing' any particular discourse: the psychological suffering of the Chilean miners or the principle of free speech involved in *Charlie Hebdo* cartoons. Mutual contingency of discourse and subject is a prior assumption of performativity in a manner that makes the politics of global events both *dynamic* and *productive* of market life.

Towards a performative approach?

One potential avenue for licensing the performative power of global events is to consider the recent rise of everyday and cultural approaches to IPE (Best and Paterson, 2010; Langley, 2008b). Such approaches highlight the way political economy is always already a product of small, local activities, cultural norms and the behaviours of everyday subjects, not the privilege of grand 'structures' or 'states and markets'. On this view, everyday behaviour like discussing an event on social media, changing a Facebook status to express sympathy or else the production of movies that otherwise elevate global events can be thought of as important dimensions of global political economy.

Thus a turn to everyday and cultural IPE can be a promising line for thinking about the politics of the global event. It increases the range of sites and practices that might be *studied as* market life beyond the prevailing discussion of meta-groupings such as 'class' or 'policy elite'. Thus we might begin to think about genres of cultural production as an important element in market life. For instance, the rise of disaster movies in the late twentieth century and recent moves towards apocalyptic scenarios that depict the end of the world – because of environmental collapse – can be thought of as important for understanding how the event is known (Fagan, 2017). More critically, it can allow a more expansive appeal to feminist, post-structural and post-colonial theoretical traditions which always already problematise the weight of power (and responsibility) involved in the constitution of market life. From a post-colonial perspective, for instance, the very idea of markets is bound up with notions of violence – through imperialism, slavery, practices of knowing – in a manner that invites a fundamental decentring of the idea of market life in IPE. For such perspectives, the very idea of 'crisis' may appear as a particularly selective reading of the history and politics of globalisation. Thus the mode and the manner of living within markets becomes a political problematic *per se*, and thus the question of what counts as 'the political' in relation to a global event is afforded a wider range of performative possibilities. This is more than a question of disciplinary positioning. It asks fundamental questions about power and discourse in order to politicise the global event as a performative element in market life.

On this view, the idea of a global event *that happens to* market life – and to which we must respond (or not) – must itself be seen as a discursive achievement. Rather than imagining a set of pre-existent, universal market logics that structure or discipline subjects in particular ways, the events that 'impact upon' a performative approach begin from the dilemma that *markets require* subjects to act upon themselves in order to enhance and/or re-shape them. Importantly, the subject does not spring forth fully formed with a set of interests or a class position, nor is it ever complete or identical with its discursive performance. As Langley and Leyshon (2012: 371) argue, there is always a gap: "The processes of identification in which . . . subjects are produced and propelled are necessarily partial and incomplete." As such, the subject is never fully disciplined or docile, but is better thought of as 'uncertain' (Langley, 2007). This mutual contingency of discourse and subject provokes interesting questions about how to engage the politics of the global event, less as some 'thing' that affects a (pre-existing) market life and more as a question of emergence.

The centrality of the politics of the subject to a performative approach can therefore prompt some interesting ethical questions: What matters in the world? How should we proceed? Who is the 'we' to which such questions apply? By linking such questions to market life, I argue, the politics of the global event presents a question about agency in the cultural political economy: How might we live differently? For uncertain subjects, I think this is not so much a question of overcoming – a class or a regime or accumulation; rather, it is an issue of self-making. Judith Butler extends this idea to argue that the subject retains the potential for a kind of *poiesis*: not that this self-making implies a subject born of nothing, but that it is part of the play and interplay of the subject with the conditions of subjectivity:

> This work on the self . . . takes place within the context of a set of norms that precede and exceed the subject. These are invested with power and recalcitrance, setting limits to what will be considered to be an intelligible formation of the subject within a given historical scheme of things. There is no making of oneself outside of a mode of subjectivation and hence no self-making

> outside of the of the norms that orchestrate the possible forms that a subject may take.
>
> (Butler, 2005: 17)

From this, my suggestion is that in order to address the affective politics of the global event, we must grapple with the norms that precede and exceed the subject – the very idea of an event that 'happens' and can result in a set of 'responses' instantiates a number of logics that are performed as part of the emotional life of market subjects. The inculcation of virtues in relation to such events – an ability to feel sympathy, solidarity or proactively plan for 'such events' – is another layer of this politics. The mediatisation and circulation of images and memes that embody the visceral, exciting possibilities of the event can produce new subjects and commonalities. Far from an interruption, or a crisis, the global event can be productive of market life.

Conclusion

The chapter developed upon the politics of the global event as an important element in market life. Rather than viewing events as the flotsam and jetsam of media narrative, it was argued that we need to explore the rise of the global event as a productive element in market life, whether as disruption, confirmation or site of meaning. It was first suggested that the global event might be seen as an empirical confirmation of the globalisation thesis. Especially, the normative component of the cosmopolitan-globalisation argument would see the rise of the global event as a signal point for recognising the need to build global forms of governance and response. However, this view was critiqued as over-determined by an ethical vision. The politics of globalisation – of hierarchy, exclusion and various inequalities of subject position – were argued to fit well into a critical perspective on the global event. The chapter therefore explored two major events, the Chilean mine disaster and the *Charlie Hebdo* attacks to uncover how particular narratives of what had happened and how to respond were elaborated. Importantly, both events were used and mobilised to downplay negative elements of market life – uncertainty, exclusion, violence, etc. – and to legitimate positive elements – bravery, heroism, tolerance. This brought forward the idea of a politics of meaning in the global event, which requires theoretical unpacking.

While a move to crisis theory in IPE was useful for exploring the role of narrative construction in manipulating or controlling a crisis, it was argued that a rational view of power and the subject acted to limit the politics of the global event. On this view, both the event and the subject are stripped of any deeper political meaning, and market life is produced as a straightforward battle of interests and ideational constructions resolving in one or another accommodation between them. Instead, the case was made for developing a performative approach to the politics of the global event.

A performative approach takes the power of discourse to produce and constrain market life as an invitation to open up questions of the political. On this view, the questions, "What is global?", "What is the event?", "Who is the 'we' that is affected?" and "How are these ideas set in relation to market life?" are understood as a discursive achievement per se. In performative terms, the agency of the subject is thus foregrounded and how discourses are taken on, problematised and enacted differently are crucial elements in the politics of the global event that I will explore in the following chapters.

Notes

1 www.bbc.co.uk/news/world-latin-america-11469025 (last accessed: 01/07/17)
2 www.bbc.co.uk/news/world-latin-america-11469025 (last accessed: 01/07/17)
3 www.huffingtonpost.com/2010/10/13/chile-miners-rescue_n_761259.html (last accessed: 01/07/17)
4 www.bbc.co.uk/news/world-europe-30708237 (last accessed: 03/07/17)
5 www.bbc.co.uk/news/world-europe-30905262 (last accessed: 03/07/17)

2 Everyday politics of the global event

Discourse, performance, subject

Introduction: the intimacy of the global event

Attempts to portray the politics of the global event as a signal point, a confirmation of a wider set of changes associated with globalisation, can underplay the contingency and performative politics involved. Chapter 1 argued that the global event is better understood as a richer concern *capable of animating* the stratified and hierarchical politics of globalisation (Beck, 2013). A critical approach would therefore seek to problematise the normalisation of scale, universality and 'equality of experience' that is sometimes assumed in cosmopolitan discourses of the global event. One way to think about the contingent politics of the global event might be to draw upon the literature on the discursive construction of crisis. Here the narration of an event in particular terms, with particular causes and a de-limited set of alternatives, can problematise the politics of stabilisation. That is to say, how does the system adjust to a new regime of accumulation? On this view, the politics of the global event might be understood as the fulcrum for the re-negotiation or extension of regimes of neo-liberal governance (Johnson, 2011). However, while such an incisive cut may yield a ready list of protagonists – class, capital, metropolitan elites, etc. – the reduction of the politics of the global event to a deliberation (albeit power laden) amongst rational agents may work to simplify and naturalise the politics of globalisation, as if the global event were just an 'interruption', a 'distraction', a 'smokescreen' for the pre-existing politics of market life to play on. Instead, I argue, we need to understand the contingent performance of the global event; the very idea of the event needs to be placed in question as something capable of affecting and involving subjects as responsive, ethical, sympathetic, etc. In short, how is the global event performed as an intimate experience? What Ulrich Beck referred to as the 'real life thriller in everyone's living room' (Beck, 2009: 11–12).

This chapter will seek to develop and consolidate the theoretical and methodological approach that will guide the argument of this book. While it is clear that the politics of the global event is related to discourses of affect, which are both located within, but also productive of norms and practices of market life, we need to provide an account of how such discourses resonate. In theoretical terms, while the previous chapter was sympathetic to constructivist theories of crisis that foreground the role of discourse, agency and power, I argued that a performative approach could go further to recognise the importance of the context and contingency of performance. By this I mean to suggest that there are certain performative conditions that allow a particular discourse to resonate (or not), which are not well accounted for by cosmopolitan theories of globalisation, on the one hand, or pre-established theories of crisis on the other. Indeed, as this chapter will argue, attention to the context and contingency of the performance of the global event can foreground the centrality and ambiguity of the market subject per se. Drawing from the work of Judith Butler in particular, as well as the secondary literature on performativity in IPE, I will argue that a performative approach to the cultural political economy of the global event can yield a clear – *and clearly political* – method of analysis that will be used to organise this book.

This argument will be developed over three sections. The section on **The media event and/as cultural discourse** engages the literature on the media event and how communications scholars understand the rise of emotion in news and media coverage of 'distant suffering'. This literature identifies an important practical context for the cultural political economy of the global event, which is that it is 'edited' and 'mediated'. Such scholarship identifies how certain global events promote a kind of 'narrative centre' for an otherwise disaggregated and globally diffuse 'mediatised' society. Two important concerns arise from this literature: 1) the importance of image and medial relay for presenting the global event (i.e. at a very basic level, 9/11 would not be the same if cameras were not present) and 2) the situation of this mediation of the global event within consumer culture (i.e. spectacles such as Band Aid blur between an ethic of solidarity and the production of humanitarian aid as a consumer item). Thus the politics of the global event is always already an element within market life, portrayed in a language that consumer subjects understand and performative of structures that agents must adapt to. For example, Lilie Chouliaraki (2013) focuses on the way humanitarian NGOs have adapted their self-image and organisation to work best within an event-driven fundraising cycle. This instrumentalisation of humanitarian discourse, she argues, further relies on a set of changes in the viewer subject to nurture an 'ironic spectatorship', which she describes a 'self-oriented morality' that is less about fundamental principles of solidarity and more about the 'minor gratifications to the self', or, simply, *feeling like* a good person. When one thinks about the role of new forms of social media in promoting images of the concerned self who responds to global events with shock, empathy or hope, say, we begin to see how the original idea of the media event must be revised to take account of the emergent agency of viewer subjects who craft their identity through such spectacles (Browning, 2017).

Building from the cultural discourses that surround and produce the politics of the global event by performing an affective viewer subject, the section on **Everyday politics of the global event?** will turn to the literature on everyday and cultural political economy to develop the theoretical and methodological framework. While still in its infancy, this emergent IPE literature helps to foreground the important role of (seemingly) small or mundane practices in the performance of market life. Thus at the risk of over simplification against a cosmopolitan vision of the global event as a 'large' thing that 'happens', we might reverse the line of inquiry to ask about the 'small' everyday 'objects' and 'practices' that make up the global event. So this might include the practicalities and technicalities of media production, say, how new technologies mean events can be mediated via smartphones, in real time and, increasingly, by everyday citizens who witness events and upload their footage on social media. Or else, as Richey and Ponte (2011) identify, we might think about the normalisation of celebrities who 'brand' certain forms of aid in response to global events. The key proposition that I take from the everyday literature is to foreground and develop the political agency of market subjects. In the work of Hobson and Seabrooke (2007), for example, this helps us to understand how everyday actors can both drive global change and practice forms of resistance that shape or subvert global market discourses to alternative ends. Attention to the everyday and cultural political economy of the global event can, therefore, problematise the assumed coherence of the spectacle on the one hand, or the 'docile' nature of the subject on the other so as to reflect the active agency of market subjects within (and against) affective discourses of the global event.

Across the everyday contexts that underpin the mediation of the global event, I argue that attention to the literature on performance and performativity can helpfully focus analysis by drawing out the mutual contingency of discourse and subject. On this view, and throughout the book, I seek to foreground the political agency of the market subject to reflect on, engage and resist the affective discourses of the global event.

The section on **Performing the global event**, therefore, outlines the theoretical framework that will structure and drive the argument of this book. By developing upon the work of Judith Butler, it is argued that we need to take account of three distinctive, though entwined, elements in the politics of the global event: discourse, performance and subject. Butler's focus on the reiterative power of discourse to produce what it names can help to identify a key problematic of this book, which is that the very idea of 'the global event' should be taken as a discursive achievement per se, iterated over time and across contexts. For author's such as Butler, but also more latterly Jack Halberstam, this discursive reiteration is understood as something that takes place in different ways *across culture* (i.e. because gender is never just gender, but a product of interdependent meanings performed, critiqued, changed, etc., over time and across genres). On this view, I argue, ideas about the global event can cross performative context(s) to include discourses of the event in psychological knowledge, news media, Hollywood cinema and comedy. The global event is avowedly not limited to the physical or existential sense of an event that happens. This is because the reiterative power of discourse identified by Butler relies on a certain interdependence between performance and subject, and the success *or failure* of a performance depends on the capacity for a subject to hear it, in the sense of having heard relevant discourses previously.

This 'thicker' notion of performativity implies a focus on the contingent emergence of discourses of the global event *across culture* and therefore implies a 'method' that is multi-sited and multi-dimensional, yet I would argue, extremely limited by a focus on a specific discourse of the event. This yields a methodological focus that can be divided into three distinct, yet inter-related, streams. 1) *The discourse of the event* (trauma or resilience): How has a certain discourse of the global event emerged? What are its logics? What are its ethics? 2) *A performance of the event* (traumatic or resilient): How does a particular performance of the event understand market life? What idea of the subject does it entail? Is the performance successful or does it break down in some way? 3) *The subject of the discourse* (traumatic or resilient): How is the market subject performed? How does this connect to or confirm existing patterns of market life? How do certain performances, resist and/or subvert these patterns?

The media event and/as cultural discourse

The idea of a 'media event' as a specific form of ritualised news practice emerges in the literature on political communication and specifically the work of Dayan and Katz and their book *Media Events: the Live Broadcasting of History* (1992). The initial idea was designed to typify and record how a particular form of media communication was emerging that sought to unite apparently disparate channels and program coverage around the singular and 'staged' production of certain events: a kind of common story that could unite coverage and viewers. Dayan and Katz identified a certain ritualised quality to the staging of such events which could serve to codify and explain how they were able to break down boundaries between viewers and the event to build a 'community of experience'.

Despite new technologies that promoted individual or atomised viewing practices, a media event could provide a form of social conversation. With regard to news coverage, for example, instead of proceeding by means of a list of distinctive items, happenings or occurrences, Dayan and Katz identified how coverage could foreground a particular event in the public consciousness, say a sporting event or an election, and in so doing allow for repeated iterations of the story in advance of and during the event. The event could therefore serve as a uniting narrative around which, in their terms, the media could present a story about a singular and 'outstanding' ritual ceremony, showing off the nation, its qualities, hopes and aspirations. This presented the media event with an affective quality to enchant and lift the otherwise mundane focus of TV news. Gone was a dry list of details, and in their place was the spectacle of an *involving* media event, which they referred to as "high holidays of mass communication" (Dayan and Katz, 1992: 1; cf. Hepp and Couldry, 2010: 3), or more concretely as a "genre" of media communication. This new genre of media communication had certain recognisable features that helped to define them as 'special' or 'outside the normal' schedule. Thus media events were conceived as an interruption that would capture attention *across different channels and programs*. For instance, a media event such as an election could be covered beyond news channels on daytime or evening chats shows, all at the same time and with different conversation points. However, for Dayan and Katz, there was usually a specific set of values associated with media events that could celebrate higher societal goals; they were, in this sense, 'historic events' that could be staged in a ceremonial way to reflect a certain gravitas.

While the media event captured the form and intention of mass communication, especially in its edited form, which was controlled by news corporations with a focus on ratings and predictability, certain critical points have been made. Firstly, the concept of a media event is quite 'rosy' in outlook; it is a wholesome celebration of historical moments – a ceremony for social values. This might suit the editorial demands of media corporations, which saw a way to provide an enchanting narrative that could attract advertising sponsors and viewer-consumers, but it misses the wide range of news reporting. Indeed, as one of the original authors went on to observe, an increasing number of media events were quite the opposite in tone. In their co-authored article, 'No More Peace!: How Disaster War and Terror have Upstaged Media Events, Katz and Liebes (2007) argued that the study of media events needed to take account of the rise of disruptive events. Global events, such as 9/11, say, or the Indian Ocean Tsunami, could not be predicted in advance and certainly did not follow a celebratory or ceremonial script. While each event could still cross channels and programs, and disruptive events could certainly enthral the viewer, a new vocabulary of disaster and suffering would seemingly destabilise the happy association between media coverage and consumer culture. Think of the near blackout of advertising during the 9/11 coverage as companies raced to pull their brands for fear of association. Editorialising such events presented a discursive challenge.

Secondly, if the broadening of the concept of the media event to include disruption was a challenge to the neat categories and concepts in the original articulation, a number of authors pointed to the role of globalisation in challenging the idea of the media event. For Hepp and Couldry (2010), the idea of the media event had been originally located in a specifically national conception of communication and news reporting, which could not account for the rapid changes associated with the rise of 24-hour news and the proliferation of global channels and media platforms. For them, media events in a global age embody a 'translocal' quality that necessarily pulls at any attempt to de-limit the narrative of the event in terms of societal values or national ceremonies. Instead, they argue that the idea of ritual itself, that there is some form of editorial control over what the event consists of, must be augmented to think about *the performative nature of the event*: that the 'process of constructing the event' must be the critical question. For example, they cite Roger Silverstone in relation to coverage of Princess Diana's funeral to identify the unstable and evolving nature of performance, whereby the audience – to some extent – is able to participate in the construction of the story:

> The Diana funeral provides, in an exaggerated but triumphant way, an example of the way in which the blurring of audience and performer takes place on a public stage, both in the media and beyond its reach (though, of course, never completely beyond its reach). It also takes place on a stage, as a result

> of its mediation, which removes it from the realm of the personal and transforms each moment into a fragment of a national or even global event. We might want, as a consequence, to think about it quite differently. To think of its participation in the funeral not as a shared and committing moment, but as a performance without responsibility; a sharing of private grief without pubic mourning.
>
> (Silverstone, 1999: 75)

On this view, they argue (2010: 15–23), translocally mediated events (that is, events whose significance is transmitted across borders) can gain a broader sociocultural relevance in contemporary societies. Instead of carefully controlled events, we must think of them as a fulcrum for the articulation of competing cultural discourses, often through the interaction between the event and the viewer subjects. The global event is always already situated within market life as both an object and subject of consumer culture: a site of emergence.

Finally, and drawing these points together, the concept of the media event has augmented to reflect how cultural discourses of market life interact with and construct different events. This performance of the media event involves a set of political questions about 'what' and 'who' performs? On what terms, and how might it be in a process of changing? For Hepp and Couldry, this involves a critical reflex to engage the various and proliferating power centres of media in a global age. For them, this necessitates a critical interrogation of the media and policy elites that would seek to control the performance of the global event to reflect and support certain interests:

> Relating media events to questions of performativity reminds us that they are power-related articulations, produced with a large amount of resources and fulfilled with certain interests in mind. But when we consider outstanding media events in their transcultural character it becomes obvious that this performativity cannot be related to just one power center. Especially if we consider conflict-orientated media events like for example terror attacks, war or the always in part politically driven Olympics, we get an understanding of the variety of interest groups and power discourses related to the performance of these events. Reflecting power is a key aspect of performativity, and a one-dimensional analysis at this point falls short.
>
> (Hepp and Couldry, 2010: 20)

This recognition of the performative politics of the global event can provoke a number of questions about how to analyse power in relation to such events. Of course, as the previous chapter discussed, one line might be to identify the discourses and agents that would seek to secure a particular regime of accumulation. Indeed, the literature on the media event can point to how cultural discourses are themselves performative of consumer culture, portraying the global event as a 'media spectacle' (Kellner, 2003) – a regular phenomenon of consumer societies organised around the consumption of images and/as commodities.

On another view, the performance of global events can nurture a far more intimate and affective relationship with the viewer subject that encourages them to 'feel' in relation to certain events, experience empathy for 'suffering' and express sympathy in new ways (Chouliaraki, 2013). By focusing on discourses of humanitarian compassion and how they emerge from – and work to shape – global politics, Lilie Chouliaraki (2013), suggests that affective discourses of the global event can perform particular responses to disaster. For Chouliaraki, this involves the revision of larger discourses of the global event from a universal form of 'humanitarian solidarity' to a more media savvy form of 'ironic spectatorship'. The global event is thus taken as productive of a new form of viewer subject. Images of suffering can provoke a 'response', but the mobilisation of this response as a normal reflex of global ethics, in turn, encourages viewers to craft themselves to feel and act in certain ways. This 'new emotionality', she argues, has specific implications for how wider values and ethics can work within market life:

> It is . . . only when we examine solidarity as a problem of communication, that is, as a moral claim seeking to reconcile the competing demands of market, politics and the media, that we can better understand how the spectacle of suffering is subtly but surely turning the West into a specific kind of public actor – the ironic spectator of vulnerable others.
>
> (Chouliaraki, 2013: 2)

From a technical affair of editorial control over the ritual and ceremony of particular events, the literature on the media event has developed to reflect the disruptive nature of many events, their situation within a complex global context and a performative question of how the very process of constructing a narrative centre can be politicised. While we might be tempted to see this as a question that necessarily focuses on media elites, or large corporations, in order to rehearse an image of market life in terms of the overwhelming structural power of capitalism, a focus on the affective discourses of the global event can broaden the scope of inquiry. Indeed, Lilie Chouliaraki (2013: 3) argues that new forms of emotionality can be performative of new modes of ethics and ethical subjectivity, which fundamentally inform how a global event is narrated:

> The personifying power of celebrity, the enchantment of the rock concert or the professional witnessing of the journalist, . . . confront us with the spectacle of distant sufferers as a cause that demands our response. In so doing, these practices form part of a dispersed communicative structure of cosmopolitan ethics that mundanely acts as a moralizing force upon western public life.

On this view, the global event is itself performative of how we are moved by, responsive to and emergent within market life. Everyday politics.

Everyday politics of the global event?

The existing literature on the media event provides some useful insights that can inform and shape the theoretical and methodological framework of this book. By raising the significance of media events as rituals of knowing and celebrating societal values, I argue, the media event can be a focal point for thinking about and practicing politics. Especially in a global context, this literature has brought forward the idea that such events are both less 'controllable' than previous work suggested and *more performative*. By this I mean to suggest that it is the politics of constructing a narrative centre, how this is achieved and through which cultural discourses of the event and subject, that is the crucial question. In this way, the politics of the global event can be more thoroughly explored through the cultural discourses of market life that are performed through the global event. To wit, as authors such as Chouliaraki suggest, we need to reflect on how media events are both situated within – and a production of – consumer culture in order to understand how particular global events resonate (or not). From the humanitarian spectacle of rock stars (or comedians) caring for famine victims, to the campaign adverts of disaster charities, a specific notion of the viewer subject as someone who might like to craft him or herself through such 'acts' of humanitarian sympathy is performed (Brassett, 2009a). And this mutual contingency of affective discourse and market subject can be rendered as the key theoretical problematic of the global event that underpins this book.

The rest of this chapter will work to situate this problematic within the emerging literature on everyday and cultural political economy. By focusing on the small and apparently mundane activities of everyday market life, authors in this emerging literature necessarily draw out the importance of actors and practices beyond the usual purview of IPE. Gone from central view are states, 'markets', institutions, corporations and 'big' global issues, to reveal the importance of non-elite actors, everyday objects and practices that make up global market life. Far from a unitary or united school of thought, however, this literature can throw up a number of important dilemmas that will serve to focus the theoretical framework of this book. Schematically, I point to the contested definition of politics, different understandings of the role of culture and cultural artefacts and wider ontological commitments to a primordial structure of global capitalism (or indeed a structure-agency problematic, more broadly) as opening the way for a turn to performance and performativity as an important theoretical route forward.

A turn towards the role of everyday actors and practices in IPE has arguably been underway for several years in the work of critical and feminist IPE that identifies the agency of class and the constitutive context of gender for normalising a particular, technical image of markets (Elias and Roberts, 2016). In different ways, feminist scholarship has pointed to the way everyday practices of social re-production, care and love have been gendered, and how this gendered performance often situates women as both intrinsic to market life, yet commonly unrecognised market categories of labour or capital. However, the central thrust for a disciplinary turn towards the everyday came in the work of John Hobson and Len Seabrooke (2007: 15) and their collection on *Everyday Politics of the World Economy*.

In that book, Hobson and Seabrooke seek to draw together a number of disparate trends in critical IPE with certain strands within the sociology of everyday life, especially the work of James Scott, to argue that IPE has been dominated by a top-down, regulatory image of the global economy that focuses on states, institutions and 'large issues' of aggregate growth, employment, trade, investment, etc. Instead, they suggest the metaphor of everyday IPE as a way of – if not uniting, then certainly – arranging the concerns of a diverse range of critical scholars alongside each other as a counterpoint to regulatory or structural ontologies of IPE. On this view, they propose a research agenda whereby IPE would seek to recognise and foreground how the everyday actions of the weak can influence the agendas of elite actors. While the weak are very often marginalised in the 'actually existing' global economy, and everyday actors are therefore very often overlooked in analysis, Hobson and Seabrooke argue that everyday spaces can be far more important than IPE scholarship commonly assumes. In terms of thinking about the everyday politics of the global event, this perspective might helpfully focus attention on the viewer subject, or, indeed, the 'distant others' affected by the event. As a first point of orientation, this is a methodological move that can emphasise the reflective agency of the market subject as opposed to any wider structural vision of global political economy. They therefore enlist the market subject as "an actor" who "uses reason to reflect on conventions and norms, as well as the interests they inform, and then chooses to act in ways which are in accordance with broader intersubjective understandings of what is socially legitimate" (2007: 17). This is therefore, and explicitly, a reflexive and (potentially) critical vision of market subjectivity.

Indeed, for Hobson and Seabrooke (2007: 16–17), a recognition of the capacity for everyday actors to 'resist' wider structures of power or indeed rationality, is a key virtue of the everyday politics perspective they favour. On this view, 'active' forms of bottom-up resistance can lead to political change through different combinations of overt resistance and subversive tactics, which challenge or alter the dominant discourse. In these terms, everyday IPE can be both a recognition of the importance of 'non-elite' actors and – at once – more reflective of the capacity and techniques of resistance available within global market life. Although the "actors concerned may not know that they are contributing to change in the local, national, regional or global contexts" (Hobson and Seabrooke 2007: 18), they can nevertheless be understood as bottom-up drivers of change.

The everyday politics of the global event can thus help us to anticipate a more dynamic, potentially radical account of the subjectivity of viewers and 'distant others' performed. However, while everyday IPE serves to focus attention on a more dynamic conception of the market subject, where agency is foregrounded and a different account of reason as something emergent within a social and political context is established, there are nevertheless certain areas of ambiguity that can further serve to underpin the approach taken here. Firstly, despite the orientation to the everyday, a number of structural precursors remain intact that serve to limit inquiry by establishing a fixed conception of politics and the political. This is reflected, on the one hand, in the founding dichotomy between regulatory and everyday IPE, and the subsequent dichotomy between everyday politics and everyday life perspectives that emerges. By this I mean to suggest that there is a suspicion that everyday IPE is simply a structural model of IPE that is turned upside down, thus the question of relevance to the discipline is still the 'big' subject of global change, continuity, etc.; it is just that the causal line now presents as 'bottom-up' rather than 'top-down'. While this clearly takes us further in understanding the detail and nuance of how a global political economy is 'possible', it nevertheless infers that everyday actors are important insofar as they act in a way that is globally consequential. Empirically, this is an important point – one which can help to identify how certain consumption decisions, savings habits or borrowing patterns can inform larger structural issues in the globally economy. However, one wonders whether the 'everydayness' of everyday IPE becomes, on this view, another form of rational market subjectivity to aggregate? For all the focus on agency in everyday IPE, a number of authors have raised the question of how spaces and people are defined as everyday in the first place. On this view, we potentially forego a deeper level of analysis that seeks to understand the everyday practices and rhythms that make up the very idea of agency within market life. Or as Matt Davies (2016) proposes, the question of the everyday might alternatively be revealed as a critical orientation, per se, in order that we might ask how a supermarket, for example, naturalises through routine, habit and architectural layout, a set of global, colonial and class hierarchies. In terms of the performative politics of the global event, then, a focus on the everyday might also be thought of as a critical question, per se, that asks how the event is portrayed as global, uniting, affective, etc., when it naturalises through performance the differentially experienced and hierarchically stratified experiences of global market life.

Secondly, building from this point, in defining everyday politics as simply a form of non-elite agency, there is a curious limitation placed on experience and politics of everyday life, not the least of which is the apparent understatement of any role for culture. By focusing on an augmented rationality in the agency of market subjects – as they reconcile to or resist wider structures of socially legitimate power – everyday IPE can distract from the thick cultural relations that make subjectivity possible. At one level, this is a question about the range of empirical subjects that can be contained within the concept of the everyday, such as cultural discourses on, say, supermarket shopping that now include discussions of fair trade, worker rights and even the morality of food waste. Where one begins and ends in terms of understanding the supermarket as a cultural artefact is a difficult question, as dependent on everyday practices of shopping as on the gendered discourses of consumption that are performed in cinema and advertising. At another level, however, in rehearsing the agency-structure dichotomy, everyday IPE might close off the complex cultural politics of market life. Analogous to crisis theories of the global event, a background concept of markets and market subjects seems to precede ideas of agency and resistance. Culture becomes one of the available discourses upon which to carry out resistance rather than a performative element in the production of market life (with its attendant conception and valorisation of everyday agency). In terms of the global event, do we 'resist against' or 'emerge through' a humanitarian discourse on distant suffering? Where does the humanitarian discourse begin and end? The rock star might legitimately claim to have been singing about solidarity throughout his or her career and the concept of distant suffering emerges from a genealogy of imperial concern that includes – and – some might argue – reproduces a discourse of 'white man's burden'.

Drawing these points together, it is precisely in foregrounding the importance of *the question of* everyday agency in the politics of market life that we can focus attention on the global event. Against a vision of the global event as something 'large' that 'happens', an everyday approach can echo the literature on the media event by asking about the politics of how such narrative centres are established, how small actors like the audience have an agency to shape the performance of the event and how discourses of the event might themselves mark out the terrain for engaging such a politics. However, in the apparent rationality of the subject, the fixity of politics in a structure-agency dichotomy (albeit bottom-up) and a general quiet-ism over thicker cultural discourses of market life necessitate reflection on the contingency of the 'everyday' in the politics of the global event. For these reasons, I argue, attention to cultural political economy, in general, and the literature on performativity, in particular, might be an important way to illuminate discussion further.

Performing the global event

In this chapter, the politics of the global event has moved from a question of mediation and editorial control – or lack thereof – to a question of performance. How does the spectacle resonate through market life? How do everyday agents engage with the affective discourses of the global event? While authors such as Chouliaraki provide an important diagnosis of the augmentation of the global event within consumer culture, providing a combination of spectacle and an arena for self-crafting spectators to 'explore themselves' through a fleeting connection with distant others, an everyday IPE perspective can focus on the capacity of viewer subjects to engage or resist such possibilities. Despite the attractiveness of this move to foreground the active agency of market subjects, it was argued that the method can risk a separation between discourse and agent, which is artificial and potentially limiting. Instead, I will argue, that attention to the cultural political economy of the global event requires a greater openness to the range of cultural discourses and cultural artefacts that can 'perform' in relation to the global event. The global event does not just happen in a physical or existential way, but is a discursive achievement per se, as dependent upon affective discourses of the event as Hollywood cinema and the mediatisation of political communication. Equally, the everyday agent is not divided from discourse, or 'instrumentalised' to resist the hierarchy of power embodied in discourse. The market subject is performed through discourse and vice versa.

What is performativity, and how can it be understood within cultural political economy? The concept of performativity has had a rapid and sometimes quite specialist uptake in IPE, in general, and the study of financial markets, in particular. Based on a fairly simple yet powerful observation that markets for certain kinds of financial product, like derivatives, did not exist before the formulae that traders use to invest in them; the idea that markets and the wider economy might be *driven* by knowledge has inspired an important set of interventions. This 'thin' conception of performativity draws on J. L. Austen's notion of 'self-actualizing' statements in order to study how certain types of economic knowledge have a constitutive effect. As Michel Callon (1998: 2) put it, "economics, in the broad sense of the term, performs, shapes and formats the economy, rather than observing how it functions". From the constitutive role of particular mathematical models, to the performativity of specific economics and business schools that educate traders, to the wider securitisation of economic policy, performativity has become influential within IPE. Indeed, the development of the concept has spoken to themes and issues in this book by focusing on the performance of financial agency, what some refer to as *agencement*, on the one hand, and the embodied, even theatrical performance of certain actors, such as central bankers, on the other (Morris, 2016; Pryke and du Gay, 2007).

However, while the elaboration of performativity in IPE has provided some interesting resources for the development of this project, I will argue that it is only by turning to the work of Judith Butler to contemplate a 'thicker' conception of performativity that we can develop a cultural political economy of the global event. To wit, I argue that existing approaches to performativity in IPE have been strongly influenced by a 'thin' conception of performativity that orientates to how specific forms of knowledge, or 'speech acts', perform particular forms of market, indeed that the question of the performance of *the economic* has been the primary, almost exclusive concern. A 'thicker' version of performativity would entertain the complex and overlapping cultural discourses of market life, where the question of what it means to live as a market subject is fundamental. In short, any performance of the global event relies on prior performances of a subject who is capable of 'hearing' such things.

In this way, I seek to echo the critical position of Best and Paterson (2010) who seek to move beyond the performative approaches of what they term 'cultural economy' to more fully engage the cultural politics of globalisation. While sympathetic to cultural economy, they argue for the development of two distinct objectives. Firstly, they suggest that this literature can "sometimes underplay the political in cultural political economy". As they surmise,

> There are clearly specific sorts of politics in many of these analyses, often drawn from Foucault's notion of governmentality, and also defined in relation to specific "left" politics, but we would contend that there is not a systematic account of the place of politics – questions of authority and power, and the way they are sustained and contested – in this cultural economy literature.
>
> (Best and Paterson, 2010: 4)

And, secondly, they observe that despite the clear focus on issues pertaining to globalisation like finance, labour and consumption, there is a need to emphasise the "specifically global dimensions to contemporary political-economic life". This is not only a question of scale but also of the cultural connections and entwinements that both emerge from and – in part – produce global market life. Indeed, with reference to the famous HSBC advertising campaign that portrayed itself as "the World's local bank", imploring customers to "think local everywhere", they discuss the cultural performance of globalisation, per se:

> [T]he cultural character of contemporary political economy is decidedly global, both in that there are a set of shared meanings across the globe which enable similar marketing strategies to operate everywhere (even while those strategies highlight cultural difference as a particular marketing ploy) and that specific management cultures become globalized through the strategies of a firm like HSBC.
>
> (Best and Paterson, 2010: 4)

On this view, it is not just a question of the technical process of performing specific markets, or the subjects capable of inhabiting such markets, interesting and analytically sophisticated as such a governmental approach might be. Instead, the task is to comprehend the multiple dimensions and forces at work in the cultural politics of globalisation. From the politics of naming and defining a subject that is, for example, 'global' or 'local', say, or 'global and local' even, to the complex webs of entwinement – political, economic, sociological, etc. – that draw them together, this implies a thicker, altogether more contingent, conception of performativity. Discourses that resonate in cultural political economy are not, in this way, limited to technical formulae, or the actions of economic agents, but may also include – inter alia – post-war documentary films that encourage British subjects to feel sympathy for people living in the colonies, encouraging them to 'buy Empire' (Aitken, 2010); the cultural 'activism' of artists who seek to subvert the idea of money by painting and circulating notes and coin (De Goede, 2005), the way migrant remittance payments emerge as both a marketised set of relations and a discursive supplement to the ethical goals of development (Phillips, 2009) or the way the everyday practice of driving a car can instigate cultural norms of market life like the mass appeal of golf (Paterson, 2017).

Rather than focus on the technical or empirical details of how one or another market discourse becomes performative, I would suggest a cultural political economy is more concerned with how different discourses and subjects emerge, come together, re-inforce, break down or transform; where the question of what it means to be global, or a global market subject, is taken as radically contingent. Beyond the everyday politics of the global event, this approach would seek to ask how a discourse of the global event is naturalised. What discourses of the event and subject are performed? And what practices and routines allow market subjects to emerge within but also produce this everyday politics of the global event? From this perspective, the performative politics concerns the contingency and instability of the discursive performance in question.

Judith Butler (2006) argues that 'gender' as such does not exist beyond the various and manifold performances of the subject of gender, especially, the heterosexual conception of male and female bodies, which – thanks to previously successful iterations of scientific discourses of biology – seems to carry a pre-discursive quality that cannot be deconstructed. However, for Butler, it is the repetition of this discursive binary across cultural discourses of, say, fashion, morality, education, etc., that combines to foreground the heteronormative social structures that read through heterosexual marriage as a social norm, while gay, lesbian or trans lives are 'queer'. It is the "reiterative power of discourse to produce what it names", through attributions of normal and abnormal, over time and across culture that Butler describes as performativity. The politics of this 'reiterative power' lie in the political insight that any attempted closure entailed in a given performative is always already contingent; as Butler (2006) argues, such closures depend on audience reception, uptake, phrasing and – under certain circumstances – the potential for subversive readings. Thus drawing on Butler's famous example, gender may well be performed in heteronormative terms – with a set of oppositions (e.g. to homosexuality and transgender identities) and regulatory hierarchies (e.g. within and between sexes), but the very fact that it depends on such exclusions means that the performative is inherently unstable. As Butler has recently underlined,

> [B]reakdown is constitutive of performativity (performativity never fully achieves its effect, and so in this sense "fails" all the time; its failure is what necessitates its reiterative temporality, and we cannot think iterability without failure). Its moments of breakdown are also important for another version of "critique".
>
> (Butler, 2010: 153)

On this view, it is the discursive performance of the global event as an everyday experience of market life – indeed the very iterability of a viewer subject who is responsive to the affective discourses of trauma and resilience – that must be foregrounded as the political question that drives this book.

Drawing these arguments together, a 'thicker' notion of performativity implies a focus on the contingent emergence of discourses of the global event *across culture* and therefore implies a 'method' that is clearly multi-sited and multi-dimensional, yet I would argue extremely limited by a focus on a specific discourse of the event. In this book, I am proposing to focus in on two specific discourses – trauma and resilience – which will be rendered through a methodological focus that can be divided into three distinct, yet inter-related, streams:

1 *The discourse of the event* (trauma or resilience): How has a certain discourse of the global event emerged? What are its logics? What are its ethics (Chapters 3 and 6)?
2 *A performance of the event* (traumatic or resilient finance): How does a particular performance of the event understand market life? What idea of the subject does it entail? Is the performance successful or does it break down in some way (Chapters 4 and 7)?

3 *The subject of the event* (traumatic or resilient): How is the market subject performed? How does this connect to or confirm existing patterns of market life? How do certain performances, resist and/or subvert these patterns (Chapters 5 and 8)?

Finally, in articulating this framework, I necessarily seek to draw out and celebrate the possibilities of resistance in performativity articulated by Butler, on drag, but as well, more latterly, by Jack Halberstam (2011) on popular culture. As such, my turn to culture – especially in relation to news media, film and comedy (see Chapters 5 and 8) – is not about simply confirming how the everyday 'makes the global'. Rather, I seek to engage the contingency and instability of the discourse/subject as an inquiry into the potentialities of resistance through culture, film and comedy as forms of political intervention per se. Thus while certain cultural products can render a hegemonic or disciplinary performance of the discourse of trauma, or resilience, say, I also seek to identify performances that subvert the established coherence of the affective politics of the global event. As such, my method is explicitly not an attempt to comprehensively reflect the empirical manifestations of a theoretical problematic, but instead seeks to argue that certain cultural artefacts 'do something' important or politically interesting with the idea of the subject at the centre of the discourse of the event.

Conclusion

By recognising the emergence of the media event in global politics, media and communications studies have done much to articulate the politics of the global event around questions of ritual, the construction of a narrative centre and the co-performance between event and consumer culture. Here the work of Chouliaraki is instructive because it draws out the reflexive component in viewer subjects that can speak and hear affective discourses of disaster or humanitarian suffering, while retaining a sense of doubt or 'irony' over their universal veracity. Situating these questions within the literature on everyday politics in IPE, the chapter argued that the relationships between market life and the global event should be understood as intimate and contingent. Understandings of the 'global', indeed of the 'everyday' and 'local', are mutually entwined via overlapping cultural performances; as such, the event becomes a fulcrum, as well as a driver, of a conversation about what it means to be a subject of global market life. In methodological terms, I argue that this points to a performative method that takes seriously the importance and instability of the discourses of the global event. The rest of this book will orientate around two such discourses – trauma and resilience – in order to unpick their various rationalities of the event and its subjects. Schematically, this implies a breakdown into three chapters on each discourse that locate discussion around 1) the discourse of the event, 2) the performance of the event and 3) the subject of the event.

Trauma and the global event

The previous chapters argued that we should take the politics of the global event seriously as an important – and performative – element in market life. Rather than thinking of global events as an 'ordinary' disruption to the 'normal' workings of market life – i.e. a crisis or not – it was argued that we should pay closer attention to the politics of meaning entailed. In this way, a politics of the global can be animated by events such as the *Chilean mine disaster* and *Charlie Hebdo* that exceeds the logics imputed by either cosmopolitan or crisis-oriented arguments. By turning to the everyday and cultural IPE literature, it was argued that a more nuanced performative relationship between discourses of the event and market subjects can be observed. Drawing from Butler, it was argued that discourses of the global event should be understood as productive of meaning and an ongoing contingency of subjectivity. As Butler (2006: xv) recounts,

> I originally took my clue on how to read the performativity of gender from Jacques Derrida's reading of Kafka's "Before the Law." There the one who waits for the law, sits before the door of the law, attributes a certain force to the law for which one waits. The anticipation of the authoritative disclosure of meaning is the means by which that authority is attributed and installed: the anticipation conjures its object.

On this view, the move to think about the performativity of the global event is not merely about adding a list of (cultural) factors to be considered in a (rational) deliberation over discourses, conducted between more-or-less autonomous agents, but rather to suggest that there is a dynamic and uncertain relation between subject and discourse. By problematising these affective relations, how they work, how they are layered over an imaginary of global market life or, indeed, the logic of event-response, we can foreground their malleability. Market subjects can be thought of as fashioning themselves *through*, *within* and/or *against* such discourses.

This section will explore the politics of the global event via an engagement with the discourse of trauma. Trauma has become a salient discourse of global events that crosses psychological theory/practice, news reporting and ethical theory (Kaplan, 2005). While news reporting on the subject of disasters and natural catastrophes has commonly used ideas about emotional shock to portray global events, there has been a step change in recent decades to focus on the idea of 'traumatic effects' (Furedi, 2004: 2). Increasingly, events such as 9/11, the Indian Ocean Tsunami, the Haitian earthquake and the Chilean mine disaster are represented in terms of first-person emotional reactions: of stress, fear and depression, but also nightmares, anxiety and pathologies such as uncontrollable anger or depersonalisation (Fassin and Rechtman, 2009).

Images are clearly an important part of the story here (Bleiker, 2006). It's impossible to think about 9/11, for instance, without the copious amounts of footage and pictures which circulated that day (and the days following). But the reporting of such stories has also begun to foreground the idea of a human 'reaction'. For example, in the immediate aftermath of the Haitian earthquake, 24-hour news coverage began to talk about the sense of shock and fear that accompanies such events. In a small segment, the *Today Program* on Radio 4 managed to interview a group of trauma counsellors who were actually on their way to Haiti, asking them about what they expected to see.[1] They expected to see large communities gripped by shock and fear, a lack of trust and feelings of anger and dread. This (expected) emotive context framed many of the early responses to the event and sought to mobilise public opinion to the needs of survivors: they are in emotional pain; they need 'our' help. On these terms, Dr Marit Brookes remarked about the need for a more expansive idea of the nature and implications of the event:

> [W]hen there is a massive disaster like this, the main concentration has to be to take care of the physical needs of the people; so this is food, water, shelter and physical safety and healthcare. Only once these are addressed can people start to process a traumatic event, to make sense out of it, and after the stage of grief and sorrow and anger and confusion, then people start to process it on a deeper level and some people develop conditions, psychological conditions, where the trauma keeps recurring in their mind.[2]

This linking of trauma to humanitarian discourses appears to be a recurrent editorial line. Taking another example, in 2008, some five years after Chechen 'terrorists' took hostage an entire school in Beslan, the BBC produced a documentary called *Children of Beslan.*[3] Survivors were interviewed against a visual backdrop of horrific images, mostly footage that was previously broadcast live and unedited (a fact which drew complaints at the time, but not in the re-packaged version). In the documentary, survivors talk about how the memories – of torture, the explosions or feeling thirsty – have remained in their minds. One boy talks of anger, another of his nightmares – the film reflects how children were made to drink their own urine. There is sentimental music throughout. By drawing on such traumatic memories – as well, nightmares, flashbacks and anger – a central message of the documentary is that the children of Beslan have post-traumatic stress disorder (PTSD). A clinical diagnosis is placed at the centre of emotive memorial to a traumatic event.

These examples illustrate how trauma can be used to think about *and know* global events in quite personal terms. Emotional language makes the event 'real' for people – viewers who may have little knowledge of the place, the situation or the experience itself. For the viewer, there is something common, even natural, about the feeling of sympathy for people involved in traumatic events. Trauma – the idea of a wound – can speak in almost universal terms about a subject, or a contingency, with which the viewer has little or no relation. Reasonably, of course, this might be a good thing: addressing global events in an emotional register appeals to more people, promoting awareness, understanding and sympathy (Hutchison and Bleiker, 2008). Memorialising such events further underlines the importance of the person, the individual, as the locus of experience. Emotional trauma crosses cultures and languages, even time and space, to make events seem more real, more personal.

The everyday prevalence of trauma in humanitarian discourses means that trauma is also becoming an important part of the political lexicon. State leaders want to be seen to respond with humanity to widespread loss of life. Bill Clinton and George Bush stood united in their visits to disaster zones like Haiti. At the same time, public discourse in America questioned Bush, in particular, because he didn't land his plane in New Orleans after Hurricane Katrina, choosing to fly over the affected areas instead. Kanye West emphasised that this was demonstrative of a lack of solidarity with the suffering of poor black communities affected by Katrina. Others questioned why Bush associated *rather too closely* with those who lost their lives on 9/11. Indeed, after Hurricane Katrina, the jazz pianist *Dr John* re-named his band the 'The Lower 9-11' to signify the hierarchy of traumatic events in public discourse. In these and other ways, trauma has become a focal point for the generation of sympathy, the negotiation of inclusion and exclusion and the judgement of political judgement. In performative terms, we might ask, what is done in the name of trauma? Who is the 'we' of trauma? Do the affective economies of the global event entailed by trauma produce meanings that might form a basis for future performances?

Rendered thus, it is interesting to return to the politics of the Chilean mine disaster. Quite apart from being a 'crisis' for market life, Chapter 1 argued that the way the event was narrated worked to silence what might otherwise be regarded as the specific origin of the disaster – underinvestment, privatisation, poor safety standards, etc. Instead, the event was portrayed as a story about heroic struggle in the face of extreme circumstances (Jimenez-Martinez, 2013). The brave miners became emblematic of the heroism of the nation, and the networks of aid and expertise that responded became an example of the global significance of Chilean development. Emotional discourses of trauma, I would argue, played an important role in this media performance:

> Last week the world rejoiced at the miraculous contact made with the 33 trapped Chilean miners who were found alive 700m underground. But now officials are struggling to keep the men from sinking into a spiral of

> depression. [. . .] "They are more isolated, they don't want to be on screen, they are not eating well. I would say that depression is the correct word," said Chilean health minister [. . .] "Following the euphoria of being discovered, the normal psychological reaction would be for the men to collapse in a combination of fatigue and stress," explained Dr Rodrigo Figueroa, head of the trauma, stress and disaster unit at the Catholic University in Santiago, Chile.
>
> (Franklin, 2010)

In this instance, knowledge about trauma is used to naturalise the event and to secure the ethical significance of a set of emotional 'reactions'. The traumatic discourse deployed here performs ideas about emotion and the event, but it does so through a certain appeal to expertise: health professionals and psychologists. The politics of such events is not just about 'solving the problem' – whether it be saving lives or surviving the storm. Instead, a cultural economy of 'knowing the event' through trauma has emerged where individuals become a subject of medical observation judged according to their 'normal psychological reaction' (Pupavac, 2004). Such knowledge is designed to bring us closer to the people involved, mediating their experience in emotional terms. Indeed, the turn to emotion can be used to relate from the individual and their experiences to the family, and, therefore, the wider community:

> Carolina Lobos, daughter of trapped miner and former football star Franklin Lobos, told reporters: "We have all changed because of this. Before it was not very common for people in my family to say 'I love you' or 'I miss you'. Now I call my mum every night, I tell her how much I love her and I send kisses. Now we are all valuing each other much more the people we have by our sides."
>
> (Franklin, 2010)

Traumatic events are thus portrayed as having an 'ethical' potential: to bring people together. The realisation of our common vulnerability, the possibility of isolation becomes a mechanism for highlighting the importance of human relations (as we struggle through the events of market life). This might be family, or the community or the nation, as per the frequent references to a 'brave nation' by the Chilean president and various staged moments, such as the singing of the national anthem by the miners. And thus on these terms, a traumatic discourse of the global event is potentially powerful. Trauma, on this view, has the ability to weave together ideas about the individual and the community, as well as emotion, bravery and political purpose. From a performative perspective, however, this is a contingent cultural political economy that provokes a further set of questions: Who is included in this discourse? Who is excluded from it? What is done in its name?

The performative politics of the traumatic discourse of the global event is the primary concern of this section, which is divided into three chapters. Taken together, the chapters present a critical analysis of the generalisation of traumatic discourses of the global event. In the wake of 9/11, Chapter 3 discusses how a range of ethical theorists turned to embrace the idea of this traumatic event as a potential opening to a more sensitive and reciprocal politics (Brassett, 2011). Traumatic events, it was argued, had the ability to reveal our vulnerability, our collective capacity to suffer, and, therefore, it might have an ethical power to displace enmities, borders or other group-based oppositions (Archibugi, 2001; Linklater, 2002). The recognition of trauma, it was supposed, might be an important basis for building global solidarity in response to this global event. Important as this ethical dimension was to post-9/11 ethical discourse, however, I argue that it risks overlooking a long tradition of critical engagement with knowledge about trauma (Young, 1995). Genealogies of trauma are contested, and their politics is by no means homogenous or clear-cut, but an over-riding proposition is that trauma has a place and a history, different interpretation, and a set of (more-or-less governmental) effects (Edkins, 2003; Fassin, 2012). On this view, I argue that the politics of vulnerability that certain ethical theorists read into 9/11 must – at some level – provoke a contingent engagement with trauma discourses themselves. A turn to the literature and practice of trauma counselling suggests that knowledge about trauma performs these emotional and ethical relations between individuals in particular and limited ways (Pupavac, 2001). In short, the chapter argues that trauma is best understood as an 'emergent language' of market life: it posits a subject, which can be affected by, and responsive to, 'events'. This existential foundation is then performative of an everyday repertoire that can generate sympathy, define insiders and outsiders, etc. How we inhabit this repertoire – this mutual contingency of discourse and subject – is a question I explore over subsequent chapters.

On these terms, subsequent chapters move beyond an exclusive focus on events that revolve around the 'actual experience' of trauma, in a clinical sense, in order to engage the more widespread and open usage of the term in everyday life as a metaphor of pain. Following Fassin and Rechtman (2009), I argue that this more metaphorical meaning of trauma – as a wound, or a general expression of pain – has licensed a generalisation of this discourse of the event through what Kaplan calls 'trauma culture'. Chapter 4 extends and animates this argument via an engagement with the discursive performance of the sub-prime crisis as a traumatic event. Elements of the discourse of the sub-prime crisis seemed to reflect similar traumatic characteristics to 9/11, especially insofar as it sought to license a quick response to this financial event that foregrounded the vulnerability of everyday financial subjects (Samman, 2016). The widespread metaphor of a 'financial tsunami' performed on helpless victims a level of shock and devastation that engulfed the 'world' and constituted the basis for an intriguing set of humanitarian governance manoeuvres. The bank bailout was conducted in humanitarian terms, financial governance was re-phrased as disaster control and the emotional plight of victims performed a curious 'financial community' (Brassett and Clarke, 2012). However, the chapter argues that this is not just a story about affective discipline to neo-liberal common sense. The political contingency of trauma – indeed, its selective application to certain events and not others – suggests a degree of malleability. The mutual contingency of discourse and subject further implies that subjects can speak the language of trauma in different or critical terms. Beyond the governmental potentialities of trauma, an acute political contestability of trauma is identified in Chapter 5 that seeks to engage the limits of these affective economies of the global event. Importantly, I argue, the contingent subjects of trauma are understood as self-reflective, even resistant, and a number of strategies for *occupying the trauma narrative* towards critical political ends are explored. These occupations can be democratic, critical or subversive, but they all play on the idea that market subjects can perform market life beyond or through a set of (apparent) performative limits. From the identification of the abject subjects of Katrina, to satirical interventions on trauma culture in comedy cinema, I seek to engage a number of ways in which we can speak trauma beyond a logic of event-response, actively politicising the categories of victim/survivor in the process. On these terms, the market subject retains a potential to occupy and engage the instabilities (and hierarchies) of the affective economies of the global event. Somewhat ironically, it is one version of this potential autonomy of market subjects, their emotional literacy or at least their adaptability in relation to events which is taken up by the resiliency discourse in the next section.

Notes

1 *Today Program*, Interview of Lizelle Howes and Dr Marit Brookes. http://news.bbc.co.uk/today/hi/today/newsid_8462000/8462906.stm (last accessed: 31/08/10)

2 *Today Program*, Interview of Lizelle Howes and Dr Marit Brookes. http://news.bbc.co.uk/today/hi/today/newsid_8462000/8462906.stm (last accessed: 31/08/10)

3 http://news.bbc.co.uk/1/hi/programmes/newsnight/8227119.stm (last accessed: 21/05/13). Full Film now available at www.youtube.com/watch?v=Nxa3SqgZ7Sg (last accessed: 07/07/17)

3 Trauma and global ethics

Affective politics of the event

Introduction: 9/11 and the politics of trauma ethics

The tragedy of 9/11 was widely portrayed as marking a traumatic event for the inhabitants of New York and America: many people, 'innocents', died in a horrific and largely uncontrollable fashion. Media images of shock and devastation – planes hitting towers, towers burning, then collapsing and smoke filling the city skyline – were relayed around the world repeatedly. The 9/11 terrorist attack was compared historically to Pearl Harbour in the US – an event marking the complete surprise and humbling of a nation. Importantly, though, the story of 9/11 was played out in terms of individuals, the poor people on the planes and in the buildings, falling bodies, brave police and firefighters and thousands covered in concrete powder (Edkins, 2002). The political significance of this global event was established very quickly – and straightforwardly – in terms of the question of *how to respond?* This traumatic event, it was argued, required a (meaningful) response (Holland, 2013).

> For New Yorkers, the events that transpired on the morning of 11 September, 2001 must have seemed like a nightmare. Immediately after the attack on the World Trade Centre that day, psychologists predicted that a wave of trauma would sweep across the country [. . .], it is estimated that some 530,000 New York City residents suffered from symptoms of post-traumatic stress disorder (PTSD) in the months following the attack.
>
> (Costandi, 2011)

While some leaders and political advocates sought to honour the feelings and memory of the dead with an aggressive display of (hyper) security, bent on revenge, justice and the assertion of power in the face of vulnerability, others had a different take. Many, adopting a broadly ethical position, sought to 'use' 9/11 as a moment to reflect on whether and how such a traumatic event could mark the beginning of a new global ethics (Archibugi, 2001). On this view, the radical exposure to vulnerability that 9/11 (re)presented could become a point of openness to solidarity: a coming together of vulnerable lives (Butler, 2004). In its capacity to reach beyond the simple fact of death and identify how people, others, loved ones, relations, even passive bystanders, could be affected, this traumatic event stood as a potential totem for mediating and understanding vulnerability. The ethical potential of thinking about the traumatic event in terms of vulnerability was reflected across a range of ethical theorists. One cosmopolitan orientation suggested that 9/11 might change the way we think about globalisation and global interconnectedness in a way that might foreground the political significance of different forms of violence (Habermas, 2003). On this view, the trauma of 9/11 challenged us to accept an important ethical context: the collective possibility for humans to experience suffering. As Andrew Linklater (2002: 303) argued,

> The violent acts of September 11 and the war against al-Qaeda and the Taliban are unique in raising profound questions about how modern societies should deal with many diverse forms of suffering. Modern societies face the challenge of ensuring that efforts to protect innocent civilians from terrorist attacks do not damage the moral ideal of freeing all human beings from unnecessary suffering.

However, for others like Judith Butler (2004), 9/11 was understood differently, as an opportunity to engage in a 'politics of mourning' where life and grief, and, specifically, the question of whose lives are *grieve-able* could become a way of finding a point of identification with the very question of suffering itself. This ethical-political question of grieve-ability ushered at the hierarchies and exclusions that pertain to concepts such as suffering and vulnerability: *Whose suffering? Whose vulnerability?*

In these ways, a politics of the traumatic event emerges whereby we must question the emotive tones of the ethical response. As the introduction to this book argued, there is an affective politics of the event. Indeed, a number of critical scholars questioned the emotional 'scripting' of public responses to 9/11. For authors such as Frank Furedi, the outpouring of personal emotion in public spaces, and through the media, became a convenient background for a wider set of governance manoeuvres that might be termed 'therapy culture' (Furedi, 2004). The adoption of trauma and suffering as the dominant frame for interpreting 9/11 therefore carried a governmental potential, whereby emotion could work as a legitimating discourse of power. In this way, I argue, trauma carries a profound ethical ambiguity that has huge potential for animating the politics of global events in critical terms. On the one hand, it makes sense, *indeed it is laudable*, to try and understand terrible events of death and destruction in a manner that emphasises their ethical possibility. In the context of the war on terror, an ethical focus on vulnerability and the reflex to reduce pain and suffering across the globe appear highly attractive. On the other hand, we must question what is done in the name of ethics. By taking trauma and the traumatic event as a basis for ethical discussion, a number of limits are produced and naturalised. In particular, we might question why this particular event? Why not another? For instance, as cosmopolitans have long recognised, many more people died across the world from poverty-related causes on 9/11 than did so in the terrorist attacks (or indeed the War on Terror) (Brassett, 2008). The emplacing of this particular traumatic event – and the widespread expectation that 9/11 would cause people to suffer from PTSD – provides an indication of how a particular medicalised version of trauma ethics was in the ascendance (Fassin and Rechtman, 2009).

My central argument is that knowledge about trauma must be understood in a contingent relation with the event of 9/11: the knowledge that surrounds trauma and the practices of governance that are perpetuated in its name. It is a particular conception of the event within knowledge about trauma that allows for – *indeed promotes* – the emotional scripts that critical scholars such as Furedi identify. Ideas about traumatic effects, normal psychological responses and collective pain are neither neutral nor universal. Their mobilisation in a political context of sovereign power, and emergent (if unclear) communities of fate, seems to endorse a range of political agendas, which require scrutiny in terms of their affective politics – i.e. us/them, hierarchies of grief, etc. Once established as a language of the event, however, trauma ethics may be performative of new discourse and relations of the global event. In short, *knowledge about* the traumatic event can spread.

This argument is developed over three sections. The section on **Trauma ethics** examines the ethical position that 9/11 can mark a point of identification with vulnerability. Cosmopolitan arguments were central to the ethical response to 9/11, and numerous reformist politicians and civil society activists promoted cosmopolitan agendas as the 'sensitive' and 'progressive' response to this event. However, developing from the argument in Chapter 1, such agendas can over-determine the role of the global event, taking it as signal for greater integration and understanding, while downplaying the political ambiguities entailed by such an ethics. In particular, the cosmopolitan reflex to promote justice and democracy on a global scale can reduce questions of vulnerability to a de-politicised logic – i.e. that justice and inclusion will tranquilise grievance, dissent or opposition. Instead, the politics of vulnerability identified by Butler suggests that we must remain sensitive to how 'certain lives' matter more than others in global politics. On this view, the mediation and interpretation of the event as traumatic becomes a central element in its politics. Indeed, emotive tones of 'national trauma' meant for some that it "was difficult to distinguish calls for a recognition of the trauma from calls for revenge" (Edkins, 2003: 19). This politics of ethics, I argue, suggests a recourse to the critical literature on trauma and specifically the governmental potentials of PTSD.

The section on **The affective politics of trauma** argues that traumatic events such as 9/11 actually present a special set of challenges for grounding an ethical response. Firstly, we encounter the general sense in which trauma is understood to afflict a group or a nation. This communal feeling of trauma is highly resonant yet deeply problematic, especially when woven to grand strategic responses. Secondly, the moral dimensions of trauma manifest prominently, yet differently, through a psychological valorisation of the individual as a moral subject. Here we must question how modern (medical) knowledge about trauma performs a number of limits. The blurring of individual and communal discourses of trauma is an important dimension in the politics of the global event. Critics of 'therapeutic governance' argue that modern knowledge about trauma reduces the ethics of vulnerability to a technology of sympathy that 1) de-politicises the subject/event via the treatment of all concerned as 'mere victims', 2) re-ifies particular norms of correct emotional behaviour via the generalisation of problem-solving rationalities such as 'Cognitive-Behavioural Therapy' (CBT) and 3) subsequently labels trauma survivors as either 'helpless' or (ironically) 'potential threats' to the security of themselves or others. The abstraction of the event from any historical or political contingency works to defer a politics of vulnerability to scientific judgement: recover or fail, express sympathy or be uncaring/hurtful, etc. Agency is diminished and communal/sovereign/governmental responses appear legitimate through their embrace of trauma ethics.

While sympathetic to both the importance and gravity of the experience of trauma, and the centrality it is accorded in the politics of global events, the section on **Trauma as an everyday language of the event** questions how we might critically engage the limits of trauma. This affective politics suggests that knowledge about trauma is clearly an important emotive register for critical engagement with the politics of global events. Rather than embrace it as 'obviously ethical', or dismiss it as 'straightforwardly governmental', I argue that the task is to engage critically its performative ambiguities. I, therefore, turn to the work of Didier Fassin, who seeks to re-imagine trauma as a 'new language' of the global event, which brings together ideas about suffering and individual subjectivity in a productive ambiguity. It is neither straightforwardly ethical, though it certainly commands ethical power, nor is it deterministically limiting, even while it prioritises so much in 'expert knowledge'. Instead, it emerges as a contingent language for understanding and engaging with difficult elements of global politics: violence, suffering, indeed market life. Key is the production of the event/response narrative of emotional ethics as an affective economy that is central to the performance of subsequent global events. The contingency of this language, though, implies that subjects retain an agency to speak and live trauma otherwise – a point developed in the following chapters.

Trauma ethics

The political significance of 9/11, and the importance of building a meaningful response, was established very quickly. In a sharp distinction to the rhetoric of mainstream political responses to 9/11 – e.g. 'with us or against us', capture Bin Laden 'dead or alive', 'the axis of evil', etc. – a range of ethical approaches were marked out by an emphasis on understanding and learning, and a set of efforts aimed at avoiding the future production of terrorism. This global event, it was argued, should have a thoroughly global response.

Cosmopolitan authors, such as Jurgen Habermas (2003) and David Held (2002), argued that the emphasis should lie with global institutions, international laws to extend citizenship rights, participatory democracy and the redistribution of wealth on a global scale. In this way, they also underlined how violence and vulnerability were not only products of terrorism but also could be read into the everyday details of market life, inequality, malnutrition, etc. However, while this approach does much to situate the global event of 9/11 within a politics of global market life, a number of limits for thinking about 'the political' in relation to trauma were also established. Authors such as Judith Butler (2004) and Jacques Derrida (2003) emphasised a 'politics of vulnerability', whereby certain hierarchies of trauma and suffering were being established. Their emphasis on the limits of such agendas raises questions about our ability to know what 'trauma' or 'vulnerability' 'is' or how sovereign assumptions that pervade global governance might entrench particular and exclusionary logics. This lays the theoretical ground upon which to engage with questions about trauma knowledge in the next section.

Trauma and the cosmopolitan response

Trauma, in the modern therapeutic sense, is used to refer to the experience of an event where our lives, or the life of someone close to us, are threatened, where we have no control over what is happening, and where basic feelings of security are put in fundamental question (Bisson, 2007). Many trauma sufferers have trouble dealing with the event and will either repress the memory or strongly dissociate from the feelings of vulnerability associated with it, using guilt, anger or radical hope as a way of 'using' the event in the life continued. As Jenny Edkins argues,

> Trauma is very much to do with the fact of survival in the face of death. The repetition that takes place in the dreams of trauma sufferers is not so much an attempt to make sense of the trauma itself, but an attempt to come to terms with the fact of survival.
>
> (Edkins, 2002: 247)

And on a societal level she says,

> In our everyday lives, we prefer to forget our vulnerability. We pretend that it is possible to be completely secure and safe. Death is an accident or a failure, something that could be avoided with better protection or better systems of healthcare. If there appears to be some threat to this security, people immediately look for ways to make themselves feel secure again.
>
> (Edkins, 2002: 247)

On this view, 9/11 can be seen as a significant event for ethics, because it brings the issue of vulnerability to the centre of America and Europe. Television images of planes crashing into buildings, people jumping from buildings, the shocked faces of passers-by and the strange looking cloud of smoke that engulfed the city generally do not tally with our generalised expectations of normal life. Equally, the intensification of security politics in the wake of 9/11, through public discussion of 'revenge' military strikes, to find Bin Laden 'dead or alive', etc., prompted an impassioned response from civil society against the War on Terror (Giardina and Weems, 2004). Cosmopolitan authors captured this mood.

Writing soon after 9/11, Daniele Archibugi set out what he termed the 'simple ethical principle' that underpins a cosmopolitan response to this traumatic event: "It is necessary to give equal value to human life, irrespective of whether an individual belongs to 'our' or to 'another' political and social community" (Archibugi, 2001: 4). In times of war, when such principles are forgotten, he argued that the deployment of certain basic agendas could help to "equalise the value of our lives with the value of the lives of others" (Archibugi, 2001: 4). The hope was, for Archibugi, that by recognising the value of the individual lives of all, including terrorists, or at least the areas and communities where terrorists might be constructed, then the production of future 'enemies/threats' will be lessened. Democratic participation, it was supposed, could work to involve disaffected peoples in debates about world politics in a way that a global war on terror could not possibly hope to achieve (Dryzek, 2006).

This faith in the power of cosmopolitan global governance chimes with the response of Jurgen Habermas (2003). Speaking just a few months after 9/11, he argued that cosmopolitanism could provide a way forward, but he tried to contemplate the political strategies that may be required. He identified the "clever, albeit fragile, coalition against terrorism brought together by the US government" that "might, in the most favorable case, be able to advance the transition from classical international law to a cosmopolitan order" (2003: 27). However, he questioned why European powers have failed to support any such possibilities. Despite the strategic elements of this proposition, it is interesting to note how the cosmopolitan response attempts to link the suffering and vulnerability of the event to a wider global problematic. The 9/11 attack is taken as a signal event to remind ourselves that suffering is an ongoing product of global market life:

> Without the political taming of an unbounded capitalism, the devastating stratification of the world will remain intractable. The disparities in the dynamic of world economic development would have to at least be balanced out regarding their most destructive consequences – the deprivation and misery of complete regions and continents comes to mind. This does not merely concern the discrimination toward, the humiliation of, or the offense to other cultures. The so-called "clash of civilizations" is often the veil masking the vital material interests of the West.
>
> (Habermas, 2003: 36)

Habermas was far from alone in this understanding of the ills of globalisation. His concern for the "the discrimination toward, the humiliation of, or the offense to other cultures" was ever present in the leftist discourses, where a mix of poverty and Palestine was often invoked to explain the emergence of terrorism (Milne, 2001). A progressive response to the trauma of 9/11 should inspire us to act to reduce such global vulnerabilities then. An appropriate cosmopolitan response is therefore ascertained as 'more global governance', albeit along more social democratic lines. Archibugi (2001: 8) argued that Europe has to rediscover the pride of guiding the world through a period as difficult as the present one, not only by hunting down the terrorists but also by promoting economic development plans in the Third World with programs analogous to the Marshall Plan. This possibility was echoed by David Held (2002: 8), who argued,

> Cosmopolitan multilateralization cannot be built on the American model of geopolitics and international engagement, especially as conceived by the Republican right after 9/11, which constitutes a new form of global unilateralism. The European social experiment – pursued on the model of social democratic values and the noble experiment in collaborative governance: the EU – points a way forward.

Trauma and the limits of response

Cosmopolitan responses to 9/11 highlight two important tenets: 1) a concern to provide an alternative response to the mainstream, US, media response and 2) a deep concern with how to prevent the production of future terrorist atrocities. This is because they identified a moral equivalence between the vulnerability exposed by 9/11 and the 'discrimination', 'humiliation' and 'unnecessary suffering' that inhibits lives and causes resentment in the world. For these reasons, there is a confident suggestion that cosmopolitan global governance is an important resource to draw from as it outlines two kinds of inclusive, social democratic principles that could be used to render global politics in more egalitarian terms. Indeed, this was an interesting blur between ethics and strategy; as David Held quipped, "Globalization without cosmopolitanism could fail" (Held, 2002: 9).

However, for a number of post-structural authors, the politics of this ethics must be placed in question. On this view, the otherwise laudable cosmopolitan responses to 9/11 may risk closing the political moment where we might question the subjectivities and rationalities that make suffering possible in the first place. Such arguments are of crucial significance for thinking through the possibilities and limits of a cosmopolitan response to trauma, because they question how ethics is political, per se. As Rob Walker argues, for these reasons "cosmopolitanism must be read as a constitutive aspect of the problems that many of those attracted to cosmopolitanism seek to address" (Walker, 2003: 268). This is not so much a rejection of cosmopolitan sensibilities as an invitation to think through their contingent ambiguity. Indeed, philosophers such as Jacques Derrida were often highly sympathetic to cosmopolitan impulse stating, "In the first place" and "as imperfect as they may be . . . international institutions should be respected in their deliberations", if only as a temper on the "serious failings of 'Western' states" in their commitment to international agreements (Derrida, 2003: 114). However, he argued that, when seeking to embed cosmopolitan norms via institutions and law, "reflection (of what I would call a "deconstructive" type) should . . . without diminishing or destroying these axioms and principles, question and refound them, endlessly refine and universalize them" (Derrida, 2003: 114). This argument about the potential limits of global governance worked to re-emplace the problem of sovereignty in political thought per se:

> I'm not unaware of the apparently utopic character of the horizon I'm sketching out here, that of an international institution of law and an international court of justice with their own autonomous force. Though I do not hold law to be the last word on ethics, politics or anything else, though this unity of force and law . . . is not only utopic but aporetic (since it implies that beyond the sovereignty of the nation-state, indeed beyond democratic sovereignty – whose onto-theological foundations must be deconstructed – we would nonetheless be reconstituting a new figure, though not necessarily state-related, of universal sovereignty, of absolute law with an effective autonomous force at its disposal), I continue to believe that it is faith in the possibility of this impossible and, in truth undecidable thing from the point of view of knowledge, science and conscience that must govern our decisions.
>
> (Derrida, 2003: 115)

Derrida's faith in the 'possibility of this impossible' ethics, this 'aporia' for the cosmopolitan response can therefore provoke us to consider the politics of trauma ethics. Even in critiquing Western state responses to 9/11, cosmopolitans perform a new violence: the sovereign logics of global governance layer up a hierarchy of political life that replaces revenge with 'humanitarian care' (Brassett, 2008). From a critical perspective, questions arise as to who is able to feel such care, who is included in the realm of care and who is excluded? The claim seems to be that – as a result of 9/11 – we now know what vulnerability is because 'we have experienced it', so now we can 'help you'. The emotional vulnerability that is embodied in 9/11 seems to be replaced by a comforting impulse that 'we can do something about it'; sovereign power is re-phrased globally through emotional sensitivity.

In *Precarious Life*, Judith Butler suggests that the potential for an ethical response to 9/11, to the trauma caused by terrorism and to suffering is curtailed by the monopolisation of the legitimate meaning of 9/11 in public discourse. The very possibility of questioning the mainstream narrative of the attacks is cut off by logics like 'with us or against us'. Even the profusion of critical and conspiracy theory-type responses that typified the post-9/11 period confirmed the centrality and self-obsession of the US with its place at the centre of the world. Deeper understandings, mourning for the loss of life, mourning for the other and the possibility of even recognising the suffering of others are curtailed. Butler, therefore, places a 'politics of mourning' at the forefront of her analysis. Such arguments are not 'anti-cosmopolitan'; indeed, they might be seen as congruent. But the politics of global ethics is foregrounded so that easy answers, simple programs of governance and other forms of sovereign politics must be placed in question. In short, laudable ethical sentiments to 'respond' should not be subsumed within a programmatic global agenda that itself closes down consideration of what 'vulnerability' might entail. As Butler (2004: 30) suggests,

> To grieve, and to make grief itself into a resource for politics, is not to be resigned to inaction, but it may be understood as the slow process by which we develop a point of identification with suffering itself. [. . .] this can be a point of departure for a new understanding if the narcissistic preoccupation of melancholia can be moved into a consideration of the vulnerability of others. Then we might critically evaluate and oppose the conditions under which certain human lives are more vulnerable than others, and thus certain human lives are more grievable than others.

By this she means to argue that certain hierarchies of pain and trauma are performatively established in public discourse (see also Zehfuss, 2009). A traumatic event like 9/11, which seems to demand a response, can overshadow the difficulty of coming to terms with loss, indeed of having life. In both the mainstream and cosmopolitan 'response' to the global event of 9/11, it is 'our trauma' that works as a straightforward foundation for a set of limited and – in Derrida's view – impossible agendas. Following Butler, the question arises as to whether and how we can know what trauma is? What is the knowledge that suggests trauma demands a response?

The affective politics of trauma

The previous section argued that the ethics of trauma and specifically the ethics of responding to a traumatic event are ambiguous. On one level, it might be suggested that cosmopolitan responses to 9/11 are 'sensitive' to trauma; there has been a clear focus on the loss of life; the indiscriminate use of violence highlighted must in some sense focus our minds on vulnerability. There is also a laudable recognition that 'others' are susceptible to suffering, whether as a result of global capitalism or the violence of Western states' foreign policy (Habermas, 2003). On another level, however, there is a danger that cosmopolitanism might efface the politics of the traumatic event via a simple narrative of global hope: hope that we can learn, hope that we can improve and hope that we can make the world a better place. Of course, such narratives are important at any time, but as a response to trauma, they perhaps overshadow the complex experience and politics of vulnerability: when faced with existential questions about 'our own' vulnerability, we respond with models of global utopias to export to 'others' (see also Ahmed, 2013: 22).

Instead, I would argue that the politics of trauma is ambiguous and complex. Attitudes towards trauma are not 'always' uniting, or other regarding, and can equally lead to divisive and alienating responses. Indeed, feelings of trauma, when performed on a mass level, are apt for manipulation, can be structured by power and can feed larger antagonisms (Pupavac and Pupavac, 2012). Thus, at some level, we must engage with the aporetic nature of trauma, that trauma is to some extent un-speakable and un-knowable. On this view, it neither 'naturally' divides nor unites, but is a subject of knowledge and therefore politics.

This section will consider the idea put forward by critical scholars that one of the key limits to our ability to understand vulnerability and trauma in the wake of 9/11 was a pervasive 'scripting' of the event through specific forms of knowledge about trauma, therapy and emotion (Edkins, 2003; Furedi, 2004). If trauma works as a form of therapeutic governance, in this way, it can have significant implications for how we are to think about the politics of the global event (Pupavac, 2001). If trauma and vulnerability have – through therapy culture – become forms of governance, then their use as critical devices for framing ethical responses is highly limited *and limiting*. Against this diagnosis, I argue that we need to recover the performative politics of knowledge about trauma, how it conceives of the event and the traumatic subjects of the event. This lays the basis for thinking about trauma as a contingent language of the event in the section on **Trauma as an everyday language of the event**.

Trauma culture

As the introduction argued, there is a contingent and ambiguous politics to affect (Ahmed, 2013). It is not simply that feeling is 'good' or 'ethical', but rather there is a social and political context for emotion. In a global context, the social and political situation of emotion can be hierarchical along racial, gendered or class lines (Pedwell, 2012). The affective politics of the traumatic event are therefore set within structures of power that privilege certain forms of market life, not the least of which, as many critical scholars argue, is the Western form of liberal individualism. Indeed, for critical sociologists such as Frank Furedi (2004: 1), affect has taken on an almost hegemonic air in contemporary capitalism: "We live in a culture that takes emotions very seriously. In fact, it takes them so seriously that virtually every challenge or misfortune that confronts people is represented as a direct threat to their emotional well-being" (Furedi, 2004: 1). In this vein, Furedi points to the increasing use of therapeutic language in everyday culture – e.g. in *The Sopranos* or Oprah – by raising the question of whether the move to emotion can actually be understood as a conservative gesture, an affective evacuation of wider political concerns. On this view, the language of emotionalism has come to pervade popular culture, the workplace and schools, indeed everyday life in a way that clouds our ability to think and practice critique. Thus rather than forming a potentially ethical take on traumatic events like 9/11, Furedi argues that the language of therapy has become somewhat populist, cheapened through its generalisation in culture, more of an element in consumption and entertainment. As Furedi (2004: 1) argues,

> The vocabulary of therapeutics no longer refers to unusual problems or exotic states of mind. Terms like stress, anxiety, addiction, compulsion, trauma, negative emotions, healing, syndrome, mid-life crisis or counselling refer to the normal episodes of daily life. They have also become part of our cultural imagination. Most viewers did not think it bizarre when Tony Soprano, head of America's favourite gangster family, went to see Pyschiatrist Dr Jennifer Melfi.

Importantly, he argues, this normalisation of emotion within 'therapy culture' can be thought of as providing a script through which emotional logics make their way into the cultural vernacular and become available for the construction of everyday reality. Indeed, Furedi examines how US responses to 9/11 focused on the emotional and therapeutic dimensions of the event, where grief was taken as the common feature of the experience: "The emotional script communicated was one that also sought to create a sense of unity around a common experience of vulnerability" (Furedi, 2004: 13). And through these affective responses, therapy culture actively mediates – indeed governs – the relationship between the community and the individual:

> The post-September 11 exhortations to mobilise collective grief to create memorials represents an important departure from previous norms of memorialisation. [. . .] Such an orientation towards remembrance reflects a powerful shift away from the more traditional affirmation of communal purpose. It represents an important shift towards encouraging people to find meaning through their individual selves. This move from a bereaved community to a community of bereaved expresses the individualising imperative at work in society.
>
> (Furedi, 2004: 14)

And here lies an important ambiguity in the discourse of trauma ethics: the elision of communal and individual trauma helps us to understand how the political economy of the global event is performative of individuality. What if by embracing modern theories of trauma, the impulse to build a global ethics of the traumatic event is productive of the very individuating tendencies it claims to question?

In order to explore the limits of trauma ethics, then, I argue that we need to engage with the production of knowledge about the trauma event. By this I mean to suggest that the modern usage of trauma is contingent upon the mobilisation of certain ideas about the individual and their capacity to experience pain, that have been generalised through what Allan Young (1995) described as the 'invention' of PTSD. For example, Alison Howell draws from Foucault to look at how certain forms of knowledge become 'regimes of truth'. She looks at how Foucault urged us to move beyond a view of madness as "something that exists outside of our constructions of it" and that; as such, Foucault was interested in historicizing the ways in which madness came to be divided from reason: "the gradual division of madmen from reasoned men in the name of public order and security, confined those deemed mad to carceral sites, and established codes of respectability and of discipline for all subjects" (Foucault, 1988: x; cf. Howell, 2011: 39). Howell therefore looks at psychology as a framework of knowledge that can work to constitute particular regimes of truth around madness, broadly understood, and PTSD more specifically. In this, she engages a politics of what she terms "diagnostic competition", whereby positive (and therefore moral) attributes are imposed. She stresses, "This stance is critical of the psy disciplines, but not antipsychiatry per se", because "[s]uch work is important in theorizing diagnoses as invented modes of reasoning, in providing critical histories of the political effects of the invention of various diagnostic categories, and in rendering the psy disciplines subject to scrutiny" (Howell, 2011: 63).

On this view, the politics of affect is more complicated than the potential conservatism identified by Furedi and asks us to reckon with the emergence and deployment of knowledge about trauma. The contemporary psychological definition of trauma is a positivist notion that rests on an identifiable combination of event and symptoms (Fassin and Rechtman, 2009). The standard criteria for classification of mental disorders, *Diagnostic and Statistical Manual of Mental Disorders* (*DSM-IV*) criteria, now involve some combination of the following: 're-experiencing phenomena' including intrusive memories, dreams and physiological/psychological distress to cues, acting/feeling as if events are recurring; 'avoidance and numbing', including avoidance of thoughts, feelings, reminders, amnesia, reduced affect; and 'increased arousal', including sleep difficulty, irritability or outbursts of anger, hyper vigilance, exaggerated startle response and difficulty concentrating (Bisson, 2007: 399). Other common pathologies include survivor's guilt: shame that others died/suffered and the survivor did not (Caruth, 1995). In common is the proposition that a trauma victim can become 'stuck in the moment' overwhelmed by fear, guilt and shame that this event could happen to them.

On the one hand, this clinical definition has clearly benefitted numerous people by providing the possibility of diagnosis and treatment. On the other hand, as a form of psychological knowledge that has increasingly generalised through therapy culture, we must be sensitive to how this 'invented mode of reasoning' comes down to earth, indeed how it attaches to wider political structures and agendas. For a number of authors, the popularity of trauma as a framework of knowledge that informs disaster response and conflict resolution in international aid agencies and humanitarian NGOs (psychiatric or otherwise) is deeply problematic. For example, Vanessa Pupavac speaks of a new form of 'therapeutic governance', suggesting that its very success is a cause for concern:

> Trauma is displacing hunger in the West's conceptualisation of the impact of wars and disasters in the South. Our attention is drawn to the psychological suffering of victims, their emotional scars, their sense of despair and helplessness. Viewing experiences through a therapeutic lens, trauma counselling, or what is known as psycho-social intervention, has become an integral part of the humanitarian response in wars. Invariably reports flag up the need for counsellors to be brought in to help the community 'come to terms' with its suffering.
>
> (Pupavac, 2001: 358)

In this way, we can see how modern knowledge about trauma can actually infuse structures of governance on a global scale (Brassett and Vaughan-Williams, 2012a). The way that knowledge about trauma is mobilised by counsellors and aid agencies allows for a complex joining together of therapeutic knowledge and global governance agendas in relation to, for example, disaster, and it works to prioritise the quality of 'response' as a key component of humanitarianism. Trauma ethics becomes a technique of response.

On this view, a particular and positivist understanding of trauma has been generalised as a universal condition: trauma and traumatisation are defined as the 'normal' response to catastrophic global events (Fassin, 2008). The politics of affect is rendered in the tensions within this simultaneous globalisation and individualisation of the event. As many cultural ethnographers are at pains to point out, differences between individuals and across cultures are effaced in this reading. It ignores the way that different people and communities have their own well-established mechanisms for understanding and engaging with what we contingently refer to as 'trauma' (Zarowsky, 2004). Performing a psychological narrative about individual trauma on societal scale renders political problems in terms of a narrative of a necessary cause/event, a set of pathological effects and a requirement to 'recover'. On an individual level, this is problematic, since it can be invasive and deterministic. As Jenny Edkins has argued, diagnoses of PTSD can depoliticise trauma in that those diagnosed

> are to accept the route to cure suggested by therapy. Political action is ruled out. Any attempt at such action . . . is interpreted as an expression of their disease. It is an 'acting out' of their symptoms, nothing more.
>
> (Edkins, 2003: 50; cf. Howell, 2011: 78)

In this vein, Young (1995) was clear to argue that part of the impetus for inventing PTSD was to tranquilise the difficult politics embodied by returning Vietnam veterans. On this view, we might question the popularity of therapeutic techniques such as CBT that both rely on and (re)produce particular understandings of the individual in terms of their ability to experience 'normal' responses to traumatic events (O'Malley, 2010). On a societal level, this generalisation of knowledge about trauma risks effacing the importance of political hierarchies, inequalities and historical injustices. By orchestrating the global governance around a logic of 'response' to the 'event', we potentially distract from longer histories of structural violence. Politics, in the sense of a contestability of power relations, becomes subsumed within an eventalised conception of the political – that is, identifiable, specific and time bound.

Trauma as an everyday language of the event

> Trauma talk is now part of the jargon of authenticity. Seemingly irresistible, it has become pure ideology, a language providing power with its refuge; seemingly responsive to real human need, it functions as a form of political administration.
>
> (Neocleous, 2012: 196)

How then should we engage with the politics of trauma? Does it remind us of our vulnerability in a way that involves us more deeply in the politics of global ethics? Or does it use such emotional registers to legitimate an individuating and governmentalizing form of power? In its simplest form, I would argue that trauma represents the idea that people can be so affected by something that it cannot be reconciled with wider notions of community, fairness, life in general (Edkins, 2002). The etymology of the term implies a wound, but the interpretation of this wound can be physical or mental (Young, 1995). In its modern construction, this inability to reconcile an event with wider assumptions about the world can manifest in certain specific symptoms: the memory of the event cannot be processed in a conventional manner, leaving the subject to return to, indeed, relive the event. Additional symptoms may include any of a range of emotional problems: fear, anger, sadness, shame, guilt. But, of course, the modern construction of trauma is exactly that – *modern* – and so it is important to recognise the plethora of analyses that seek to uncover and critique the historical emergence of the contemporary form of trauma (Caruth, 1995; Fassin and Rechtman, 2009; Young, 1995). Importantly, whereas early understandings of trauma saw it in negative terms, a weakness, a stigma, most genealogies of the concept would argue that a far more positive connotation has emerged over time.

The genealogy of this idea of trauma can be traced to early studies of 'railway spine', where survivors, or so-called malingerers were found to present with recurring memories of an accident, nightmares and wider pathologies (Young, 1995: 16–19). The negativity of the idea was related to the frequent claims of compensation and sickness benefit against the train companies. Another common marker in the literature was the growth of army veterans presenting with emotional and psychological issues after the first and second world wars. Labelled at the time as shell shock, it was suggested that soldier experiences of the war could be understood in terms of the effects of being near explosions (Edkins, 2003). Finally, a range of studies have drawn from the psychoanalytic tradition of Freud to look at early childhood memories of sexual abuse (Caruth, 1991). These historical precursors are an important touchstone for thinking about the ethics of trauma as – in different ways – they bring to light the possibility of a trans-historical dimension to trauma – i.e. that it was always there, a natural trait, which we have simply come to know. A common refrain of trauma counsellors is that trauma is a 'normal' or 'natural' response to a particular type of event (Royal College of Psychiatrists, 2013).

However, for all that these earlier tropes anticipate contemporary understandings of trauma – especially the range of associated symptoms – it is not clear that they tapped into widespread public or moral debates of the time. Indeed, a recurrent theme in the history of trauma studies suggests a general difficulty with understanding trauma in public terms. It is represented very often as a private experience, even a social taboo, a sign of weakness or even a stigma; at the very least, something that we don't talk about. Theoretically however, the study of railway spine and shell shock, in particular, did plant the seed of external causation. Whereas before psychological issues, delirium, hysteria and so forth, might be understood purely in terms of subject pathology, or malfunction, ideas about railway spine and shell shock, began to associate such patterns with a causal event external to the subject (Young, 1995).

The historical event(s) which drove trauma into the realm of being a *public* moral question were the Holocaust and Vietnam. With the growth of knowledge about the details of the Holocaust, ideas about trauma took on a concern with the mass – of community and of experience (Alexander, 2004). Given the context of large scale state sanctioned death camps, the idea of a mass social wound took on a moral weight in the public mind (Gieson, 2004). And an idea that came forward was that trauma might be so large, so painful, as to be un-express-able. In different ways, the appropriate response to trauma became one of documenting, cataloguing, remembering and memorialising traumatic events. Indeed, trauma and traumatic events often portray the idea that the (public) politics of trauma is primarily concerned with the memorialisation of communal tragedies (Edkins, 2003). Thus, 9/11 did not just arrive as an embodiment of a traumatic event, but captured an interesting element in the discourse between public and private.

If the Holocaust did much to shape thinking about the communal nature of trauma, then Vietnam was a key moment in the generation of knowledge about private trauma (Young, 1995). With Vietnam ideas about trauma took on a concern with developing medical treatment of the individual. In simplistic terms, if the Holocaust oriented studies of trauma to the 'victims' of violence, then the treatment of US army veterans for traumatic symptoms focused on 'the perpetrators' (Edkins, 2003). Psychiatrists sought to deal specifically with Vietnam veterans who displayed a host of symptoms including nightmares, flashbacks, as well as emotional responses, such as fear, anger and shame. Through a range of treatments, in house and residential, it was proposed that something called PTSD could be diagnosed and treated. This 'invention of PTSD' as a medical issue could present a new ethics of *trauma as individual*: one of a range of ailments that health professionals had a professional duty to treat (Young, 1995).

While we might see these different histories of trauma and the traumatic event as somewhat opposed, divided between psychology and counselling, between the study of (mass) public trauma and the (treatment of) individual experiences of traumatic symptoms, I would argue that it is important to remain sensitive to the nuances and ambiguities that carry through them to the present. As Dider Fassin argues, it is productive to think about the modern sense of trauma as a "moral problematization": that "trauma is not only a clinical description of a psychological status, but also the political expression of a state of the world" (Fassin, 2008: 533). Or as Alexander (2004: 1) describes: "It is by constructing cultural traumas that social groups, national societies, and sometimes even entire civilizations not only cognitively identify the existence and source of human suffering but 'take on board' some significant responsibility for it."

By recognising the socially constructed nature of the traumatic event, how it both produces and is produced by forms of knowledge about trauma, it is also possible to recover the ambiguity and malleability of the individualised subject of trauma. As Fassin argues, this is because the (constructed) idea of the trauma victim can then be thought of as a particular mode of subjectification:

> This way of thinking about subjectification contrasts both with the essentialist conception that reduces the experience of trauma to the reified "condition

> of the trauma victim" – always the likely result of the psychological account – and with the moralist critique that demagogically denounces the "victimization of victims" [. . .]. The issue is thus both theoretical and ethical. It is inscribed in a tension that Judith Butler articulates when she writes that subjectification "consists precisely in this fundamental dependency on a discourse we never chose but that, paradoxically, initiates and sustains our agency" and "signifies the process of becoming subordinated by power as well as the process of becoming a subject".
>
> (Fassin, 2008: 533–4; cf. Butler, 1997: 2)

On this view the individual subject of the global traumatic event is never quite defined, but is – as Chapter 1 argued – 'uncertain' between governance and some from of sympathy or empathy in the public discourse on trauma. Like all moral systems, I would suggest, it leaves room for growth. Imperfect and contingently developed through binaries of negative/positive, public/private, etc. the discourse of trauma is nevertheless susceptible to politics:

> From this perspective, humanitarian psychiatry is itself another instance of power that [. . .] prescribes a certain discourse: its compassion for trauma produces a particular form of subjectification that is imposed on individuals, but through which they can also exist politically.
>
> (Fassin, 2008: 534)

Thus, the critical discussion of trauma moves beyond questions of the correct genealogy, or the appropriate critique of power and asks how trauma is a discourse through which politicisation might be happening in different, perhaps new ways.

> Rather than a clinical reality, trauma today is a moral judgement . . . . more a feature of the moral landscape serving to identify legitimate victims than it is a diagnostic category which at most reinforces that legitimacy. It speaks of the painful link that connects the present to the past. It identifies complaints as justified and causes as just. Ultimately, it defines the empirical way in which contemporary societies problematize the meaning of their moral responsibility in relation to the distress of the world.
>
> (Fassin and Rechtman, 2009: 284)

This generalisation of trauma as a moral category is an important development in the genealogy of the term. If trauma has moved to a position of dual significance both as a (contested) psychological category and as wider metaphor of moral judgement (Alexander, 2004) then it makes sense to question how the morality of trauma is articulated. This is also partly a question of its translation into everyday usage. If trauma has moved into a wider arena of public knowledge, an everyday discourse of suffering, where pain, guilt, shame, and vulnerability are rendered 'knowable', indeed conversable, this begs a question of how this everyday discourse is given meaning and how are we to interpret this political economy of the global event?

Conclusion: the ethical performance of events?

The chapter discussed how global ethical theorists attempted to enlist a particular notion of trauma and suffering in the event of 9/11. Cosmopolitan approaches sought to take the traumatic event as a signal point for coming to terms with and managing 'global' vulnerability via overlapping communities of fate – i.e. global governance. These progressive responses were contrasted with post-structural critiques of our ability to know vulnerability. Hierarchies of grief potentially layer with sovereign power to legitimate an emotive/tragic realism on the one hand, or a more governmental and individuating form of therapeutic governance on the other. Moving beyond these limits, it was argued that the task was to grapple with the ethical performativities of trauma in historical and social context. A certain production of victims, community, normality and pain across the genealogy of trauma raised an important binary of public/private that seems to express something of the current meld between psychology and morality in the discourse of trauma ethics. This ambiguity was neatly encapsulated in Fassin's suggestion that trauma has come to provide a new language of the event, an imperfect, inexact discourse that allows expression for pain and empathy in the current conjuncture. The language of trauma ethics draws together ideas of the individual, pain, meaning, community, suffering, and sympathy in a manner that carries rich potential for thinking about the affective politics of the global event. It is a framework of knowing the event, but also a moment of subjectification through which subjects can speak against violence and hierarchy.

4 Trauma and the sub-prime crisis

Governing the financial event?

Introduction

Trauma can present an inclusive, everyday language of the event that weaves together moral relations, subject positions and notions of urgency. While elements of this discourse carry a cosmopolitan or humanitarian dimension, seeking to foreground human suffering so that response can be comprehensive and immediate, there are equally problematic dimensions concerning governance. One strain of critical thought in this area points to the disciplinary possibilities of 'therapeutic governance', whereby modes of response are enacted according to certain rationalities of psychological knowledge. A public language of 'trauma governance' can therefore segue into a pervasive and totalising form of politics. Indeed, Chapter 3 argued that the genealogy of trauma reveals a curious overlap between theories of private trauma and a more communitarian discourse of public trauma. On these terms, trauma culture is layered over more problematic ontologies of sovereign power and neo-liberal individuality (Edkins, 2003; Furedi, 2004).

Rather than accept the extremes of these two approaches, trauma ethics versus trauma governance, it was argued that the instability and malleability of the discourse of trauma should be foregrounded. Drawing from Fassin, Chapter 3 suggested that the ambiguity and malleability of trauma means it is better regarded *as a language* of the global event (through which we can converse). Trauma defines a certain sense of pain in the world and nurtures a moral consciousness of whether and how we might respond. Understood as a language, we might better ask questions such as what is done in the name of trauma? How does trauma produce the politics of specific events? How do subjects speak the language of trauma? On this view, it was argued that the possibility for subjects to speak 'otherwise' against or through the discourse of trauma is retained.

This more performative approach will now be developed by situating the political language of trauma through the performance of a specific event in market life – namely, the sub-prime crisis. I will argue that the sub-prime crisis was distinguished by a widespread focus on its traumatic qualities and characteristics in the media and policy discussion of sub-prime (Samman, 2016; Brassett and Clarke, 2012; Brassett and Vaughan-Williams, 2012b). Pace Chapter 1, this was not simply a smokescreen that enabled a new regime of accumulation to legitimate itself. Rather, it entailed a set of political and ethical possibilities and limits that were of significance in the constitution of a form of market subjectivity that emerged. The traumatic market subject is vulnerable, affected and in need of salvation, help and understanding.

The section on **Financial crisis and the discourse of trauma** foregrounds the humanitarian dimensions of the traumatic discourse of sub-prime by pointing to the normative and emancipatory possibilities that were read into the event. While much of the global discussion of sub-prime centred on the shocking and devastating elements of this financial event, numerous commentators used the scale and profundity of the debate as an opportunity to reflect on how to improve global finance and how to develop fairer terms of global governance. Trauma emerged as an important element in this wider ethical discussion because it underlined a certain zeal in the media and policy discourses of sub-prime: the crisis was variously described as an epochal earthquake, a tsunami, a latter-day Pearl Harbour, etc., performing notions of dramatic urgency. By orienting to shock and the plight of the apparent 'victims' of sub-prime, indeed of finance, more broadly, the humanitarian discourse of trauma established a relatable narrative that performed the nature of the event in terms that identified a credible and urgent 'response' – namely, bailing out the banks and 'saving' everyday market subjects.

The section on **Event/response: the humanitarian discourse of trauma and its limits** traces this tendency to excite in more critical terms. The effort to build everyday emotional attachments between arcane financial products and abject economic subjects can be viewed as a governmental move: to 'save' such 'victims' of the traumatic event. Traumatic emotions of shock, guilt, blame and even anger stoked a broad governmental consensus that something must be done to save global finance. In this way, trauma arguably worked as an ethical origin of a more humanitarian vision of finance, whereby far from a/the problem, finance is performed as a potential agency of salvation from poverty and destitution in the world (Brassett and Vaughan-Williams, 2012b; see also Andreu, 2016). On this view, the way in which the crisis was narrated *as an event* with certain traumatic qualities permitted a set of responses akin to therapeutic governance: intervention on behalf of victims who are emptied of agency. The irony of this 'humanitarian' response to the trauma of sub-prime was that banks were bailed out by the taxpayer – i.e. the salvation of finance was underwritten by the 'victims' most affected by the ensuing policy of austerity.

Finally, the section on **Performing the traumatised financial subject (differently)** contends that the politics of this traumatic narrative of the sub-prime crisis can/should be further disaggregated. At one level, there are forms of politicisation ongoing within the traumatic narrative of the sub-prime crisis: by making finance and financial markets into something political, I argue that trauma can bolster an important set of critiques of finance – e.g. inequality, foreclosure. The ambiguity and malleability in the trauma discourse saw a number of instances where market subjects drew upon alternative visions of trauma and therapy in order to contest or resist the governmental potentials of the traumatic narrative of sub-prime. At another level, I will argue that the traumatic spectacle of 'financial apocalypse' also gave birth to a host of satirical and subversive critiques of finance and financial crisis. From cartoons, to satirical news programs, the grandiose rhetoric of sub-prime allowed for a number of interesting interventions. In particular, I address the role of one British satirist, Charlie Brooker, in terms of a wider politicisation of how finance and the state are portrayed in the public sphere. In the process, I argue, we can uncover an everyday form of political agency that creatively unpicks the moral weight and seriousness of sub-prime in a way that can hint at potential routes beyond the governmental narrative of trauma.

Financial crisis and the discourse of trauma

A notable component of the media, policy and academic discourse of the sub-prime crisis was a general sense that whatever we were witnessing was a massive and unexpected traumatic event. One press article referred to the 'Financial Tsunami: The End of The World as We Knew It. (Engdahl, 2008), while academics pondered how

> the subprime crisis that began in the summer of 2007 may rank as one of the most traumatic global developments since World War II. Unlike wars and famine, this crisis and how it was caused seems to have caught the governing elites in rich countries completely unawares.
>
> (Sinclair, 2010: 64)

While initial reports suggested that this was a northern trauma, indeed, mostly originating in the US, albeit understood as a specific risk element in Anglo-Saxon capitalism, the magnitude of the event was portrayed in terms of its likely 'global effects'. As Ngaire Woods (2009, emphasis added) proclaimed, "Just when many of the world's poor countries have fought their way back – and started building democracies that work, businesses that grow, exports that sell – *a tsunami is swelling up out of the banks of the rich world*." This popular metaphor of a financial tsunami joined equally apocalyptic scenarios – earthquakes, volcano eruptions, death spirals, etc. – to produce an image of a massive natural disaster that would affect the whole globe. For an economic sector that is often typified as cold, calculative, almost arcane in its operations, the traumatic discourse of the sub-prime crisis became an impressive example of the affective politics of the global event. Gordon Brown called for a 'global early warning system' akin to those that were proposed for (actual) tsunamis only a few years previously, seeking "a new Bretton Woods with a new IMF that offers, by its surveillance of every economy, an early warning system and a crisis prevention mechanism for the whole world" (Sparrow, 2008). In this sense, attempts to manage the sub-prime crisis echoed wider systems of disaster response that were becoming increasingly popular in global politics (Brassett and Vaughan-Williams, 2012a).

Discourses of unexpected traumatic events, early warning systems and so forth require some engagement, I think, since, ultimately, the declining value of financial investments and assets *is not the same thing* as a tsunami. That to say, the invocation of trauma *does something*; that is, it performs knowledge about trauma – with an important notion of 'cause', 'event' and 'response' – yet it also requires a certain context, which works as a contingency of its success.

Ontologies of trauma: event-subject-response

> In our everyday lives, any of us can have an experience that is overwhelming, frightening, and beyond our control. We could find ourselves in a car crash, be the victim of an assault, or see an accident. Police, fire brigade or ambulance workers are more likely to have such experiences – they often have to deal with horrifying scenes. Soldiers may be shot or blown up, and see friends killed or injured. Most people, in time, get over experiences like this without needing help. In some people, though, traumatic experiences set off a reaction that can last for many months or years. This is called Post-traumatic Stress Disorder, or PTSD for short.
>
> (Royal College of Psychiatrists, 2013)

Knowledge about trauma rests upon the construction of an intimate relationship between the individual and the 'traumatic' event. The trauma narrative presents human ethics as a question of individual and collective agency in direct relation to an extreme event: a situation where our lives, or the life of someone close to us, are threatened in some uncontrollable way. Certain reactions – fear, anger, guilt, shame, avoidance – are expected. Certain responses – sympathy, solidarity, bearing witness, memorialisation – are promoted. This narrative can be used and deployed across a range of subjects and issues within global politics: from mass disasters, through terrorist attacks, to personal tragedy. But as Fassin and Rechtman (2009: 6) note, the constitution of this language of the event was by no means a simple or linear movement:

> This turnaround is played out simultaneously on two stages. On the one hand, we have the professional circles of psychiatry and psychology, which [. . .] have been substantially influenced by social movements demanding rights, particularly for veterans and women who have suffered violence. It was the convergence of these disciplines and movements, as well as alliances between them, that gave rise to the diagnostic category of post-traumatic stress disorder, which was to become the keystone in the construction of the new truth. And it was in this context that further developments in psychiatric victimology and humanitarian psychiatry emerge. On the other hand, the more generalised and global idea of trauma, designating an irrefutable reality linked to a feeling of empathy, has spread throughout the moral space of contemporary society.

While the scientific background and content of knowledge about trauma fits in well with a governmental image, it is this generality of trauma – as a moral relation between individuals and events – that renders it with so much potential: by deploying the trauma narrative, an ethical concern for individual and collective suffering finds common cause with institutions and actors, translating into a viable political project (often in a matter of hours). One possibility that the trauma narrative presents, therefore, is the idea of rapid and credible response. Indeed, humanitarian NGOs have emplaced trauma as a central motif of disaster response. However, such generality can also be associated with particular *limits*. As Fassin and Rechtman (2009: 6) go on to discuss:

> This trend is independent of opinions as to the validity of the diagnostic category as a way of accounting for the painful experience of tragic events in other cultural contexts. In fact, although there has been much criticism of what some see as a form of psychological ethnocentrism, the critics do not question the moral importance of trauma.

This indicates an important politics of trauma, the recognition of which can serve to unpick the contested politics of the global event. The modern understanding of trauma that has been generalised as a universal condition through its inclusion in the *DSM-IV* and widespread promotion by professional 'guilds' of trauma counsellors must be understood as a contingent product of Western history. As Chapter 3 argued, it depends on scientific criteria on the one hand, but also a generalisation and popularisation as a moral category driven by far more public traumas such as the Holocaust and Vietnam. This poses problems of definition, not least since there seems to be some slippage between private and public genealogies of trauma – e.g. many people seem to be comfortable that a nation might be traumatised, for instance, without being troubled by the work of personification that goes into such a move. Yet, moreover, as many cultural ethnographers have pointed out, there exist vast cultural differences in the way different individuals in different cultural contexts might understand or experience trauma. It seems to efface the possibility of alternative and sometimes well-established mechanisms for understanding and engaging with what we contingently refer to as 'trauma' (Zarowsky, 2004). Thus the governmental effects of producing a psychological narrative about individual trauma on societal scale is that it renders political problems in terms of a narrative of a necessary cause/event, a set of pathological effects and a requirement to 'recover'.

In terms of the individual, the generalisation of trauma counselling is problematic because it can be invasive and deterministic, seeking to portray people as 'known' psychological units. The popularity of therapeutic techniques such as CBT and its correlated more generalised practice of 'talk therapy' rely on and (re) produce particular understandings of the individual in terms of his or her ability to experience more 'resilient' responses to traumatic events. However, if we begin to imagine the generalisation of therapeutic governance on a societal level, then it risks effacing the importance of political hierarchies, inequalities and historical injustices. For example, the Haiti earthquake might raise the issue of Haitian suffering in the consciousness of the West, but such events are unlikely to stimulate a more critical discussion about the histories of formal or informal colonial subjugation. Politics, in the sense of a wider contestability of power relations, becomes subsumed within an eventalised conception of the political – that is, identifiable, specific and time bound.

While knowledge about trauma arguably contains such ethico-political limits; however, it should be stressed that for the most part, it has been understood more broadly as an important mechanism for understanding and addressing suffering. Despite the critiques levied in Chapter 3, it is hard to shake the view that there is something good or ethical in the recognition of trauma and traumatic events in global politics. To this end, we should note the role of radical political movements and humanitarian NGOs, and the growth of disaster management practices as an important mechanism for consolidating the humanitarian dimensions of trauma (Fassin and Rechtman, 2009; Howell, 2011). For example, trauma has been a popular trope with radical social movements that see it as an important strategic device to promote their particular cause on the political agenda. From its inception, itself partly because of the critical energy generated by Vietnam vets seeking proper compensation and recognition for their plight (Young, 1995), the moral power of 'victimhood' enshrined in the trauma narrative has made it an important strategic discourse for emancipatory groups. In particular, feminist organisations have used it to place rape and child sex abuse on the legal and political horizon. Such campaigns both draw upon and re-signify knowledge about trauma. In this way, they help to normalise the trauma narrative that we read from psychological knowledge, while also redeploying it for political purpose.

Drawing these points together, there is a sense in which the normalisation of the trauma narrative and the entrenchment of the event within discourses of global politics is fusing to a set of instrumental and managerialist discourses of global governance. There is coalescence of problem-solving logics between psychology, disaster management, humanitarianism and global governance. For instance, Vanessa Pupavac (2001: 360) talks about how such overlapping logics can be understood to produce the common sense of "therapeutic governance" in which

> politics becomes . . . about appealing to and regulating the vulnerable id. Under therapeutic governance, rights are being reconceptualised in terms of psychological recognition and custodianship rather than freedoms, that is, as protection by official bodies, rather than protection from official bodies.

Contingent, limited, yet persuasive and seemingly moral, trauma has become an important and popular language for understanding and responding to global events.

Quintessentially, past decades have been marked by several large-scale, globally mediated 'traumatic events' including – inter alia – the terrorist attacks of 9/11 and 7–7, the 2004 Indian Ocean ('Boxing Day') Tsunami and Hurricane Katrina. Such events have been understood, represented and 'governed' according to the logics of therapeutic response. As Frank Furedi (2004: 12) argued in the case of 9/11, "There has been an emphasis on perceiving an attack on a nation as an assault on society's collective and individual mental health." Indeed, a primary reference point for American commentators after 9/11 was the invasion of Pearl

Harbour, which was produced as a comparable historical precedent of collective pain. Fassin and Rechtman (2009: 1–3) recount how, in the days following 9/11, an estimated 9,000 mental health specialists intervened to provide counselling for trauma, and a number of professional websites were set up or modified to deal with the demand for psychological support. They note that this occurred despite a number of surveys indicating that there was no significant increase in levels of PTSD in the population of New York. For them, such contradictions imply a *consolidation* of the trauma narrative in the popular imagination:

> From the literal sense in which the term is used by psychiatrists (a psychological shock) to its metaphorical extension disseminated by the media (a tragic event) [. . .] the idea of trauma is thus becoming established as a commonplace of the contemporary world, a shared truth.
>
> (Fassin and Rechtman 2009: 2–3)

On these terms, the performative politics of trauma can be understood as an important contingency of the discourse of the sub-prime crisis, whereby the humanitarian elements of finance were elevated and nurtured.

Event/response: the humanitarian discourse of trauma and its limits

A key element in the performance of a traumatic narrative of sub-prime was the use of tropes of disaster across media and policy circles. It was variously referred to as a 'financial tsunami', like the 'eruption of Krakatoa', or even the 'end of the world' (Mattli and Woods, 2009; Mason, 2009; Engdahl, 2008). In the early period of the crisis, one economist referred ominously to the problem of sub-prime as the "tip of the iceberg" (*BBC News*, 2 April 2007). Another British journalist referred to a "full on financial heart attack" (Legrain, 2008).

While we might be tempted to think about this in rather general terms – i.e. the media were simply drawing on common tropes of urgency to direct and focus public opinion on something that was quite significant, such imagery developed through repetition to perform the crisis in quite specific terms. For example, the use of imagery such as 'tsunami', or a financial tsunami, is important because it plays on popular understandings of mass casualty events such as the 2004 Indian Ocean Tsunami. The implicit suggestion is that the sub-prime crisis was not only an example of the awesome natural power of finance but also an 'event' literally capable of threatening the lives of hundreds of thousands of people. This threatening relationship, once established, could then be worked through the more humanitarian dimensions of the trauma narrative: "It is going to be a very challenging task . . . we're not going to be able to save everybody", said Sheila Bair, chairman of the Federal Deposit Insurance Corporation (*BBC News*, 17 April 2007).

The trauma narrative permits a large amount of emotional license, yet structures it around the fundamental co-ordinates of an event, with a concomitant need for a response. In this vein, the performance of the sub-prime crisis as a traumatic global event allowed for the performance of 'victims' who needed to be saved. This is a significant discursive move, focusing away from structural problematics inherent within finance – scale, risk, securitisation, etc. – towards the victims on the receiving end of the tsunami. It therefore serves to individualise the 'event'. Individualisation is an important technique of media relay, because it allows journalists to tell relatable stories about individual human suffering, rather than boring, complicated stories about Collateralised Debt Obligations. In turn, as Chapter 3 argued, trauma can permit an interesting and politically consequential slippage between individual psychological stories and collective or sovereign responses. In the UK, attention turned to the plight of Northern Rock, which was suffering what was widely reported as the "first run on a major bank in the UK" in over a hundred years (Peston, 2008a: 159). Members of the public were seen queuing round the block in an attempt to withdraw their money. They were interviewed, telling their stories of lifetime savings, worries over their future, insecurity about their ability to even see their money. Importantly, though, this was portrayed as very much a national story. While sub-prime might have initially appeared as something of an American issue, the plight of Northern Rock savers related a British dimension. This was not only about poor 'victims' but also entertained a number of difficult emotions about Britain, of guilt and shame at how we had allowed this event to happen.

In this context, the event-response dynamic is not instantaneous, but requires an engagement with the traumatic qualities and characteristics of the event, what Furedi might refer to as an 'emotional script'. Performativity is not a straightforward or structural process, but relies on repetition, change and even failure. Importantly, the audience for any performance can be invited in, so to speak, to accept or not particular elements. In the UK, this coalesced around a certain set of societal debates. A specific victim of the trauma was constructed – in the form of poor innocent savers – bearing witness to the unexpected tragedy that was befalling them. In keeping with the humanitarian dimensions of the trauma narrative, the audience was widely encouraged to feel sympathy for these innocent victims of the sub-prime crisis. But at the same time a certain moral division emerged between responsible savers and irresponsible borrowers:

> It was the financially literate, financially aware and financially conscientious members of the middle classes who could claim to be the genuinely innocent victims of a sub-prime crisis that was the result of other people's poor decision-making.
>
> (Watson, 2009: 433)

Thus at the same time as the human interest was evoked through sympathy for victims, so too a degree of *blame* emerged for irresponsible borrowers on the one hand and the greedy and predatory sub-prime lender on the other (Montgomerie, 2008: 3). While there was some muted discussion of the nature of sub-prime lending itself, that referred to the low incomes and (often) black and Hispanic origins of borrowers, the public mood seemed to focus rather more on the lenders. Commentators sought to identify the perpetrators of this traumatic event and as, is now well known, they quickly came to focus on the activities of bankers (Widmaier, 2010).

In the UK, the scope of such blame became a rather pointed and vindictive narrative; bankers were castigated across a wide spectrum of public opinion, and for a period, it seemed like the status of banking may never recover. Importantly though, this did not so much entail a critique of the structural power of finance as a very specific focus on the person of individual bankers. 'Fred the Shred' became a 'bogeyman' for a vitriolic media, with MPs openly discussing rescinding his knighthood, while protestors actually camped outside his house and strung up effigies of him. Again, such trends were in line with the wider effort to individualise the event: Who had done it? Who were the victims? In this way, I would argue, the anger and animosity that ran through discourse of blame, while no doubt a form of critical energy, were themselves harnessed to confirm the performative idea that a traumatic event had 'happened'. Rather than initiating a more thoroughgoing period of moral and ethical reflection on the structure of finance, anger and blame at the bankers served to confirm the original performance of a traumatic event. The emotion they licensed, the identification of perpetrators to be blamed, implied, in ever more vitriolic terms, that a traumatic event had happened.

Emotional responses to the event were not only individual experiences but also gradually mobilised by the media and interpellated as collective categories – sub-prime borrower, predatory bankers, innocent victims. As Mat Watson argued, the media discourse of the sub-prime crisis, particularly as it manifested in the UK, nurtured and mobilised a generalised sense of angst. Particularly important here was the focus on individual homeowners. The active production of a middle-class panic became a politically significant factor in the emerging response: "The continued newsworthiness of the sub-prime crisis was facilitated by the ease with which a focus on house prices was used to turn a public financial event into a personal struggle to survive global economic pressures unscathed." This weaving of a traumatic event to individual experiences that could then be used to categorise and re-frame sub-prime as an epochal challenge of global proportions meant that few if any argued with need for a 'response'.

In line with Furedi's notion of an "emotional script" that "sought to create a sense of unity around a common experience of vulnerability", there ensued a generalised reflection upon the predicament that we all found ourselves in. Everyone's wealth and health, including governments', were invested in the possibility of an ever appreciating property market. In a US television interview, former treasury secretary Henry Paulson (2008) claimed that the USA had "in many ways humiliated [itself] as a nation with some of the problems that have taken place here". Personal fears could be writ large into a broad sense of doubt about the economic and political settlement in general, its viability and its potential excessive harm. Senator Mel Martinez, then a member of the US Banking Committee, told the Financial Crisis Inquiry Commission about a September 2008 meeting with Paulson and Ben Bernanke:

> I just remember thinking, you know, Armageddon. The thing that was the most frightening about it is that even with them asking for extraordinary

> powers, that they were not at all assured that they could prevent the kind of financial disaster that I think really was greater than the Great Depression.
>
> (Cited in United States Financial Crisis Inquiry Commission, 2011: 372)

An event, unpredictable and awesome, and beyond our control was performed. In humanitarian terms, victims were identified and emotional renditions of the traumatic effects of the event were licensed. Interestingly, there was some instability in the performance whereby negative emotions of anger and blame, which might potentially have seemed critical at the time, were rendered according to a further individualisation of the crisis. Rather palpably, a sense of fear and angst stalked the coverage of the event in a way that demanded a response, even as it was unclear whether it might be enough to 'save us'. This was an affective narration of a global event *par excellance*, with local manifestations, epochal and scalar implications, individualised logics and a clear slippage to imply a collective wound. In short, a politics of response was being established in advance.

Therapeutic response: governing the event

The traumatic narrative of the sub-prime crisis established a shocking, unexpected event and quickly wove it to the performance of stories of individual victims, helpless in the tide of this financial tsunami. In media and policy coverage, here was no escaping the effects of the event; in the UK, there was a literal barrage of stories about how individual lives had been affected, how savings had been lost and how houses might be re-possessed. Again, while this might have seemed like a critical moment, where the balance between capital and labour, and between finance and the state, might be re-negotiated, the performance of traumatic emotions, anger, fear and blame worked to tranquilise such possibilities in a series of rather morose ruminations. Following Judith Butler's understanding of performativity, I would argue, in this moment of rumination, financial subjects came to anticipate the object of finance and financial authority, just at the point when it was most a threat. It was not finance, per se, that had caused the problem, but a traumatic event itself with universal implications.

When the blame game began in earnest, there was a divergence between the aforementioned anger at greedy bankers and a more generalised lament about the state of our society. This inner-directed evaluation arguably suggested deeper possibilities for reform. Values came to the fore as the *Financial Times* (2009) ran 'The Future of Capitalism' editorial series which asked "what can – and should – replace it?" and even the normally mainstream *Newsnight* began to seriously contemplate the re-organisation of global capitalism to prioritise ethics, rather than greed (Denman, 2008). Yet, again, such responses allowed for a further nurturing of the centrality of the 'traumatic event' by promoting a form of self-judgement. The layperson viewer who had just gotten used to the idea that this was a personal crisis, that we should both feel anxious for ourselves and angry at greedy bankers, was asked to contemplate the historical shape and scale of global capitalism.

Some truly epochal imagery began to circulate. Paul Mason (2009: 38, emphasis added) observed,

> There's a lot of catastrophic imagery being thrown around about this crisis, but I think I have finally found one that fits: with the 15 September meltdown, the stock market panic and finally the economic chill that is falling on the world and depressing growth. **It's like the eruption of Krakatoa**. On 26 August 1883 the Sumatran volcano exploded so big that the sound was heard in Perth, Australia. That wiped out about 3,000 villagers and the local ecosystem. That's like the week of 15–19 September. Then, a tsunami killed 30,000 people. Nobody had ever seen one before so they were not prepared. But it was still basically a regional not a global tsunami. That is the credit freeze and the stock market crash of last week combined. Finally, in the year after Krakatoa erupted, global temperature fell by 1.2 degrees centigrade because of sulphur dioxide emitted into the atmosphere, and sunsets were red for years. That's the global recession that is intensifying and feeding back into share prices and bank solvency

Such metaphorical work is clearly interesting in terms of an academic study of performativity, the lines of reification – of time, geographical scale and nature – all speak to previous critical work in IPE. However, what is so interesting about these affective economies of the global event is how they link so seamlessly to the gaze of market subjects: "Then comes the volcanic winter: the immediate chilling of the real-world economy, felt from the floors of Chinese export factories to the bars of British pubs" (Mason, 2009). Market subjects are not just anticipated as a potential audience, they are actively interpellated as participants in the performance. Their emotions are directly appealed to in the narratives that individualise the crisis (e.g. the threat of declining house prices/savings), suggest its world-historical scale (e.g. the threat of 1930s-style investment loss) and legitimise managerial governance response (e.g. the threat of devastation if faith in financial markets is not restored by the state).

Event history became acceptable discourse of financial commentators. Just as Pearl Harbour had previously been promoted as the historical comparison point from which to understand 9/11, so too were the Wall Street Crash and the Great Depression performed as the historical mirror points for the sub-prime crisis (Samman, 2016). In his widely read BBC blog, Robert Peston (2008b) declared that the sub-prime crisis "can now be classified as the most severe and intractable malfunction of the banking system since the late 1920s". We were reminded that the Wall Street Crash was so bad that people threw themselves out of buildings (e.g. Cohen, 2008), the Great Depression so severe that thousands in the first world starved or lived homeless (e.g. Gregory, 2008). The world-historical scale of events became infused to a discussion of 'progress', or lack thereof. Had we sold out the promise of modernity by refusing to learn the lessons of the past? In terms of the narrative of trauma, being asked to feel guilt at personal excesses is one thing, but being complicit in a selling out of the promise of modernity is of a slightly different order. The (modern) world was ending, and we were all quite personally to blame. We had lived beyond our means, borrowed more than was feasible. And now the historical comparison points were looking quite dark indeed. A sense of shame was nurtured – at greed, at irresponsibility and, in some cases, at 'being Iceland' or just using too many credit cards.

In this way, the global event is very much more than an economic crisis in need of a political resolution. Read as a traumatic narrative, the performance of the sub-prime crisis had actually very little to do with finance – or least the performativity of financial knowledge, which dominates in the literature (Brassett and Clarke, 2012). Instead, it was about tsunamis, tidal waves, heart attacks and death spirals. Although these different metaphors might mobilise a range of quite different emotions, what unites them is the sense of fear and panic they produce: they are traumatic in the sense that they involve the performance of an event where life – and a way of life – is threatened. In the context of the sub-prime crisis, they suggest the helplessness of the victims, the emergence of guilt and shame amongst survivors, the mobilisation of anger towards the bankers (that is, away from financial capitalism) and the emergence of world-historical gravity that asked whether we had collectively sold out the promise of modernity. The politics of the performativity of sub-prime crisis was less about the repetition of financial knowledge, the iteration of numbers and the relaying of equilibrium based theories of price. Instead, I would argue, it was more about the construction of a traumatised financial subject who was in need of help, in need of governance. As Gordon Brown reassured the UK on the eve of the recapitalisation of the banks: "I want you to know that we are doing this for you."

Just as Pupavac understands therapeutic governance to involve the rendering of victims as *in need of help*, requiring "protection by official bodies, rather than protection from official bodies", so too did the performance of the traumatic narrative of the sub-prime crisis involve the production of essentially passive and needy financial subjects. In the context of the repetition of traumatic emotions such as shock, fear, anger and shame, I would argue that such financial subjects were performed as either *in need of help* or, in part, *to blame*. Indeed, this form of uncertainty was arguably an important component of the governmental logic because, *either way*, they were emptied of the political agency necessary to question or otherwise resist the mode of response. The particular knowledge and rationalities associated with psychological and humanitarian practices of trauma ethics, thus served to legitimate a therapeutic governance response to the sub-prime crisis which, as part of the wider overlapping performativities of finance – as central to modernity and 'our very way of life' – ultimately denied the 'victims' of the crisis their political agency.

Performing the traumatised financial subject (differently)

The sub-prime crisis could have been a great opportunity for public education on the nature of hierarchies pertaining to global finance. Daily news coverage created a widespread awareness that decisions in one part of the world directly affect lives in other parts of the world, indeed, that our welfare is bound up with a particular form of financial market life. This was a potentially democratizing moment. What took centre stage, however, was a particular(ly) catastrophic *event* that carried a number of traumatic qualities and characteristics. The performance of this event seemed to focus on a set of negative emotions – blame of bankers, shame of irresponsible borrowers/nations – that served to individualise the event. And this link between the global event and market subjects set in train an event/response logic that effectively emptied individuals of political agency and legitimated a therapeutic response: *bail out the banks*.

Recent work in IPE has highlighted the importance of the performance of financial subject positions (e.g. Langley, 2008b), how they are both enlisted to, and actively ascent to, various social discourses of debt and aspiration – e.g. the 'entrepreneurial debtor'. In Langley's (2006: 922) terms, it is precisely those "subjects who, self-consciously and responsibly, further their own security and freedom through the market in general and through the financial markets in particular" that were performed as 'participants' in, or 'victims' of, the traumatic logics of the sub-prime crisis. That is to say, at some level, the performance was visceral: market life is embodied by financial subjects who engage in certain rationalities, but who can also produce a form of life through those rationalities. On this view, it is a logical extension to suggest that financial subjects might have been particularly sensitive to the emotional logics that were appealed to in the traumatic narratives of the traumatic event. Therefore, the emotional intimacy performed between financial subject positions and the wider politics of the event was a key element in the performative politics of this global event.

But a critical analysis of the traumatic narrative of the sub-prime crisis must also engage with the politics of exclusion. Who is unable to claim trauma for their cause? Who or what is othered by the trauma narrative? Broadly, we might argue that history and imperialism are effaced in the focus on trauma and the traumatic event. After all, low wage work, unemployment, precarious welfare systems and massive levels of human poverty and malnutrition all existed *before* the sub-prime crisis. Yet questions about these broader social problems was cut off by the urgency of finding the appropriate response to the traumatic 'event' at hand. As the introduction suggested, this move to fret about comparatively wealthy citizens in the north, who might not profit quite as much from their speculative house purchase, or, indeed, that they might receive less benefits from one of the pre-eminent welfare systems in the world, could be rendered as a somewhat privileged perspective on moral suffering in a wider global context. Indeed, it is remarkable just how little the trauma narrative was contested in media, policy and academic debates.

More attention was directed towards finding the appropriate governance responses to this 'traumatic event', often along the lines of Robert Shiller's (2008b) 'Subprime Solution', which essentially suggested that rather than question securitisation, the task was to *make it work again*. Indeed, even the most critical of the many 'commissions' on the sub-prime crisis conducted by Joseph Stiglitz was ultimately concerned with making securitisation work better rather than questioning its role in producing the crisis (United Nations, 2009). Thus the way in which the trauma narrative worked to *eventalise* the sub-prime crisis was a potent instance of the performative power of finance: it was not finance that was the problem, but a traumatic event that – *in threatening (good) financial subjects so directly* – demanded certain responses to shore up a system that produced the very problem in the first place. What is lost in this logic is a strategic adaptability. So, for instance, if we forget the dramatic and world-historical scale of this event, we might ask a different set of questions. For example, in all the media and policy discussion of the sub-prime crisis – even as it addresses predatory lending, and practices of securitisation that allowed such massive leveraging of risk – there was scant attention paid to the idea that sub-prime lending, per se, is actually a progressive agenda to provide practical ways in which low-income market subjects can begin to build a wealth base. More critically, I would argue, discourses of trauma that surrounded the sub-prime crisis have underpinned a wider consensus around the 'too big to fail' logic of financial regulation. Gone is a strategic focus on how to build financial relations that benefit specific market lives – e.g. through practices of alternative finance, local banking and patient finance. Instead, trauma seemed to set the tone for a macro-prudential common sense that ensued where financial regulation became the avoidance of disaster.

However, perhaps most problematic about the dominance of the humanitarian and governmental logics of the traumatic narrative of the sub-prime crisis is the way it distracts from the agency of actually existing market subjects. That is to say, despite the apparent completeness of the trauma narrative, possibilities for intervention did exist, and they were explored. It is therefore important to highlight the manner in which the trauma narrative of the sub-prime crisis was actively brought into question and turned to alternative possibilities. Accepting the contingency of how traumatic narratives are performatively overlaid in moments of financial crisis, one route that was explored was to push the logic to its end point. Writing in the *New York Times*, Robert Shiller (2008a) also argued,

> It is important to consider the psychological trauma of foreclosure. No one is likely to starve or sleep on the streets as an immediate result of a foreclosure, and the authorities no longer dump a family's furniture on the sidewalk when it happens. Nonetheless, there is deep trauma. Homeownership is a fundamental part of a sense of belonging to a country. The psychologist William James wrote in 1890 that "a man's Self is the sum total of all that he can call his, not only his body and his psychic powers, but his clothes and his house, his wife and children, his ancestors and friends, his reputation and works, his lands and horses, and yacht and bank account." Homeownership is thus an extension of self; if one owns a part of a country, one tends to feel at one with that country. Policy makers around the world have long known that, and hence have supported the growth of homeownership.

Pragmatically speaking, while Shiller's move is clearly performative of the traumatic narrative, it poses the intriguing suggestion that if losing a home is traumatic, then building lines of accountability might be a key objective of ethical intervention. In terms of rhetoric, we might seek to re-describe elements of the traumatic narrative of the sub-prime crisis to argue that 'victims' might require not just rapid humanitarian responses, but also ongoing and long-term support. By adopting the language of 'recovery', rather than blame and shame, it might be argued that social support is required to build trust in order that victims can 'move on'. For example, Wharton business school (2009) engaged an account of the crisis by psychologist David Webber:

> Helping an individual recover from a traumatic experience provides a useful analogy for understanding how to help the economy recover from its own traumatic experience . . . The public will need to "hold the perpetrators of the economic disaster responsible and take what actions they can to prevent them from harming the economy again." In addition, the public will have to see proof that government and business leaders can behave responsibly before they will trust them again.

This brings a more strategic edge to trauma. By taking the example of political movements in the US that have sought to 'claim' trauma for their cause, should Shiller's intervention be re-described in emancipatory terms? Defining issues such as foreclosure and unemployment as 'a traumatic event' would arguably generate a symbolic, even a *legal* wedge. If home foreclosure could be defined as traumatic, then 'victims' could potentially claim legal compensation in circumstances where it could be proved that the process was avoidable. Such a move is clearly problematic in terms of affirming the status of victimhood and potentially encouraging abuse; however, it might represent one pragmatic re-description of the trauma narrative that re-calibrates the balance of agency in relation to the financial event.

More critically, the traumatic narrative of sub-prime was also a subject of satire. For instance, Charlie Brooker questioned the traumatic narrative, placing it in terms of a wider critique of the new media and its melodramatic approach to the economy:

> Unemployment now so huge it has to be depicted by plummeting monolithic numbers. [. . .] The news itself is becoming less of an easily digestible summary of events and more a grotesque entertainment reality show with heavy emphasis on emotion and sensation and a swaggeringly comically theatrical sense of its own importance . . . [. . .]

Brooker:	The world of global economics makes less sense than me going bibble bibble, but nevertheless when it goes wrong the news can make it seem terrifying.
Jeremy Paxman:	Today stock markets across the world tumbled, imploded, continued to collapse like deflated dirigibles.

Brooker: After all if the boom of the last decade was all a dream the current situation is a nightmare rendered in calculus, meaninglessly huge numbers, sliding graphs, a CGI red arrows display team crashing repeatedly to the floor, and one frightening prognosis after another. It's so bad leaders of the G20 are having to get together in the worlds most disappointing razzle pile up in **a desperate bid to save the world from global cash-pocalypse.**

(*Newswipe with Charlie Brooker*, 2009)

I would argue that such interventions undermine the very idea of a financial event by placing it in the context of the bizarre nature of mediated society. Brooker charts the invocation of the French Revolution, of an episode of *Loose Women* and parodies the litany of flawed metaphorical devices used to explain quantitative easing: these include spanners, petrol cans and railways tracks. Brooker further satirises one highly problematic attempt to individualise the crisis: Dermot O'Mernahans's Economic Cycle, where he 'rides a bicycle' around England attempting to interview 'individuals' who were bearing the brunt of the downturn in the economic cycle. Unfortunately, in the program, it seems the majority of the individuals interviewed were actually doing pretty well and were mildly optimistic about economic prospects. In such interventions, the individualisation of the crisis, its world-historical scale and the existential need for intervention are all undermined as the very notion of a traumatic event is placed within the context of the entertainment logics of a sensationalizing news media. In this way, the traumatic narrative of the financial subject can be resisted. Such a resistance may well work in a piecemeal and non-linear fashion; that is to say, the proposal is not simply to replace the traumatised financial subject with a less traumatised and less financial subject. Rather, such (problematic) modes of subjectification are themselves cast as a site for thinking and imagining alternatives.

Conclusion

This chapter has argued that the politics of the global event is increasingly narrated in terms of a series of traumatic qualities and characteristics. From terrorist attacks, through natural disasters and on to financial crises, the moral depth of the global event is performed in relation to specific, identifiable, individual experiences. In various ways, it was argued, the idea of trauma can be used and deployed to communicate the human scale of such events, the pain and suffering, the requirement for understanding and sympathy. Such narratives of the global event constitute a complex of political possibilities and limits, and the ethics of trauma carry a mix of humanitarian and governmental possibilities. The limits of the trauma narrative, it was argued, include the possibility of a governmental response, whereby the event becomes the political foundation for a set of knowledge practices to define and order the lives of individuals qua 'victims'.

The traumatic narrative of the sub-prime crisis carried a set of disciplinary and limiting dimensions that effectively cast the sovereign response – i.e. 'bailout the banks' – as a humanitarian, therapeutic response. On this view, the discursive performance of the sub-prime crisis was addressed in terms of market subjects themselves. It was argued that the traumatised financial subject was encouraged to feel shock and fear at the scale of the event, and yet, through the deployment of related traumatic emotions – of blame and shame – subjects were also encouraged to think about the crisis in terms of individual responsibility. However, while the performance of sub-prime as a traumatic event suggested a diminution of political agency on the part of financial subjects, the chapter concluded by pointing to two potential examples of how the discourse might be politicised. While such problematisations of the traumatic event do not exhaust the politics of the sub-prime crisis by any means, they do, nevertheless, point to the possibility of agency. Quite apart from the totalising potentials of the humanitarian and governmental versions of trauma, an alternative critical path might point to the capacity of subjects to perform events otherwise. The next chapter will now pick up where this one leaves off to open up and scrutinise the politics of the traumatic event as an ongoing and everyday moral dilemma for reflexive market subjects to engage. In this way, I hope to identify important ways in which we might pragmatically reclaim the contingency of trauma in order to suggest alternative ways of *living with, through and against* its ethics.

5 Trauma and the market subject

Performing vulnerability

Introduction: the event as a pervasive dilemma

Previous chapters have considered the elevation of traumatic events in media and policy narratives of global politics. The 24-hour news and social media run through a seemingly endless stream of natural disasters, industrial accidents, mass shootings and financial crisis. As humanitarian organisations, moral theorists and celebrities seek to interpret such events in ethical terms, a certain humanitarian imperative infers we must 'respond' in some way to the pain and suffering caused. Trauma has become a touchstone for the wider ethical dilemma of how we understand and seek to mitigate pain in global market life. The performance of global events such as 9/11 and the sub-prime crisis in traumatic terms can play on particular emotive and individual stories in order to animate 'larger questions' of suffering, global inequality, violence or greed. The ethics of a global market life is eventalised; the traumatic event requires a 'response', be it understanding, sympathy or intervention. However, while elements of the ethical discourse of trauma are clearly attractive, in that it can provide an affective language through which political issues are discussed and addressed, nevertheless, certain limits pertain. It was questioned how narrating global events in terms of trauma can condition a limited politics of response? For instance, aspects of the therapeutic response to individual trauma can arguably provide a scientific legitimacy for what many critics regard as a more governmental set of interventions. The identification of helpless 'victims' who need to be saved, and who have a certain requirement to recover, can equate to a form of *therapeutic governance* that both strips individuals of agency and – on some arguments – can work to overlay wider forms of sovereign power. On this view, the weaving together of individuating logics of trauma with wider metaphors of a wounded community can fundamentally shift the nature of politics and the political within *therapy culture*.

However, in line with a performative approach to the politics of the global event, previous chapters also sought to situate and unpick the terms of this political dilemma by foregrounding the historical emergence of trauma as a *new language* of the global event (Fassin and Rechtman, 2009). Trauma has a place and a history; indeed, the genealogy of trauma in Chapter 3 suggested that this new language of the event was contingent upon the confluence of different trends, medical, political and personal. Beyond the binary of humanitarian versus governmental discourses of trauma, Fassin and Rechtman discern an ambiguous movement from the concept of a psychological wound to a wider social metaphor of pain, and the historical elevation of the idea of community trauma seems both conceptually distinct, yet politically resonant with, modern theories of PTSD. Trauma is thus a 'shared truth' – a wider register for 'moral judgement'.

Throughout, I have argued that these different lineages of trauma foreground the terrain upon which we might re-politicise the global event. The idea of trauma as a 'language of the global event' provides a conceptual mechanism whereby both the event and victim of trauma are rendered as contestable – *and therefore political* – subjects. Developing from the examples given in the previous chapter – of turning trauma to more critical/emancipatory ends, and the (related) possibility to subvert the politics of the event via satirical interventions – this chapter will now contemplate a performative politics of trauma culture. The performance of the traumatic market subject is not limited to one or another discourse that circulates at the time. Indeed, successful performances require a context, a lineage, a repetition and, following Butler, an audience that can anticipate the disclosure. On this view, I argue that the aesthetic terms through which cultural producers have interpreted and contributed to the language of trauma are also an important site of its politics. From popular moral plays on the self in an 'uncertain world', through shock treatises on the horrors of war and romantic fantasies of cartoon heroes who are empowered by their suffering, this chapter will pragmatically engage the cinematic portrayal of trauma. Returning to the dilemmas of performing the event within consumer culture discussed in Chapter 2, I argue that we need to take account of plural iterations of the trauma subject. Different films can do different things with trauma, re-telling moral stories in new and changing circumstances. Quite apart from an event-focused politics of response, then, a performative approach can lead us in the direction of problematising how the event is performed in popular culture: How are its subjects known? What relations are foregrounded? And how do they support or contest wider rationalities of global politics?

Following the genealogy of trauma from a contested psychological category to its current emergence as a wider metaphor of moral judgement, I argue that certain cultural performances can negotiate and instantiate new meaning(s) in trauma. The section on **Batman and the moral self** will interrogate the role of trauma in Christopher Nolan's *Batman* trilogy. These films explore how trauma has a particular(ly) productive power to weave together the logic of a moral individual with notions of contingency (the event) and universal community (i.e. anyone who may be affected by the event). Developing from this, the section on **Trauma as a register of social critique** addresses two critical documentaries – *The Wounded Platoon* and *When the Levees Broke* – which employ tropes of trauma to elicit a form of social critique. In these productions, trauma 'requires' a range of political responses from empathy to radical engagement. This critical dimension of trauma cinema provides an alternative register for the moral assessment of the event: one that might extend beyond therapeutic governance to entertain the abject and sentimental dimensions of trauma.[1] Finally, the chapter turns to a critical discussion of sentimentality and resistance in order to outline the parameters of a more subversive ethics of trauma. The section on **Trauma comedy** takes a lead from films such as *The Big Lebowski* and *Team America* in order to think about *trauma comedy*, questioning how comedy might subvert trauma ethics in a manner that can reflect political critique and provoke alternative imaginaries of the global market subject. A productive agency in relation to the politics of the event.

Batman and the moral self

Batman Begins opens with a young Bruce Wayne innocently playing hide and seek; he crouches over a disused well; it gives way; he plummets to the bottom. He is left in shock at the bottom, in darkness and scared. Then the darkness erupts with thousands of bats that fly over him, screeching. He then awakes with a jolt in a prison cell.

"A dream?" his cellmate asks.

"A nightmare" he replies.

"Worse than this?" his cellmate quips as the scene reveals the dire nature of their life.

By use of flashback, the traumatic event, the subject of trauma and the wider world are placed in a conversation about pain and moral response. The *Batman* trilogy performs trauma as a 'normal' framework for thinking about market life as a set of choices made by the moral self. The films are structured around the traumatic events of the childhood of Batman, introducing a complex discussion of how to respond, both personally and as a society. The idea that traumatic memories recur is woven into the film's cycle of flashbacks that attribute a certain driven quality to Bruce Wayne. When he is confronted in a prison fight, the attacker exclaims, "This is hell," and "I am the Devil."

But Wayne retorts, "You are not the devil, you are just practice."

Such drive is often taken as a coping mechanism for trauma sufferers, but in Batman, it is held up as a potentially positive attribute in the wider social world.

The conceit of Batman is to take a fictional cartoon character, a super hero, and turn him into a real human being, placed in extreme circumstances. Nolan's Batman is placed into a tragic world where his own personal questions about how to respond to trauma become the fulcrum of wider social issues. Trauma places Wayne in a moral struggle with himself and the world, a world that could both hurt him and bring pain to millions. However, this pain is also positive – a prerequisite for the dynamism and strength that drives Wayne. As his mentor Ducard says, "I often wonder at the riches in dark places." The reversal is telling: the traumatic narrative can produce a superhero; trauma may be a source of moral edification. Indeed, Ducard even sees a story of honour:

> Fear has been your guide. But now you must advance or fear will keep you on your knees. We will help you conquer your fear: "Death does not wait for you to be ready. . . . Death is not considerate, or fair. Facing death you learn

> the truth . . . You are weak . . . You are alone . . . And you are afraid . . . But not of me. Tell us, Wayne . . . What do you fear?"
>
> (*Batman Begins*, 2005)

More flashbacks inform the audience that his childhood confrontation with the bats, led to nightmares and insecurity. Such fears led him to ask his parents to leave an opera performance they were attending. When outside the opera house, a mugger shot his mother and father in the alleyway. Thus Batman's confrontation with crime is also partly a responsibility drawn from the guilt of 'causing' his parents' death. Fear and guilt interact with the aforementioned drive to produce a superhero weighed down by power and questions over whether and how to act.

An altogether more Nietzschean moral world is inhabited by the Joker: "What doesn't kill you, simply makes you stranger." In his first scene, he arranges for a group of thieves to rob a bank and tells each of them a different story about how they can benefit by killing one of their accomplices. By the end of the operation, he has managed to use them all against each other, and they are all dead (leaving him with the money). The Joker wears make-up, war paint, to scare people. Like Wayne, his power is based in the reality of trauma, but it is a reality so gruesome, he seems unable to recall it except in 'battle', often different versions on different occasions. The trauma he suffered was intentional:

> Wanna know how I got these scars? My Father was drinker and a fiend. He beat mommy right in front of me. One night he goes off crazier than usual, mommy gets the kitchen knife to defend herself. He doesn't like that. Not. One. Bit. So, me watching, he takes the knife to her, laughing while he does it. Turns to me and says "why so serious?" comes at me with the knife – "why so serious?" Sticks the blade into my mouth – "Let's put a smile on that face" and . . . "Why so serious?" [as the Joker kills Gambol]
>
> (*The Dark Knight*, 2008)

The heroism of Batman's response to trauma is therefore contrasted with the Joker's. His method is to *spread trauma*, setting people against each other: the robber clowns who kill each other in the bank raid and two gangsters who are given a pool cue and asked to see which one of them can survive to join his organisation. On a broader scale, he tells the city he will kill a different person every day until Batman turns himself in; he puts a bomb on two boats full of people and gives the passengers each a button that will blow up the other ship and save themselves (they don't do it).

Significantly, the Batman trilogy departs from a binary division of trauma into *either* a private concern requiring a medical/psychological response, *or* a public issue of collective memory. Instead, Batman blurs this divide to treat trauma as a register of ethical engagement, per se. For example, when Wayne and Dent meet, their discussion crystallises the moral framework of trauma as a discourse of politics. Taking Wayne's personal struggle with 'why he should do good' and how this is possible when it involves doing bad things, the restaurant scene presents the struggle as fundamental to democracy. Wayne questions, "Who appointed the Batman?" Dent replies, "We did. All of us who stood by and let scum take over this city." When questioned about the democratic status of Gotham, he continues, "When their enemies were at the gate the Romans would suspend democracy and appoint one man to protect the city. It wasn't considered an honour. It was a public service." His suggestion is that the Batman exists as an interim protector, waiting for someone else to "take up his mantle" (*The Dark Knight*, 2008). This sentimental understanding of trauma is partly humanitarian, but it lacks the therapeutic dimension. Indeed, the sentiment ties directly with Wayne's hope that his personal moral response to his trauma can serve as a way of spreading good, even as it indulges in a form of despotism. Thus Batman uses trauma to overlay an argument for exceptional politics. This exception is underlined by the reality of the Joker, whose Nietzschean ethics works as a constitutive outside for what be regarded as the liberal trauma of Wayne and Dent. As he retorts,

> Don' talk like one of them – you're not, even if you'd like to be. To them you're just a freak like me . . . they just need you right now. But as soon as they don't, they'll cast you out like a leper. Their morals, their code . . . it's a bad joke. Dropped at the first sign of trouble. They're only as good as the world allows them to be. [. . .] when the chips are down these civilised people . . . they'll eat each other.
>
> (*The Dark Knight*, 2008)

While much of the action and adventure of the trilogy can be read as a standard Hollywood battle between good and evil, this perhaps underlines how trauma has become normal and weaved to an acceptable mainstream moral framework. If the traumatic events of the individual can be woven to a story of good and evil that spans the individual/community divide, then democracy and justice can be thought in terms of the event. Trauma can serve as a language of social critique both upholding the cause of the state in exceptional times (as Batman initially supports) and questioning the state's response to traumatic events (through the character of Dent). From the reflexive questioning of the self and how it responds to trauma in Batman to the wider moral question of defending the dominant mode of community, trauma invests the liberal narrative with a romantic power.

From a critical point of view, the moral-selving of Batman is problematic on a number of levels. As suggested, it can be woven to a form of exceptionalism that justifies the actions of a superhero on a social scale. But there is a sense in which it also works to 'govern' the self through an ethics of trauma. Fassin and Rechtman (2009: 97) suggest that the "expansion of the concept of trauma seems to indicate a general approval of the concept that something of the human resists all forms of moral destruction". This humanitarian foundation is rendered through the moral self of Batman as a moral play where the 'good' response to trauma involves a gradual engagement with the meaning of 'events'. This works through the identification of 'negative' responses to trauma. The Joker seeks to spread trauma, succeeding in provoking a similarly 'negative' response from Dent. When things go wrong for Dent, the Batman chooses to take the blame for his violence and his negative responses to trauma in order to shore up the myth of the state. As the Joker predicts, the city is happy to turn against Batman. Batman's will to self-sacrifice is exposed as the central problem, an issue that is ultimately resolved in personal/therapeutic terms: Wayne's character 'let's go' and 'moves on'.

Trauma as a register of social critique

For all that, trauma can be woven to an imaginative narrative of comic-book heroism, the previous section argued that the possibility of critique is foregrounded. The problematic potential engaged by Batman, that how we respond to traumatic events is an instructive moral dilemma, is a political question insofar as it touches upon the state. Developing on that theme, this section will address a number of critical documentaries that have sought to use the traumatic event as a critical foundation for a political narrative that questions state power and violence. Here again, trauma works as a moral framework, but it turns that moral framework to explore a more emancipatory form of politics. In this way, we might recover the radical potential of trauma as a critique of violence in an everyday context. Beyond a critical emphasis on the saccharine dimension of trauma and recovery – where trauma is woven to a sovereign story of memorialisation and remembrance – we can begin to question how the lived experience of trauma can remain a critical foil in cinema. While fictional works such as Batman use trauma in figurative terms, suggesting through flashback, creating drama through fear, guilt and anger, documentaries can engage more directly (and contingently) in the medicalised language of PTSD. Two films that stand out are *The Wounded Platoon* and *When the Levees Broke*, which both use trauma and PTSD as basis for questioning the politics of traumatic events. Rather than portray the state as the fulcrum for remembrance, each film, in different ways, seeks to identify the role of the state in the violence that causes trauma. This critique of the state is something that critical scholars often overlook in their rush to diagnose therapeutic knowledge.

Critical documentaries

> We give up part of our morality to go to war. We accept what the military gives us as our morality, our sense of right and wrong. It allows us to survive. It allows us to kill. The trick is coming back and living in a civilian world that doesn't have the same thoughts and feelings as we do.
>
> (*The Wounded Platoon*, 2010)

The Wounded Platoon is a critical documentary produced by the American television program distributer Public Broadcasting Service (PBS) that addresses the experiences of the Third Battalion fighting in the Iraq War. It draws on their experiences to develop ideas about trauma and war, but then uses these ideas as a factual critique of US army policy towards soldiers. In line with the cinematic performance of trauma, the documentary emplaces an event, one which killed the 'charismatic' Sergeant Huey, at the centre of analysis. As Ryan Krebbs recalls,

> I'm still having nightmares, flashbacks. There's nothing but smoke and dust everywhere. And I remember looking over to the left and seeing two kids completely just torn apart. And I kept running through the smoke, and the first guy I saw was, you know, Sergeant Huey, covered in blood. His uniform was just covered in blood. And that's about all I remember of that incident.
>
> (*The Wounded Platoon*, 2010)

Several other soldiers recall seeing body parts in the road, people on fire and the memory of watching fellow soldiers die.

In this way, *Wounded Platoon* echoes a set of moves within the armed forces in the US and UK to foreground the traumatic realities of war. In the UK, this has seen NGOs such as Combat Stress and Help for Heroes embrace the idea of trauma as an 'invisible wound'. Teasing at this discourse, however, *Wounded Platoon* juxtaposes such wounds ("they still had Iraq inside of them") with the experiences of returning soldiers to develop a critique of the military. Since the Iraq war began, we learn that a total of 18 soldiers from Fort Carson have been charged with or convicted of murder, manslaughter or attempted murder, and 36 have committed suicide. Retired military psychiatrist Stephen Xenakis argues that the links are obvious: "We have someone who's been emotionally traumatized, and they've got PTSD. [. . .] They can't think as clearly. They are really vulnerable to just overreacting" (*The Wounded Platoon*, 2010). And thus the documentary moves on to use the idea of trauma to critique the army. It reveals a military mental health system overwhelmed with soldiers suffering psychological injuries – at Fort Carson, the rate of PTSD diagnosis has risen 4,000 percent since 2002 – and the widespread use of prescription psychiatric drugs both at home and in combat.

Again, Ryan Krebbs suggests, "Everybody was on Ambien, everybody. It was hard to find somebody that wasn't taking Ambien, . . . It helps you sleep, and it also fucks you up. It gets you pretty high." (*The Wounded Platoon*, 2010). After returning home, Krebbs was also prescribed the antipsychotic medication Seroquel, on which he purposefully overdosed in a suicide attempt. By the time of the surge, more than 20,000 US troops in Afghanistan and Iraq were taking antidepressants and sleeping pills. It is argued that these drugs enable the army to keep soldiers with PTSD on the battlefield. In this way, almost counter-intuitively, the documentary uses PTSD and psychological expertise to develop a critique of the governmental dimensions of therapeutic governance within the military. Against certain strains of critical thought, then, the *Wounded Platoon* animates the language of PTSD as site of divergence and disagreement, in order to refocus its critical potential. Quite apart from the sometimes monolithic image of psychological knowledge, it is interesting to conceive of knowledge about trauma as a contested domain. Trauma knowledge does not begin and end at DSM criteria. Different counsellors can do different things with knowledge about trauma, often disagreeing over, sometimes even campaigning for, certain interpretations of trauma. In critiquing the military, *Wounded Platoon* suggests one way in which PTSD can be mobilised in emancipatory terms.

A similar line of argument can be found in Spike Lee's *When the Levees Broke*, which presents a highly politicised reading of the 'disaster' of Katrina to make the case that the event can be interpreted in terms of 'wilful neglect' along class and racial lines. Again, emotion licensed as trauma becomes a language for making a set of moral and political points. Indeed, a highly concentrated section of the documentary focuses precisely on the psychological experiences of survivors, with one psychologist stating, "This is a Post-Traumatic Stress Disorder Situation." People are filmed returning to nothing; their houses are gone; perhaps, their families are gone. While they are all educated and employed, the post-Katrina landscape makes it almost impossible for them to start over again. One man refers to his own personal experience of trauma, that you cannot prepare for the emotional impact: "Like if your momma were violated" or "if one of your parents die". Medical professionals list the psychological symptoms they observe in the population: agitation, nightmares, people cannot sleep and the resulting growth of prescription medication.

On the one hand, elements of this analysis suggest that the form of 'problematisation' of Katrina in terms of trauma is a straight case of 'diagnosis'. The use of trauma, especially in the medical vernacular of PTSD, can sometimes work as a mere extension of therapeutic governance. As Jenny Edkins argues, diagnoses of PTSD can depoliticise trauma in that those diagnosed

> are to accept the route to cure suggested by therapy. Political action is ruled out. Any attempt at such action . . . is interpreted as an expression of their disease. It is an "acting out" of their symptoms, nothing more.
>
> (Edkins, 2003: 50; cf. Howell, 2011: 78)

On the other hand, however, this section of *When the Levees Broke* culminates with the story of a mother who lost her daughter, which seems to exceed such terms. The daughter had been staying with her father and his wife during the flood, and they had chosen not to leave. The woman says her daughter came to her in a dream, she said, "Momma, I'm falling. I'm falling." The woman says she wanted to help her baby, she was only 5 years old, but that she never even got a chance to say goodbye. Such relationality in death, and life, restricts from simple answers; it lays bare the abject experience of trauma in Katrina. The absence of a resolution is arguably *an opening to politics*.

Drawing these points together, I would argue that these are unstable performances of trauma. Both films make a clear turn to the personal experiences of survivors in their critique of the state. For the most part, this is done using PTSD as the central narrative. Indeed, the range of symptoms, nightmares and flashbacks are used to 'testify' to the violence of war and of disaster. Thus there is a contingent use of medicalised knowledge. Unlike Batman, trauma is not deployed as an ethical framework, where recovery becomes the ideal/moral option. Instead, trauma is used to communicate the pain of events; private trauma is enlisted to a form of public critique. Such documentaries suggest there is scope within PTSD to communicate something of the violence of power; by reducing events to management – through 'drugs' or 'recovery programs' – the state is exposed as insufficient in relation to the personal pain, which exceeds such governance. This might be thought of as a kind of strategic essentialism, whereby the positivist invention of PTSD, with its gamut of 'observable symptoms', is taken as useful vocabulary for addressing the violence of market life on its own terms. More importantly, the documentaries allow subjects to exist and speak politically. A suicidal veteran and a poor black mother are translated by the deployment of PTSD as abject moral subjects, in pain – human.

Trauma comedy

The genealogy of critical knowledge about trauma identifies two somewhat distinct perspectives: humanitarian and governmental. In the first, trauma plays the role of a radical challenge to normal politics, working to make us step outside of our normal frame of reference, to think and feel deeply about difficult topics. This performance of the market subject as an affective being can fulfil a number of diverse functions, allowing for empathy, communication and potentially mobilising resources to support affected subjects. In the second, we encounter an altogether more critical view: that the generalisation of positivist knowledge about trauma *should itself* be understood as a recuperation of the radical power of trauma within knowledge. On this view, it is argued that the widespread recognition of the moral significance of trauma can be read as a form of humanitarian technology: trauma therapy, the invention of PTSD, CBT, etc., all coalesce in a form of therapeutic governance that is increasingly governmental – an affective evacuation of the political. But this is a rather stark – indeed universal – binary.

On this view, either trauma works as a fundamental and radical challenge to normal politics within market life, or the very invention of knowledge about trauma is an expression of the governmental potentialities that underpin such life. The production of market subjects with forms of political agency that work in the affective terms of trauma is *either* a radical critique, *or* a disciplinary technique to secure market life. As I have argued, the missing step in this genealogy of critical thought about trauma is a recognition of the everyday production of knowledge about trauma through culture. By identifying a blur between the psychological definition of trauma and a broader, more everyday category of pain, a performative approach can suggest that there is more at stake in/with this emergent language of the event. We require, in short, a critical engagement with the everyday politics of how trauma is performed, how it educates and how subjects learn to live through *and against* its moral precepts.

Beyond the binary of humanitarian versus governmental, the everyday performance of trauma can provide techniques for critical intervention in the politics of market life. In Hollywood movies such as *Batman*, trauma can be used to provide a definition of heroism: far from a 'magical superhero', the Nolan trilogy tells a story of an ordinary boy facing up to a series of traumatic events – being trapped down a well, the experience of fear and insecurity and witnessing the murder of his parents. Trauma here becomes a moral narrative about how to respond positively to difficult events in life. This can be contrasted with the character of the Joker, who responds badly to his own childhood trauma, and who then seeks to 'spread trauma'. *Batman* is therefore re-imagined as a complex moral play, whereas in the critical documentaries *The Wounded Platoon* and Spike Lee's *When the Levees Broke*, trauma is instead used as a critical device. Abject and marginal subjects are seen telling their stories of war and loss, rendered up against the diverse forces of state power that seeks to subject soldiers to *highly inadequate* forms of therapeutic governance, or which can simply ignore the trauma of Katrina victims. The contrast is important. In *Batman*, trauma is woven to the sovereign power of liberal ethics; making the right choices in relation to adversity can be a spectacular embodiment of moral bravery. In the critical documentaries, trauma is used to identify and critique the state's failure to provide a secure market life. So trauma is mobilised as a critical foil to unpick the terms of political life for the market subject.

In this last section, I would like to examine the rise of *trauma comedy*. Comedy about trauma, gallows humour, holocaust jokes, etc., present an interesting line of thought that may at first strike as offensive or extreme. However, by engaging with the terms of trauma comedy as exhibited in films such as *The Big Lebowski* and *Team America*, as well as jokes by people like Matt Berry, I will argue that there are important potentials for subverting the very subject of trauma. Again, different elements of this traumatic performance do different things. For instance, in *The Big Lebowski*, there is an affectionate chiding of the PTSD victim, a kind of 'warts-and-all' embrace of Walter by the Dude suggests an alternative way of living with trauma. Here trauma comedy provides a kind of pluralist acceptance 'for the freaks'. Yet the comedy of Team America arguably explores darker territory about traumatic flashback.

In these and other ways, trauma comedy offers an interesting way to think about the everyday politics of trauma, how it infuses market life and how it might be subverted. This can be a critical and sentimental form of education. Extending from the moral reflections of liberal heroes, through the abject empathy of critical documentaries, comedy can play on the instability of trauma ethics: public mourning, the subject of PTSD and therapeutic governance. This might infer a more sophisticated version of trauma ethics, for the freaks and the apathetic. Yet it might also, in certain circumstances, allow for a recognition of governmental dimensions of trauma and the ethical relations implied by trauma/comedy. Such reflexivity, I argue, is performative of a market subject that is at least able to question the affective terms of their market life.

While comedy about dark subjects is perhaps nothing new, recent years have seen a growth of comedies that focus on the subject of trauma and, more importantly for this chapter, the satirical portrayal of the trauma victim. In *The Big Lebowski*, in the character of Walter, the subject of the Vietnam vet is held up for gentle ridicule. Despite his obvious instability and public outbursts of anger – such as pulling a gun during an amateur bowling competition because "there are rules!" – it is clear that Walter is still loved and tolerated by his friends. Indeed, Walter's PTSD comes across in the form of an exaggerated series of social faux pas. For example, in one argument in a café over the menu, Walter argues, "Lady, I got buddies who died face down in the muck so that you and I could enjoy this family restaurant" (*The Big Lebowski*, 1998). The comedy explores an altogether different narrative of how to live with a subject of PTSD and how trauma can be quite funny when compared to what we might regard as 'normal life'. Perhaps most poignantly, Walter attempts a eulogy at Donny's funeral: "Donny was a good bowler and a good man. He was one of us. [. . .] He died as so many men of his generation before his time. [. . .] so many bright flowering young men at Kai Son, at Lon Dak, at Hill 364. These young men gave their lives. So did Donny, Donny who loved bowling" [the ashes scatter all over the Dude]. Afterwards the Dude shouts at him asking, "What the fuck does this have to do with Vietnam?" (*The Big Lebowski*, 1998). They embrace.

The Big Lebowski suggests a warmth and reconciliation to PTSD in liberal America. Even after the most chaotic and difficult burial for their friend, a hard emotional dilemma is smoothed with a typical line from Walter: "Fuck it Dude. Let's go bowling" (*The Big Lebowski*, 1998). A more direct parody of the trauma narrative can be found in *Team America*, which satirises the hubris of post-9/11 America and the War on Terror, with its thumping rock back track: "America, Fuck Yeh! Coming along to save the Mother fucking Day, yeh!" (*Team America: World Police*, 2004). While all the characters in *Team America* present with complex emotional lives, whereby they see the world in terms of 'feelings' for each other, it is the lead character who has the closest relationship with trauma. Gary is the unlikely hero of the film, a famous Broadway star called upon by Team America to use his special 'acting powers' to infiltrate a terrorist network. While Gary has doubts about his ability to save the world in this way, he eventually opens up to recount an early childhood trauma when he lost his brother Tommy:

> We were all out at the zoo one day. I was doing some acting, walking on the railing of the gorilla exhibit. I fell in. Everyone screamed and Tommy jumped in after me, forgetting that he had blueberries in his front pocket. The gorillas just went wild. They jumped all over his body and threw him around like a rag doll to get to those blueberries. One gorilla would throw him to another gorilla who tossed him to another. Everyone panicked and cried out for somebody to help but it was too late. The gorillas beat him to death before the zookeepers could gas them all.
>
> (*Team America: World Police*, 2004)

Much like the hero narrative of *Batman*, it is this early childhood trauma that is both the source of Gary's impressive acting skills and a crippling guilt about his role in life. When Gary expresses such feeling to Lisa though, she reassures him: "Gary, you didn't kill your brother. Those gorillas did." From here on Gary resolves to commit his acting powers to saving the world by infiltrating the terrorists by pretending to be one of them. Almost immediately, he faces a challenge to prove his credentials to one of the terrorists who doubts he is genuine, recalling the noise of the Gorillas, Gary 'acts':

> I was just a boy when the infidels came to my village in their Blackhawk helicopters. The infidels fired at the oil fields and they lit up like the eyes of Allah. Burning oil rained down from the sky and cooked everything it touched. I could only hide myself and cry as my goats were consumed by the fiery black liquid death. In the midst of the chaos, I could swear that I heard my goats screaming for help. As quickly as they had come, the infidels were gone. It was on that day I put a jihad on them. And if you don't believe it, then you'd better kill me now, because I'll put a jihad on you, too.
>
> (*Team America: World Police*, 2004)

Comedy and satire can play an important role in the performative politics of the subject. In her discussion of 'drag culture', Butler argues that in "imitating gender, drag implicitly reveals the imitative structure of gender itself – as well as its contingency" (2006: 187). While parody can only serve this subversive role in a problematic way, as it can always be rewoven to market logics, she celebrates its potential, arguing, "In place of the law of heterosexual coherence, we see sex and gender denaturalized by means of a performance which avows their distinctness and dramatizes the cultural mechanism of their fabricated unity" (2006: 187–8). In this vein, I would argue that the subversion of trauma through Walter and Gary presents an important possibility; that the fabricated unity of trauma with heroism, with self-discovery, with righteousness, might be teased apart.

Such emotional literacy is a mainstay of both the humanitarian narrative and the governmental critique and it is therefore crucial to recognise performances that directly tease at its foundations. On one level, the moral depth of trauma is undermined in trauma comedy. Trauma is an important affective discourse, in part, because of its ability to command silence; trauma cannot be questioned, or even understood fully; it can only be experienced or witnessed. Such weightiness is undermined by trauma comedy; the idea of victim-hero, and their emotional growth, is directly placed in question. On another level, however, it is possible to conceive of such forms of satire as form of politics that works with the contingent language of trauma. It is not a critique 'of' trauma. Much like the critical documentaries in the previous section, it is better to think of such satires as a form of critique in the language of trauma. However, if trauma and PTSD are provocative territory for comedians, nowhere is this more acutely demonstrated that in a British satirical short *Action Man: Battlefield Casualties*, produced by Veterans for Peace UK (2015), a campaign group which seeks to raise the British age of conscription to war. The short is presented as an '80s-style advert for children's toys and is voiced by British comedian Matt Berry, who narrates a satire of a toy advert where children are playing with the Action Man figures. Three adverts are spliced together and concern a visual presentation of children play with PTSD Action Man:

Advert 1

Voiceover: Action Man: Battlefield Casualties. For PTSD Action man, danger lurks at every turn. He never feels safe, not even in his own home. Do what you can to block out the memories. [He drinks special brew] With no support from HQ, it's up to you to find a way.
Action Man: 'Looks like we're on our own' [He snorts cocaine]
Voiceover: PTSD Action Man now comes with 1000 yard stare action. With time running out, only you can stop the pain.
Action Man: 'Let's get out of here.' [Hangs himself]

Advert 2

Voiceover: Here comes paralysed Action Man. Legs really don't work. His spine shattered by an enemy IED. Action Man is crippled by constant pain. With his bowels out of action, only a colostomy bag can save him from disaster.
Action Man: 'Reloading' [as child places new colostomy bag on toy]
Voiceover: But despite his injuries there can be no rest. [He receives a 'Benefits Cancelled' notice]
Action Man: 'Back to work for me!' [Seen struggling to stack a shelf in a wheelchair]

Advert 3

Voiceover: Make the ultimate sacrifice with new dead Action Man [on the battlefield Action Man is seen covered in blood with no legs] Blown to bits by bombs, its up to you to pick up the pieces.
Child: 'We've lost him'
Voiceover: Identify the body with dog tags.
Child: 'Private Smith, 19 years old.'
Voiceover: Reward him for valiant effort.
Child: 'You've been promoted.'
Voiceover: Can you dig the grave in time??
2 Children: 'Let's do it!' [High five each other]
Voiceover: Bury your dead Action Man with full military honours. 'Present Arms, Fire'. [Trumpet plays] Coffin sold separately. (*Action Man: Battlefield Casualties*, 2015)

The comedy of this piece is clearly quite dark, playing on the disconnect created between a child's toy and the experience of trauma and PTSD. In some ways, it touches on the same themes as Walter's character in *The Big Lebowski*, where the PTSD victim is portrayed a helpless human, reconciled to life back home. But the humour is more cutting and suggests that no such resolution is possible. Action Man is reduced to alcohol and drugs to bury his flashbacks, eventually committing suicide in the first advert, or being reduced to menial labour in the second. Veterans for Peace campaign to increase the age of military conscription, because they don't think war is fitting place for children. In this sense, the use of a child's toy, with child actors, evokes the innocence of young fantasies of action heroes and war, yet this is juxtaposed with the very real consequences of such military culture. The satire works to enlist trauma as both a radical critique of state violence and a subversion of the role of advertising in market subjectivity.

Conclusion

The argument of this chapter is contingently situated and engaged. To wit, if the popular language of trauma is linked to the (emergent) buttresses of neo-liberal government – the media, the event and the hero – this does not infer that trauma must of necessity, form an apology (or an escape). Against the image of trauma as either humanitarian or governmental, I have engaged the possibilities and limits of how it might work as a contingent language for engaging the politics of the event/subject. While the potential violence of these emergent subjectivities echoes past dilemmas – of 'victimhood', 'recovery', indeed the very 'know-ability' of pain – cultural producers (and everyday subjects) might also 'use' and 'subvert' these limits in novel terms. Occupying the narrative of trauma in this way requires that we re-phrase it in pragmatic terms, less as a universal truth of global ethics (which fails to contain the excess of suffering it claims to reflect) and more as contingent vocabulary within which subjects and moral arcs can be written critically, lived imaginatively.

Beyond trauma?

While trauma has clearly worked to augment and structure knowledge about the global event, the forms of resistance considered in this chapter are by no means the only ways in which the politics of the global event might be conceived. Indeed, over recent years, the popularity of trauma has begun to wane in the institutions of global governance and national media and policy circles (Howell, 2011). While the event/response logics of trauma theory have been read into the politics of vulnerable market subjects, they have also perpetuated a mood to 'learn from' major global events so as to prepare for them.

In psychological circles, this has been typified by an interest in 'giving space' to people who experience traumatic events. Illustrative here is the debate about Critical Incident Stress De-Briefing (CISD) (Bisson, 2007). For many years, it was supposed that a key issue in the rapid response to trauma victims was to try and 'prevent' the onset of PTSD. In practical terms, this was interpreted as requirement to intervene quickly, often on the day, to interview trauma victims and to educate them about the kinds of symptoms they may experience. While this form of intervention was considered a major advance on historical problems of ignorance, denial and/or stigmatisation, a range of anecdotal critiques of this method quickly emerged. Victims appeared to consider the practice invasive and humiliating in itself. At the same time, a number of evidence-based studies suggested that CISD was associated with a higher chance of victims developing PTSD compared to those who did not receive such interviews. One body of opinion began to form that such proactive forms of counselling carried the capacity to 're-traumatise' individuals. A new practice began to emerge around the idea of 'watchful waiting' – a technique that suggested it was better to assume that people might have healthy or 'resilient' responses to traumatic events. Interestingly, this less invasive idea seems to counter many of the stronger critiques of therapeutic governance by placing the adaptive capabilities of the individual as the prior assumption. While it is accepted that trauma might happen, it was by no means considered to be the 'normal' or 'inevitable' outcome of every extreme event.

Note

1 It should be noted that my reading of these cultural products is exclusively concerned with the way trauma is understood and performed in everyday terms. I do not seek to make an intervention on film studies, nor do I draw from the tradition of psychoanalytic studies of film that has variously drawn upon 'trauma theory' as a way of deconstructing films (see Antze and Lambek, 1996; Radstone, 2007. See also Leys, 2000).

Resilience and the global event

Previous chapters looked at how the modern discourse of trauma and the traumatic event can be performative of a certain set of relations between the global event and the market subject. Trauma was introduced to the discussion of the global event as a critical discourse. Authors such as Habermas and Beck sought to conceive of the traumatic event of 9/11 as an instructive moment, something that could demonstrate the shared vulnerability between a privileged West and a dominated and immiserated 'non-West'. This use of trauma as a critical entry point to the hierarchies of global capitalism is both curious and ethically productive, using one rationality of the global (cosmopolitan sympathy) to hail an economic subject in affective terms (the reflexive liberal subject). Thus the traumatic discourse of the global event performs a market subject with broader, global concerns by *promoting* a sense of shared vulnerability and (potential) solidarity. As an affective economy, however, it was argued to perform a mix of humanitarian and governmental rationalities that coalesce around an event/response logic. On this view, the traumatic market subject emerges as problematically 'vulnerable', perhaps helpless and in need of 'governance', whether it be through empathy, understanding or counselling. The humanitarian governance of market life, therefore, carries a potential to diminish the agency of market subjects in order to 'save them' and restore order. However, despite the disciplinary dimensions of this affective economy, it was argued that such performances should be understood as unstable. Indeed, Chapters 4 and 5 pointed to a number of ways in which the traumatic discourse might be engaged and/or resisted, whether by turning to a politics of empathy – e.g. using trauma to critique market governance – or by subverting the terms of subjection inherent in the discourse – e.g. through comedy. Across these different lines of thought, I drew from Foucault, Butler and Fassin in order to emphasise the capacity of self-making subjects to speak through and against the traumatic narrative of the global event. In this way, I argue, an alternative politics of global market life can be imagined.

Of course, trauma and the traumatic narrative are by no means the only discourse of global events, and indeed, their moral depth and emotional weight may even lead to a form of 'compassion fatigue'. Aspects of the trauma narrative infer a different order of media coverage, long-term healing and understanding, whereas news media can sometimes seek out more visceral or dynamic arcs.

Indeed, as the conclusion to Chapter 5 suggested, recent decades have perhaps seen a turn away from the trauma narrative as the pre-eminent discourse of the global event to embrace an altogether more flexible and managerial postulate in resilience (Howell, 2012). While trauma remains in the mix, a corollary discourse of resilience has emerged that steps away from the negative and emotive dimensions of trauma to promote a positive attitude to the event, moving 'from a state of vulnerability to one of resilience' (Béné, Wood, Newsham, & Davies, 2012: 15). This second section of the book will therefore address the idea of resilience as an affective discourse of the global event that works in a number of different ways to trauma, performing a more positive set of relations between the market subject and an 'uncertain' market life (Chandler, 2014b).

What is resilience? Representations of resilience abound in news and popular culture (Grayson, 2017). In the aftermath of the Boston bombings, city leaders affirmed that Boston was a resilient city that would survive and come back stronger. An event that would normally be performed as traumatic, a shocking wound, very quickly emerged with a set of positive qualities: bravery, recovery, solidarity (Brassett et al., 2013). News reporting on the eventual manhunt for the bombers seemed to focus on the deployment of a complex network of agencies. Such 'first responders' came from multiple agencies and knew how to co-operate, indeed had sophisticated techniques of co-ordination in a fast-moving event scenario. Yet it was actually the widespread awareness of the nature of the unfolding event that led to a tip off from a member of the Boston public about the whereabouts of the bomber – media, public agencies and Twitter hashtags seemingly combined to produce what many deemed to be a positive outcome (Brassett et. al., 2013). Resilience on these terms is at once a proactive and inclusive discourse of the global event. Quite apart from the weighty tones of trauma, the discourse of resilience seems to carry an aesthetic of speed and adaptive response. Instead of reeling from the shock of an event, resilience suggests an adjustment, a re-orientation to live with and through the event. Against the governmental dimensions of therapeutic governance, resilience allows for unconventional forms of co-operation and agency. Indeed, it seems to embrace the same kinds of reflexivity – about the limits to knowledge and the contingency of life – that are normally encouraged by critical approaches. Contingency, uncertainty and imagination, so often the clarion call of critical scholars against the structural necessities of global capitalism, are incorporated into resilient agendas as founding assumptions (Chandler, 2012). For some, this all represents a major shift in the ethical politics of the global event from trauma to resilience (Howell, 2012). Gone is a focus on the disarming power of events; instead, we begin to see a reversal: by all means, events do happen, but the important thing is to prepare for such uncertainties by fostering adaptability (O'Malley, 2010).

Trauma and resilience coalesce around a similar problematic of the global event and how it affects (and is affected by) individuals, but there is an important augmentation. While trauma addresses the affective impact of events, resilience develops a more proactive treatment: the event is yet to happen, and we can therefore build qualities and characteristics of preparedness and adaptability into our systems of governance. Thus while seemingly distinct, this book will emphasise the continuity and mutual performance of trauma and resilience. Resilience agendas often involve knowledge and practitioners directly linked to trauma and trauma counselling; indeed, the everyday performance of resilience through scenario planning is intimately involved with knowledge about trauma (Aradau and Van Munster, 2012). Instead of a decisive shift from trauma to resilience then, I would argue that trauma and resilience can be better understood as *linked* discourses of the global event.

In his responses to the UK vote to leave the EU, for example, the governor of the Bank of England (BOE) Mark Carney was quick to diagnose a form of trauma that would likely affect global markets: "All this uncertainty has contributed to a form of economic post-traumatic stress disorder amongst households and businesses and in financial markets," he argued. "People have become more cautious about their futures and they're more averse to making irreversible decisions that may be exposed to some future disaster risk" (cited in Sculthorpe, 2016). He therefore noted that the BOE had been making a number of important contingency plans for just such an event in order to build up the underlying 'financial resilience' of the UK. While we might wish to debate what 'economic trauma' actually is, and how an event such as Brexit might cause it, Carney's discursive move captures something of the eventalisation of Brexit. The discourse of trauma served to foreground the weight and seriousness of the event in affective terms. The symbolism performed – of a 'vote against the establishment', a 'working class protest' and the widely cultivated fear of a 'rise of racism' – meant that the event promoted a set of emotional reactions. Andre Spicer (2016) suggested,

> There is a sense of trauma. Pay careful attention to how people talk about the referendum and you will notice it is often in very visceral and disturbing terms. They talk about it as "a body blow", "a catastrophe" or even "a death".

Much like the performance of the sub-prime crisis as a traumatic event in Chapter 4, Brexit conjured an important politics of identity about the vulnerability of a British role in global politics: we were all quite personally involved in global politics. But if trauma has migrated into the mainstream of the public sphere in this way, serving as a readily available emotional register for communicating about global events, its discursive counterpoint in resilience has arguably performed an altogether different and more diverse set of functions. Set up as the reverse positive of trauma, discourses of resilience speak to a more forward-thinking set of agendas. Indeed, strictly speaking, Carney's association of economic PTSD with a backdrop of financial resilience should not be possible, since resilience agendas effectively aim to 'avoid' the potential for traumatic effects by engendering a set of positive coping strategies, adaptability and a capacity to 'bounce back' (Chandler and Coaffee, 2017).

Indeed, this juxtaposition of resilience to trauma can serve to highlight some of the central critical dilemmas in the politics of resilience, about it its effectiveness *and desirability*. Firstly, for policymakers such as Carney, resilience serves as a managerial discourse of governance that provides a practical orientation to an uncertain reality. On this view, we might think about resilience as a form of adaptation to the possibility of extreme events so as to reduce the negative consequences. In this policy-oriented vein, the discourse of resilience is taken as a positive attempt to foster a sense of preparedness and adaptability in relation to extreme events. Uncertainty is taken as a pervasive existential reality of interdependent systems, where shocks or asymmetries in one network can provoke unintended consequences in others. The managerial objective then is to foster co-operation within and between networks that recognise and plan for the inevitability of extreme events such that when they occur, the optimum level of proactive response is possible (Braithwaite, 2013). On this view, resilience is a good thing, if done well.

Secondly, an altogether more critical line of scholarship regards the discourse of resilience as an epitome of neo-liberal governmentality. Thus the resilient demand to foster self-reliance and adaptability amongst market subjects should be taken as heralding a retreat from public responsibility for welfare. And the recognition that 'extreme events' might impact the economy infers a burden of adaptation within networks and individuals. This critique emerges from the wider literature on neo-liberal governmentality that charts the responsibilisation of market subjects as a key mechanism for 'governing' individuals – by 'guiding their conduct' (Foucault, 1997b: 203; Dean, 2010). Indeed, authors such as Jonathan Joseph (2013) further identify the shift to resilience thinking as a fitting counterpart to austerity, an embedding of neo-liberalism through the kind of proactive self-governance required to deal with a roll back of welfare. Rather than an affective *response* to an event, as per trauma, resilience is better understood as the nurturing of a set of affective dispositions and proclivities *before the event*. From self-help books that encourage positive thinking, to the quantified-self movement that overlays new technologies with an ethos of constant improvement, resilience is argued to perform an affective discipline of neo-liberal market subjects (O'Malley, 2010). The resilient market subject is not so much defined by any particular event – as per the traumatised subject – but has rather been encouraged to define themselves in relation to the inevitability of different events by proactively fostering 'resilience'. Whether this marks a progressive improvement of the circumstances of the liberal market subject or a governmental completion of the politics of the global event appears to be a central dilemma.

Yet across these large narratives of resilient governance, there seems to be a common disconnect: resilience is *uncontested*. Those who take resilience as an important and progressive policy agenda suggest that it can be straightforwardly applied to yield a set of 'positive' outcomes. Equally, the more critical scholarship on resilience appears to regard the expansion of resilience into almost every area of global politics as basically inevitable. Much like the globalisation discourse that proliferated before it, resilience seems to carry a productive ambiguity; while it manifests everywhere, its potential local connotations are endless. As Cavelty et al. (2015: 3–4) playfully remark on the theme of resilient security:

> Have you heard? There is a new superhero in town! Her name is Resilience and she has quickly made herself indispensable to the Security Empire.

> Resilience materializes in crisis situations and fights against Complete Breakdown by granting the vulnerable means and responsibility to help themselves. Her nemeses are Contingency and Uncertainty – yet, they also give her reason to exist. At a certain point, she was reported to be in a league with Risk and Preparedness, but that is unconfirmed. Others are in a clearly ambiguous relationship with Resilience. Prevention suspects that she might be an imposter, Precaution eyes her warily, and Resistance wonders whether he should become her sidekick or start a campaign against her. Resilience is mysterious: she can be in many places at the same time, takes on various forms, slips into different subject-bodies, and eludes clearly-defined dimensions of time – some say she is only ever emergent in essence. She is a typical postmodern heroine, existing in different universes, with various stories of origin – her multiple personalities imbue different characteristics, normative concepts, and ways of interacting with subjects.

Rather than proceed with a definition of the substance of resilience – whether positive, emancipatory or totalising and governmental – I will argue that it is productive to ask what does resilience do? What relations and subjectivities does it permit or encourage? And what possibilities and limits does it create for politics, agency and change?

This section will be divided into three chapters that each develop a critical take on the role of resilience as an affective economy of the global event. Chapter 6 is entitled 'Resilience and Neo-liberalism', and seeks to understand the discourse of resilience and how it fits within, produces or resists market life. Discussion engages the predominant managerial and critical readings of resilience within liberal market life. The resilient market subject is produced as a straightforwardly self-making, adaptable subject that is capable of dealing with, or bouncing back from, extreme events. The 'beauty' of this construction, I argue, is to enshrine the (un)certainty of the event as a kind of *deus ex machina,* which conditions a vision of market life as management and planning, rather than politics. A number of criticisms of the totalising nature of this way of thinking will be addressed including an engagement with the arguments of David Chandler (2012), who identifies an avowedly anti-liberal discourse in resilience. Indeed, even the resilience agendas of the BOE – by no means a hotbed of anti-capitalism – can reveal a range of critical positions on concentration, inequality, and the importance of local banking. Much like the resistant subjects of trauma identified in Chapter 5, there appears to be an important reflexive possibility in the idea of a responsible, self-making, resilient subject. Therefore, Chapter 7 will develop on an important performative instability in financial resilience – namely, by fostering adaptability – and values of systemic interdependence, the discourse of financial resilience seems uniquely malleable. Indeed, a number of alternative finance initiatives seem to speak directly to the aims of the major financial institutions that advocate for resilience (Brassett and Holmes, 2016). Whether alternative finance practices like local banking, peer lending or alternative currencies are resilient and/or resistant is a question addressed via an engagement with *Bank of Dave*, a critically oriented local banking initiative that seeks to publicise alternative modes of finance (cf. Fishwick, 2012). Against those who would point to the generalisation of the global event in resilience, how uncertainty and contingency become the affective drivers of the responsible market subject, I argue that it is the particular and detailed performance of financial resilience in *Dave* which actually politicises the sub-prime crisis and allows for financial agency.

Finally, Chapter 8 will revisit this question of the politics of resistance. Against those who would see resilience as a triumph of neo-liberal forms of governance, I argue that resilient market subject can also be thought of in resistant and imaginative terms. This chapter draws on the work of Jack Halberstam (2011) in order to develop a critical engagement with the everyday performance of resilience in Pixar movies and popular culture more broadly. By situating resilience as an element within a wider cultural political economy of the event, I argue, a performative approach retains a sensitivity to the diverse and overlapping ways in which the contingency of this discourse about contingency can be recognised and engaged. Far from a stultifying triumph of neo-liberal governance, resilience can be understood as a terrain of politics like any other. Engaging with the specific and particular ways in which it hails systems and performs, subjects can therefore shed light on how such performances are subverted and changed.

6 Resilience and neo-liberalism

The *deus ex machina* of the future event

Previous chapters have identified an affective politics of the global event in terms of a logic of response that is inculcated through market subjects. While trauma presented itself as a critical discourse that – especially in relation to 9/11 and the sub-prime crisis – sought to foster concern for the humanitarian dimensions of the global event, a politics of affective discipline was drawn out and engaged. Here the idea of 'response' was portrayed in terms of a potential hierarchy of values – *whose trauma matters?* – and how they might order, or produce, particular ideas about global market life. Indeed, the importance of victimhood, empathy and therapeutic governance were taken as an emerging – if problematic – register of political agency within market life. But what happens when we consider more proactive discourses of the global event like resilience? How is the idea of the global event/market life performed? And what subject positions does it license?

Against traumatic imagery of shock, fear, emotional wounds, and empathy for victims, the discourse of resilience seeks to proactively plan for 'extreme events' by fostering networks and subjects with a capacity to bounce back. Far from a traumatised victim, the subject of resilience appears with a more positive set of attributes: preparedness and adaptability. Rather than a reactive politics of the global event, provoking shock and empathy, the affective dimensions of resilience have an altogether more pervasive orientation to market life, seeking to use the existential uncertainty of the event as a foundational justification to condition a range of practices and emotional dispositions. This represents a step change in the logics of governing and living within market life. From the more aesthetic and mediatised image of the global event discussed in the first section on trauma, this section will therefore encounter an altogether more *theorised* and bureaucratically pervasive version of the event – *an event to be anticipated.*

On this view, resilience *does things* to market life. Thinking in terms of resilience pitches global market life as complex, made up of interdependent systems that must adapt to a range of uncertainties. Part of this adaptation involves regulators – and network agents alike – beginning to model the likelihood of system wide 'events', such as terrorist attacks, financial crises or floods, in a manner that supposedly enhances both their predictability and the efficacy of contingency planning. But part of it relies on a certain performance of the world – an ontology of global market life that foregrounds the relationality, which traumatic events were previously thought to expose. Thus, for a number of critical theorists, especially those working in a post-Foucauldian line, resilience must be placed in the context of wider rationalities of neo-liberalism that seek to discipline subjects to certain logics and norms of market life.

While elements of a resilience agenda certainly map onto existing policy areas such as systemic risk and global security, and though resilience is clearly a practical policy orientation, a more critical reading would point to how assumptions about the ontology of market life – as complex, emergent, uncertain – can carry a set of governmental implications. Like trauma before it, then, while resilience clearly pitches as a critical discourse, attempting to reflect and promote the positive capacities of individuals and communities, its everyday performance requires an orientation to craft market subjects in new ways – e.g. via resilience agendas in schools, financial education, self-help books, wellness agendas. On this view, the increasing use of the term resilience across diverse policy areas reflects and engenders a wider and more endemic set of changes in rationalities of neo-liberalism (Lentzos and Rose, 2009; O'Malley, 2010; Walker and Cooper, 2011); it is part of a general trend to 'responsibilise' individuals and legitimate power relations through invocations of uncertainty in relation to 'future events' (Dean, 2014; Zebrowski, 2009). Resilience thus becomes a supplement to the general scaling back of state responsibilities that accompanies neo-liberal reforms, engendering attitudes, practices and agendas to underpin the adaptability that is sought, not least, in relation to austerity (Joseph, 2013a). This is a powerful diagnosis of resilience that identifies how an apparently practical, even progressive discourse can work to reify a set of (what are exposed as) political assumptions; an emphasis on resilience can act to 'normalise' the existential uncertainty of the extreme event, reducing 'crisis' or 'disaster' to a natural and expected part of global market life. In turn, this can mute a wider critique of the configurations of political and economic power that both produce and rely on this (apparently) necessary logic of the future event. From a governance response, to an existential condition, resilience can become a totalising political discourse of complex market life.

Despite the attractiveness of this more critical approach to resilience, this chapter will interrogate the position in terms of its own potential for reification. That is to say, many critical approaches to resilience run the risk of handing an easy 'victory' to neo-liberalism as the dominant formation within market life. Ironically, much like the policy variant of resilience that it targets, the critical approach to resilience seems to assume that that resilience actually 'works'; resilience is portrayed as a logical and successful completion of neo-liberal governmentality. Instead, by drawing on the politics of performativity identified in previous chapters, I will argue that the contingency and instability of various 'practices' made in the name of resilience is sometimes understated in the critical literature (Brassett and Vaughan-Williams, 2015). And this can be explicitly illustrated by reference to the everyday politics of the global event. In the case of finance, for example, we live in a period of unprecedented public engagement with finance and financial practices, precisely because of the way the sub-prime crisis was eventalised in the public sphere. As a direct result, sophisticated critiques of finance are increasingly available online, in social forums and – thanks to organisations such the Tax Justice Network and UKUncut – in mainstream media. Such engagement and contest prefigures the ability to think and practice financial resilience in other ways.

This argument will be developed over three sections that seek to draw out and problematise the political discourse of resilience. The section on **Resilience and market life** will consider the dominant framings of resilience that exist in the literature. Both policy oriented and critical approaches foreground the politics of the global event in somewhat monolithic terms whereby a pervasive uncertainty in relation to the future event seems to condition a host of logics and rationalities, both progressive and governmental. The section on **Towards a performative critique of resilience** will then develop a performative critique of this politics of resilience. Against both the policy and critical approaches, it is suggested that scholarship should be more concerned with developing analyses of the *actual practices* of resilience. Indeed, we might distinguish between resilience and neo-liberalism by arguing that a resilient focus on complexity and emergence may actually challenge significant aspects of neo-liberal governance, not least the sanctity of interactive market outcomes. Finally, the section on **Performative agency** will draw these points together in a discussion of Butler's (2010) concept of performative agency and the question of whether and how discourses of resilience succeed, break down or misfire. Recognising the contingency of these discourses of contingency can open up a performative politics of resilience that will be engaged in subsequent chapters.

Resilience and market life

An important theme of this book is to question how apparently 'non-economic' discourses of affect can have resonance and become constitutive within market life. In the case of trauma and read from an emotive and sometimes explicitly psychological discourse of the subject, this was an avowedly hybrid form, which explored how a critical promotion of empathy and humanitarian concern for suffering was mobilised in relation to global market life, financial crisis and as a critique of disasters such as Katrina. In the case of resilience, there is arguably a more direct path. On the one hand, the rise of resilience in psychology has promoted certain qualities and characteristics of coping, adaptation and reliance on social networks that fits quite naturally with a functioning market subject. On the other hand, the emergence of resilience as a pervasive discourse of global governance, deployed in policy areas as diverse as terrorism and flood defence has direct implications for the governance of market life. Policymakers now conceive of interrelated governing networks, the systemic importance of critical infrastructure and the qualities and characteristics of a resilient economy. As Walker and Salt (2006, cf. Chandler 2014b: 19) argue, resilience has an expansive logic which means it

> should appeal to anyone interested in dealing with risk in a complex world. This includes business leaders, policy makers, resource managers and politicians. It also includes . . . members of the public . . . This is because at its core,

> resilience is about risk and complexity, things that impact all of us. We live in a complex world. Anyone with a stake in managing some aspect of that world will benefit from a richer understanding of resilience and its implications.

The discourse of resilience appears to be both pervasive and important, yet its meaning seems somewhat underspecified. Although we have witnessed an impressive growth in the use and spread of the discourse across policy areas such as critical infrastructure protection, financial stability and education policy, the idea of resilience emerges from an equally diverse range of disciplines and traditions. Often loosely referred to as the ability to 'bounce back', it carries a genealogy that draws from engineering and the capacity of certain materials to return to their former shape after pressure is applied (de Bruijne et al.,, 2010), from psychology and notions of the 'resilient individual' who displays cognitive coping abilities in relation to traumatic experiences (Seligman, 2011) and, most influentially, from the study of ecological systems as they adapt to external shocks.

Ecologists are responsible for identifying the reflexive component of resilience that arguably makes it particularly suitable for contemporary practices of governance within complex market life. By observing ecological systems as they adapt over time to external shocks like disease or environmental shifts, certain authors have described resilience in terms of qualities such as flexibility and adaptability over time: resilience as an emergent system property (Holling, 1973). Indeed, this notion of emergent adaptability has been enthusiastically drawn out and engaged across the social sciences and especially in relation to organisational and community resilience – i.e. "the capacity of a social system (e.g. an organization, city, or society) to proactively adapt to and recover from disturbances that are perceived within the system to fall outside the range of normal and expected disturbances" (Comfort et al., 2010: 9, emphasis added). Thus resilience is figured as a positive, emergent quality of social systems in relation to the event (to come). If trauma privileges the shocking element of the event – i.e. that 'falls outside the range of normal or expected reality' – resilience almost seems to accept such shocks before they happen in order to privilege the qualities and characteristics of adaptation to them.

Across these different genealogies, I would argue, resilience carries an elliptical quality, somewhat akin to the way trauma blurs between a clinical diagnosis and a wider metaphor of pain. Resilience seems to conjure an image that combines physical attributes of strength, as well as more relational qualities – social and psychological – of adaptation and 'improvement'.[1] This ability to combine traits and qualities gives resilience a certain constructive ambiguity, which makes it readily applicable to alternative and diverse policy agendas. The 'successful' spread of resilience in governance practices has spurred a burgeoning and, typically, inter-disciplinary literature which roughly divides over whether or not resilience is a 'good thing', which can/should be improved and a more critical set of arguments, which focus on the disciplinary dimensions of resilience and how it fits within wider patterns of neo-liberal governance. While these different strands of thought clearly diverge in terms of their normative evaluation of resilience, this section will argue that they actually share quite a bit of common ground over both the conceptual rendering of resilience and the likely, continued growth of resilience agendas and practices.

Policy and managerial approaches

In the policy and managerial literature, resilience is taken as a straightforwardly good thing that should be fostered (e.g. United Nations International Strategy for Disaster Reduction, 2012; Zolli and Healy, 2013). It is a quality defined by active metaphors of 'bouncing back' or 'pulling together' in the face of shocks, extreme events or other forms of rupture to 'normal life'. In this way, resilience is understood as a positive and proactive quality in light of pervasive existential uncertainty; whereby shocks, death, catastrophe and all variety of extreme events are taken as a normal element of life that systems (whether ecological or social) may be more-or-less *resilient to*. Within the global political economy, this approach has typically focused on the rhetoric of stability in relation to economic shocks. In line with the comments of Mark Carney, the Bank for International Settlements has sought to promote "the road to a more resilient banking sector" (Bank for International Settlements, 2013: 52). Equally, Ben Bernanke has called for the production of communities resilient to recession (Bernanke, 2013), while economists affiliated to both the World Bank and the International Monetary Fund can now be found comparing economies and regions on their capacity for resilience to financial crises (Didier et al., 2012; de Gregorio, 2013).

While a concept of crisis and, more latterly, ideas of systemic risk have a clear trajectory in IPE and global economic governance, the invocation of resilience has spawned a growth of systems modelling that derives from ecological studies (Brassett and Holmes, 2016). This carries distinctive implications for how we think about ontology of the subject at hand, in this case, market life. Broadly speaking, the concept of ecology refers to a system of alliances between entities in a radically interconnected milieu of interaction. In its initial phase, such approaches aimed to think scientifically about how ecological systems adapt and change over time and in relation to external shocks. As C. S. Holling argued,

> Individuals die, populations disappear, and species become extinct. That is one view of the world. But another view of the world concentrates not so much on presence or absence as upon the numbers of organisms and the degree of constancy of their numbers.
>
> (Holling, 1973: 1)

On this view, resilience is produced as one possible response to a disturbance or extreme event such as flooding, fires and human activities such as deforestation. Holling critiqued the notion of a naturally occurring equilibrium, understood in terms of a balance to which life will eventually return through self-repair. And he therefore introduced a key distinction between engineering resilience, which refers to the time it takes for a system to return to its previous state after an external disturbance, on the one hand, and *ecological resilience* relating to a more open and complex ability of a system to sustain productivity under pressure, while not necessarily 'returning' to any primordial state. Holling, therefore, argued that resilience should be associated with qualities *within* a system rather than any end point, or goal; thus, "if we are dealing with a system profoundly affected by changes external to it, and continually confronted by the unexpected, the constancy of its behavior becomes less important than the persistence of the relationships" (Holling, 1973: 1) Importantly, by turning to a focus on relationships, Holling's view of ecological resilience becomes extendable to contemporary social systems. Concepts such as uncertainty, shock and importance of adaptive relationships arguably map well onto problems of governing market life where uncertainty and risk seem pervasive. Indeed, in their influential genealogy of the concept, Walker and Cooper (2011; 6) argue,

> Under the sign of resilience, this is an approach to risk management which foregrounds the limits to predictive knowledge and insists on the prevalence of the unexpected, *seeking to absorb and accommodate future events in whatever unexpected form they may take.*
>
> (Walker and Cooper, 2011: 6; emphasis added)

By taking the quality of adaptability and locating it in relation to unexpected (and unknown) future events, resilience arguably creates a closed theoretical loop that complements other managerial tropes of 'continual improvement' and ideologies of constant 'change'. For instance, Norris et al. (2008) survey a number of ecological approaches (Holling, 1973; Waller, 2001; cf. Klein et al., 2003; Carpenter et al., 2001; Longstaff, 2005; Resilience Alliance, 2017) in order to define resilience as "a process linking a set of adaptive capacities to a positive trajectory of functioning and adaptation after a disturbance" (Norris et al., 2008: 130). However, beyond this emphasis on 'everything always getting better', it is important to note that the emergence of a reflexive dimension to resilience studies. As the concept has travelled from engineering through ecology to management and policy approaches, a critical orientation within scholarship has sought to foster and encourage resilience. Thus through activities of bodies such as the Stockholm Resilience Centre, it is assumed that interactions between humans and ecosystems can seek to build ecological resilience *through* "resilience analysis, with a simultaneous focus on adaptive resource management and adaptive governance" (Walker et al., 2004). A once emergent quality is thus imagined as reflexive quality to be inculcated. According to the Organisation for Economic Cooperation and Development, resilience agendas maximise the "ability of households, communities and nations to absorb and recover from shocks, whilst positively adapting and transforming their structures and means for living in the face of long-term stresses, change and uncertainty" (Mitchell, 2013, p. 4).

Common across these approaches then is the notion of society as a set of relationships. The system is not directly founded on any particular subject – be it the (rational) individual or a particular set of (liberal) values, say – but on the *characteristics* of the system as a whole. That system is not equivalent with any particular state or equilibrium, but is merely adapting and changing over time. While initially defined as an emergent quality of individuals or systems, the managerial discourse has gone on to conceive of this quality as something that can be *actively engendered.* Thus while resilience can be defined in terms of the capacity of an individual, community or system to bounce back from, or adapt to shocks, this is only one – somewhat metaphorical – element of the discourse. Indeed, where resilience is found to be absent or diminished – a managerial view would posit that the qualities of resilience can be proactively developed by making it a priority for individuals, organisations and states. This might be done through training, specific resources, capacity building or the pooling of knowledge. Resilience can be further developed through the repeated running of resilience practices themselves – i.e. by learning from various experiences of adaptation and identifying how such learning can challenge/improve existing practices. Adaptation thus feeds further adaptations in a process of recursive learning, resilience as an emergent reflexivity – within individuals or organisations – to cope with the contingent and uncertain realities of market life.

Resilience as governmentality

While the managerial approach has proved highly successful, spreading easily across issue areas, organisational and policy agendas, a range of critiques have identified the absence of a historical, cultural, or political dimension to such analyses. Resilience – on a managerial account – is taken as an inherently good thing that needs to be developed in virtually all areas of life (Lundborg and Vaughan-Williams, 2011). Against this view, critical approaches argue that the widespread deployment of resilience agendas should itself be questioned: *Why is resilience so successful? Why now? With what effects?* More broadly, the critical approach ushers at a deeper politics of resilience in terms of power, governance and nuanced processes of legitimation and re-legitimation associated with neo-liberal forms of governmentality. Whereas managerial and policy approaches see uncertainty and the potentiality of extreme events as the primary existential problematic to be responded to (in better or worse ways), critical scholars question how this ontological idea of uncertainty *constitutes* a particular set of conclusions within resilience discourse. Simply put, there appears to be quite a bit of certainty about what uncertainty implies. To wit, the inevitability of extreme events can be understood as a de-politicising move, which both reduces our ability to question the causes, power relations and structural injustices that permit them and defines an appropriate set of 'proactive responses'. On this view, for critical scholars, the adaptability that managerial approaches celebrate and foster must be viewed as, *itself*, an adaptation within neo-liberalism: resilience as a supplement to neo-liberal restructuring, part of a more generalised trend to *responsibilise* individuals for the vicissitudes of market life (Dean, 2014; O'Malley, 2010).

In many ways, the governmental approach to resilience echoes the centrality accorded to adaptation by managerial perspectives. However, rather than replicate the assumption that levels of resilience can be improved in a quantitative sense, the governmental approach looks to resilience as disciplinary logic, framed as way of coping with uncertainty. Distinguishing between risk and uncertainty, Lentzos and Rose (2009: 236) argue,

> [A]ttention to uncertainty poses problems for rationalities of risk management, nonetheless these uncertain futures must be rendered thinkable, prepared for and pre-empted or mitigated. . . . this does not entail a resort to 'non-rational' ways to bring the future into the present, but rather requires the use of different modes of rationalization.

Indeed, they point to the rise of scenario planning, whereby practitioners seek to imagine different forms of catastrophe. This future preparedness is encapsulated in the discourse of resilience which, they argue, "has become something that can be engineered into systems, organizations, perhaps nations and persons" (Lentzos and Rose, 2009: 243). And thus a governmental approach places a critical spin on the logic of adaptation identified in managerial and policy approaches by portraying it as an *engendered logic* rather than a straight problem-solving exercise:

> A logic of resilience, then, is not merely an attitude of preparedness; to be resilient is not quite to be under protection nor merely to have systems in place to deal with contingencies. Resilience implies a systematic, widespread, organizational, structural and personal strengthening of subjective and material arrangements. . . . Perhaps the opposite of a Big Brother state, a logic of resilience would aspire to create a subjective and systematic state to enable each and all to live freely and with confidence in a world of potential risks.
>
> (Lentzos and Rose, 2009: 243)

Thus the issue of uncertainty is essentially folded into the governmental logics of liberal society via discourses of resilience. It is not a disciplinary logic in the sense of 'orders' or 'sanctions'; instead, the production of subjects capable of living with (a particular rationality of) uncertainty is promoted as a new framework of governance. Indeed, this argument that resilience is tied to *the production* of particular subjects is given a further embellishment by Pat O'Malley, who suggests that resilience planning is not simply a logic of 'large scale' or 'state' governance, but actually entails building upon diverse logics and techniques of the self. In particular, he emphasises how the self is increasingly encouraged to nurture or train resilient traits understood as anything from self-help books that teach individuals to 'survive through chaos', to the widespread prevalence of cognitive-behavioural techniques in Western society. Indeed, he suggests that this 'resiliency manoeuvre' "takes much of its impetus from compatibility with advanced liberal approaches to government in what are constituted as particularly uncertain times" (O'Malley, 2010: 490):

> The new resilient self is . . . to be achieved rather than taken as natural. Closely linked to a "duty to be well", it is part of a move to "empowerment"

> that displaced ongoing "dependence" on professionals. As with "markets" and "communities", "resilience" has shifted from being a natural given to being a technique to be applied wherever advantageous, built up, or assembled in ways that resonate with Rose's description of advanced liberal consumers who assemble their lives from an array of commodities.
>
> (O'Malley, 2010: 505)

At the same time as resilience governs individuals through 'empowering them' to respond to and cope with extreme events, therefore, it also perpetuates a set of individuals capable of succeeding within neo-liberal market life. Indeed, Jonathan Joseph (2013a) has argued that resilience can be read as a form of *embedded neo-liberalism*, whereby the responsibility for dealing with the excess of politics in neo-liberal agendas is re-embedded through individuals and communities.[2] Uncertainty, therefore, becomes a supplement for the governmental logics of liberal society via discourses of resilience that seek to foster subjects capable of living with the existential condition of the 'future event' (Evans and Reid 2014; O'Malley 2010). As Mitchel Dean (2014: 160–61) argues, the foregrounding of such events in the neo-liberal imagination works to legitimate, rather than critique, that system:

> [W]e witness the emergence of a regime of government that no longer promises an omniscient market order enhancing human welfare but simply accepts the evolution of complex systems and the inevitability of catastrophe. . . . crises and catastrophic events can do nothing to undermine this regime. Indeed, they confirm its narrative; the only possible policy direction is to prepare against their inevitability.

From an existential uncertainty to a systemic precondition of the very logic that governs the resilient vision, the global event has moved from a position of exteriority to everyday market life, to an internalised logic – a *deus ex machina* that locks in the politics of neo-liberal governance via engendered logics of adaptation. Interestingly, the global event becomes both magnified in this account – a fundamental condition of nearly all aspects of market life – and hollowed out of any distinctive substance. The global event as opportunity to observe the emergent quality of resilience.

Towards a performative critique of resilience

The critical literature on resilience does much to situate and problematise the assumed apolitical nature of the discourse. It situates resilience historically in relation to both the restructuring of certain states along neo-liberal and/or austere lines; it provides a political diagnosis for the widespread focus on extreme events in public discourse, and it problematises the apparently apolitical nature of norms of individual responsibility (for emotions, for welfare, etc.). In this way, the critical literature points to the disciplinary element of resilience beyond the more pragmatic or practical orientation of the managerial and policy approaches that is potentially attractive.

Despite the importance of this move, however, I would like to place in question some of the assumptions and implications that follow from it. While sympathetic to the way a governmental approach to resilience captures important linkages between the (future) global event and the everyday subjects of (neo-liberal) market life via a logic of complexity and uncertainty, there is a sense in which resilience is figured as a curiously determinate force. Simply put, I wonder if resilience could ever be as coherent or complete as is sometimes supposed? To follow the line of argument, neo-liberalism appears to be successful because of its ability to expand rationalities of neo-liberal governance, and resilience seems to stand as a matter of 'completion' for this form of governance, tranquilizing critique by deferring all political contest to the logic of the future event. By way of example of the formidable power attributed to resilience, in one passage, Walker and Cooper (2011: 157) suggest,

> In its tendency to metabolize all countervailing forces and inoculate itself against critique, "resilience thinking" cannot be challenged from within [. . .] but must be contested, if at all, on completely different terms, by a movement of thought that is truly counter-systemic.

While this somewhat monolithic image of resilience is presented as a reason for seeking out more radical 'counter-systemic' visions of politics and political contest, there is a danger of ignoring other potential frailties of resilience that may exist. Arguably then, certain accounts of resilience within neo-liberalism may actually work to reify *what resilience is*, in turn fostering a totalising diagnosis of its success that can distract us from alternative modes of politicisation.

Building from this, it is important to emphasise the prior and apparently ongoing victory of neo-liberalism that is doing the work in some, otherwise critical, accounts of resilience. For many working in the literature on governmentality, neo-liberalism is itself an incredibly successful and expansive set of rationalities that both accord with and progressively govern nearly all elements in global market life. As a result, by weaving the totalising logic of resilience to equally expansive and successful account of neo-liberal governmentality, it is conceivable that we might downplay certain nuances, internal dilemmas and ambiguities in how resilience agendas are actually performed. Resilience, it should be remembered, is a relatively new discourse that is being deployed in different ways across different sectors and issue areas. In that sense, we should retain sensitivity to what is doing the work in any critical account that reads resilience as a completion of neo-liberalism.

In this vein, David Chandler argues that we may also need to conceive of the '*anti-liberal*' dimensions of resilience: that resilience can also function as a critique of neo-liberal forms of governance. Indeed, for Chandler (2014a: 48), it should be foregrounded that resilience thinking can actually be seen as a "*radical critique* of the knowledge claims of actually existing neoliberalism, suggesting that the hierarchical causal structure and assumptions of socially determined interactive outcomes still clings too much to a liberal modernist ontology". Whereas a neo-liberal vision of market life would defer fundamental questions of politics and ethics to the unintended outcomes of the price mechanism, on a strict reading, resilience would be sceptical of the assumed rationality implied by such an ontology. Instead, by emphasizing relationality and emergence, resilience arguably operates with a more comprehensive appreciation of the limits of rationality and the radical uncertainty that conditions life within different systems, of which markets are only a part. As Chandler (2014b: 19) argues,

> There is . . . little point in attempting to understand resilience as a core concept at play in discussions about policy problems and policy solutions today without considering what is assumed in the assertion that the world is now more complex. To understand the demand for resilience-thinking as a potential answer or a solution, we must first grasp what is already implied in the question of the ontology of the world or life itself as "complex". Without complexity there would be no demand for resilience.

On this view, it has been argued that critical scholarship on resilience may need to pay more attention to the particularities, nuances and contradictions of its current emergence (Lundborg and Vaughan-Williams, 2011). Equally, emerging empirical studies of resilience could do more to reflect the contingency of its performance, instabilities and contradictions (Cavelty et al., 2015). Importantly, this does not mean that resilience is not supportive, potentially of neo-liberalism, but rather that we need to provide an account of how specific performances of resilience may or may not play such a role. Indeed as Joseph argues,

> Although not wanting to reduce the idea of resilience to neoliberal governance, in policy terms it fits extremely well into this environment. The effects of the use of the concept are more important than theorising its precise meaning. Its place within neoliberal discourse is more meaningful than any philosophical or scientific interpretation.
>
> (Joseph, 2013a: 44)

In different ways, then, I would argue that we need to recover the contingency of this discourse on contingency by addressing its performative politics.

For Judith Butler (2010), the performance of something called 'the economy', including its separation from society or state, is part of a continual (and unstable) process, that depends upon repeated iterations, elisions, and exclusions. For Butler, performativity, indeed a performative approach to global market life, is distinctively political because it is incomplete; it often fails or misfires, in Austin's words, necessitating change or contest. Thus while resilience might well, in certain circumstances, overlay a set of neo-liberal governance techniques, what if we instead conceived of such a scenario *as a failure* to iterate the radical component identified by Chandler? Or more productively, what if we began to conceive of how "marginalized forms of resilience can challenge dominant forms" (Cavelty et al., 2015: 12)? On this view, the performative politics of resilience is rendered as a set of open questions for research: How is economic or financial resilience performed in different contexts? What possibilities and limits are performed in its name? Drawing from the critical literature, how are individuals and communities conceived/produced? But then also problematising some of the implications of these questions: How do the anti-liberal dimensions of resilience manifest? Thus how might we conceive of the productive elements of failure: What instabilities, breakdowns or misfires can be identified in the performance of resilience? And can such failure be taken as ground for re-politicisation where the marginal form of resilience might be read as a resistance to the dominant?

Performative agency

Drawing these points together, a performative politics of resilience would question how the event is performed, what does it do, *in context*. Large and sweeping diagnoses of the nature of resilience in both the managerial/policy and governmental approaches clearly offer important signposts for what is at stake in the discourse of resilience and how a logic of adaptability in relation to a pervasive uncertainty over future events is both emergent and a quality to be reflexively fostered. But such diagnoses can work to downplay the potential for politics in resiliency discourse. To recall Fassin's idea that trauma provides a form of subjectivity through which people can nevertheless exist politically, turning humanitarian concerns to a critique of power and violence, my suggestion is that similar, albeit different, potentialities exist in resilience. Understood as a discourse that is potentially critical of actually existing neo-liberalism then, I aim to draw out how new forms of market agency are performed within resilience. Indeed, as Chandler (2012: 217) sets out,

> The resilient subject (at both individual and collective levels) is never conceived as passive or as lacking agency (as in the case of 1990s understandings of victims requiring saving interventions), but is conceived only as an active agent, capable of achieving self-transformation.

On this view, the performative politics of resilience may contain within it the seeds of a form of agency that *exceeds*, so to speak, the expectations of neo-liberal or governmental visions. Just as resilience can critique the ends of market order, retaining a radical or emancipatory potential, so the active fostering of resilient agency might lead to alternative or anti-market forms that contest the political logics of neo-liberalism. Again, these are not necessary components of resilience discourse, but are empirical questions to be asked about how it is performed, whether such performances are successful, and what possibilities and limits for agency they instantiate. As Butler (2010: 151) notes, this "implies risk, wager, and the possibility of having an effect, but without any strong notion of probability or any possible version of necessity". Such a view puts in play both the potential for failure and the normative components of any discourse that is iterated. And this implies a concerted move beyond the pronouncements of economic policymakers and regulations that typify diagnoses of neo-liberal governmentality – important as they are:

> It is not only the explicit speech act that exercises performative power; other exercises include (a) the mundane and repeated acts of delimitation that seek to maintain a separation among economic, social and political spheres, (b) modes of prediction and anticipation that constitute part of economic activity itself, and (c) organizations of human and non-human networks, including technology, that enter into specific economic activities such as price-setting [. . .] performativity implies a certain critique of the subject, especially once it is severed from the Austinian presumption that there is always someone who is delegated to speak or that performative discourse has to take the form of discrete verbal enunciation. Such a view strikes me as important in all kinds of ways, especially when we seek to consider situations of performative breakdown, when the effects of a performative operation fail to work. Similarly, once performativity is no longer the discrete action of a subject, we can rethink as well the normative status of such a theory or, rather, the role of norms in establishing the best direction for agency.
>
> (Butler, 2010: 150)

On this view, the performative politics of resilience includes, but is not limited to, the networks and actors that re-iterate the demand for – inter alia – resilient governance, resilient response and resilient subjects. However, Butler is keen to emphasise the 'perlocutionary' element of performativity, by which she means the 'felicitous' conditions which allow for one or another performance to be successful or to be heard. This is because she wants to change the emphasis within studies of performativity within the economy from a cultural constructivism that emphases how current models of economic agency became sovereign, to reflect the importance of breakdown, misfire and, ultimately I would suggest, a critical resistance that might seek to imagine other ways of being a market subject:

> In his "Signature, Event, Context", Derrida . . . argued that we can only think the process of iterability by understanding the rupture or failure that characterizes every interstitial moment within iteration. This view set his theory apart from cultural construction, which presumes that performativity describes the process by which certain kinds of phenomenon are made or brought into being, and deconstruction, which assumes that the process of making something introduces failure and undoing as a necessary part of that operation. If one remains within the presumption that performativity works (and that we only trace the ways in which economic life is "made"), then performativity is assimilated to the notion of cultural construction. An example of this would be the oft-cited formulation found in Callon . . . that economic theories and models accordingly contribute to the phenomenon that they seek to explain, and we are left with a hermeneutic reading of performativity.
>
> (Butler, 2010: 152)

For Butler then, we must retain a sensitivity to the role of breakdown and misfires in the performance of the economy because this is a condition of politics. By this I mean to suggest that – at its strongest – the cultural constructivist vision, or, indeed, accounts of neo-liberal governmentality, present a kind of (informal) structuralism; "My worry is that the cultural constructivist position thinks performativity works and that it imputes a certain sovereign agency to the operation of performativity that foregrounds the illocutionary over the perlocutionary" (Butler, 2010: 153). By emphasising failure, breakdown and misfires, Butler suggests that we might refound performativity as a critical theory of capitalism; indeed,

> its moments of breakdown are also important for another version of "critique". Under what conditions do the theories of finance produce impossible scenarios that are bound to backfire and fail? They are not "bound" to do this for causal or dialectical reasons, but because they seek to derive endless possibilities from limited resources.
>
> (Butler, 2010: 153)

By emphasizing the precarious and political nature of performativity, Butler provides important signposts for developing a critique of how political agency emerges and is reproduced. She crystallises an important limit in how the critical literature on resilience conceives of the way the discourse works as an almost inevitably successful completion of neo-liberal governmentality. For sure, resilience cannot rely on the performative agency of a sovereign subject, since this already ignores the way resilience is made up of a set of assumptions about complexity and the limits to knowledge that would undermine such a sovereign subject. However, if the overlapping rationalities of neo-liberalism, wellness, adaptability, etc., can perform a logic of resilience that connects and conditions the resilient subject to the uncertainty of the future event, then the nature of politics must be read as expansive, not diminished. This is partly because – proponents and critics alike – "seek to derive endless possibilities from limited resources". But equally, I would argue, because every breakdown, failure or misfire can be read politically as the felicitous conditions for another kind of performance. Performativity is not simply a story of government through discursive reiteration, it also provides "the resources from which resistance, subversion, displacement are to be forged" (Butler, 2013, p. 23).

Conclusion

The discourse of resilience can animate an important performative politics of the global event. By foregrounding the existential uncertainty of the extreme event in a proactive discourse of governance, resilience presents – and potentially reifies – an ontology of complex market life that proponents and critics alike regard as both important and expansive. Absent foundational claims about rationality, or the liberal individual, resilience seems to work in 'light touch' in an almost apolitical way, whereby *the limits to knowledge* are recognised in order to foster co-operative and adaptable relationships over time. While proponents and critics diverge over the attractiveness and, indeed, the politics of resilience, there is a general acceptance that the discourse is pervasive in ever more areas of life. Indeed, the chapter engaged a number of theorists of neo-liberal governmentality that diagnose a significant disciplinary dimension to resilience, which seeks to fuse between the logic of uncertainty over extreme events and a requirement for market subjects to make themselves 'resilient' in preparation. Affective governance thus relies on a *deus ex machina* of the future event to nurture a particular form of market subject capable of endlessly fashioning him or herself to cope with (an ontology of) complex market life.

In developing a performative critique of this affective discourse of the global event, I do not intend to simply re-state the virtues of resilience that are identified in the managerial and policy approaches. Indeed, my argument is reflective of the disciplinary potentials that exist within resilient rationalities, not least in relation to the progressive cultivation of a responsibilised subject that is simultaneously prepared for, and, therefore, constitutive of neo-liberal market life. This appears to be an important and evocative development in the theorisation of governmentality that can certainly open new research avenues. However, I do intend to tease out the politics of performativity identified by Butler, whereby we must remain attuned to both the empirical details of specific discursive performances of resilience and how they succeed or fail, *as well as* the potential for a new form of critique that is more reflective of the performative agency that may be emergent in the process. On this view, at least one way in which resilience might be thought differently is via Chandler's emphasis on its anti-liberal dimensions: that resilience is partly conceived through a problematisation of actually existing neo-liberal governance – i.e. top-down, market-based solutions, individualism, etc. While Chandler interprets this as a moment of de-politicisation, whereby the very (postmodern) critiques of modernity are recuperated within its prevailing rationalities, I will argue that there is potentially more at stake. Crucially, the previous chapter argued that one way in which to think through the performative politics of this (anti-liberal) discourse might be to reflect on the performance of agency that flows from the resilient market subject. To wit, an adaptive, self-making subject may not necessarily craft him or herself to fit neo-liberal projects; indeed, he or she may be critical of such projects, or may find a way to live otherwise in the face of certain (constructed) uncertainties such as the global event.

Notes

1 This reading echoes David Chandler's (2014b), who distinguishes between a classical and a postmodern discourse of resilience, whereby the classical version 'used' to carry connotations of strength and fortitude because of its reliance on a subject/object distinction, whereas the postmodern vision assumes an embedded and relational subject, denoting an emergent conception of resilient adaptability. While an important and insightful argument, I find it difficult to retro-fit or extract the contemporary discourse of resilience to/from classical ideas of the subject, which had their own distinctive attributes (that were not known in terms of resilience) in order to denote a 'shift' to contemporary usage

of the term. Instead, I find it interesting how the contemporary discourse of resilience 'succeeds' through the combination of a postmodern relational emergence with everyday tropes of 'bounce-back ability'.

2 As Joseph argues, "In the process of constructing and interpellating neoliberal subjects, neoliberal discourse and practices appeal to them as citizens or consumers who are 'free' to take responsibility for their own life choices, but who are expected to follow competitive rules of conduct. Governmentality works by telling us to be enterprising, active and responsible citizens. Neoliberalism works through the social production of freedom and the *management and organization of the conditions in which one can be free*." Resilience contributes to this through its stress on heightened self-awareness, reflexivity and responsibility. It encourages the idea of active citizenship, whereby people, rather than relying on the state, take responsibility for their own social and economic well-being. In particular, it focuses on the risk and security aspects of this by encouraging preparedness and awareness (Joseph, 2013a, 42)

7 Resilience and (everyday) finance

Performing adaptability differently

Introduction

In order to engage the performative politics of resilience within market life further, this chapter will engage in a reading of the discourse of financial resilience and how it is performed and what forms of agency it might inculcate. While recent years have seen a proliferation of the resilience discourse in policy and academia, the movement to finance has been less well reflected. From a relatively little known idea in engineering and ecology, resilience is fast becoming the predominant governance frame for thinking about a range of 'event-oriented' issues from floods, through terrorist attacks and now financial crisis (Brassett and Vaughan-Williams, 2013). In academia, the study of resilience has become something of a cottage industry, akin to the growth of globalisation studies in previous decades. This has spurned numerous articles, books and even one or two journals on the subject (Chandler and Coaffee, 2017). Within the discipline of politics, early work on resilience has been dominated by a focus on critical security studies and environmental politics (Cavelty et al., 2015); however, its role in economic issues of development and finance is receiving more attention in recent years (Williams and Vorley, 2017). Indeed, this is apt because a growing trend in post-crisis global financial governance has been the spread of policy agendas and theoretical models designed to build a *resilient* financial system (Brassett and Holmes, 2016). Institutions of financial governance, banks, financial subjects and, increasingly, the media now conceive of resilient business models, resilient risk profiles and resilient managers.

How should we think about this turn to resilience in financial governance? In some sense, of course, the turn to resilience in the governance of global finance is a fairly logical development. After a period of crisis, bank failures, credit instability and a plethora of 'unknown unknowns' on the risk profiles of financial houses and central banks alike, the desire to build some resilience into the financial system is understandable. However, this chapter will argue that the drive towards economic and financial resilience must be situated within wider patterns of resilience thinking in other areas of policymaking, where the ability to 'bounce back' and 'adaptability' in relation to 'extreme events' are also emphasised. This is not just an appeal to the relevance of the wider literature, but also a recognition of the contingency of the application of resilience to finance. Thus when Mark Carney (2015) remarks that "real markets are fair, resilient, and effective" he is performing something of the wider context within which resilience functions. Since the financial crisis, economists and policymakers have attempted to update their understandings of financial stability through a recognition of resilience thinking with its emphasis of systemic interdependence and the possibility of unforeseen 'shock events'. In keeping with the wider context of resilient knowledge, this chapter will argue that the discursive work done in the name of building financial resilience invests heavily in a concept of 'the event' as a significant – *indeed inevitable* – feature of market life. How this is known, performed and *resisted* within the everyday discourse of financial resilience is the subject of this chapter.

The section on **The rise of financial resilience** recounts how the general shift to resilience discourse in global finance has emerged across the major institutions of global governance in recent years. Critical IPE studies of global finance have tended to address these changes, if at all, via standard debates over financial regulation, stability and risk. Instead, this chapter questions the discursive work done in the name of resilience, that we should reflect the specific ways in which resilience has been narrated within financial governance, in general, and the policy thinking of the BOE, in particular. While much of the turn towards resilience agendas can be located in a post-crisis search for stability amongst policymakers, it is interesting to reflect on the discursive work of policy actors such as Andrew Haldane that provides important substance. His work on complex systems analysis and his 'vigorous' use of metaphor suggest a creative component to financial resilience that exceeds the idea that financial resilience can work as a straightforward 'supplement' to neo-liberal governance.

Indeed, this possibility is taken up in the section on **Financial resilience: conservative *and* radical**, which looks at the everyday politics of financial resilience in the UK. At one level, certain 'alternative practices' flow quite naturally from financial resilience with its emphasis on diversity and local organisation in the development of financial networks. For example, Haldane's work with certain prominent social finance NGOs can be read as an everyday practice of financial resilience that steps outside of the neo-liberal mainstream of macro-prudential regulation. By encouraging reflection on the everyday make-up of a resilient financial system, on the actors and on the networks that constitute it, resilience can point to alternative forms of finance: local, autonomous, less risky. At another level, however, the turn to everyday finance also represents a contest over the question of what resilience is – a point forcefully articulated in terms of critical protests against finance and the politics of the financial event. Far from an 'exogenous shock' or a 'traumatic event', the sub-prime crisis is narrated by numerous everyday financial subjects as an indictment of neo-liberalism that requires a politicisation of finance and a democratisation of banking and lending. Protests against austerity by NGOs, grass roots movements and the general public can point to a questioning of the dominant narrative of the global event of sub-prime, but also the elaboration of alternative financial models, local currencies, local banks, peer lending and so forth, that actively respond to the uncertainty of the 'event' with their own vision of financial resilience.

This potential continuity between resilience and resistance plays on Chandler's idea of an anti-liberal component, yet seeks to explore further how the performance of resilient agency can anticipate new forms of market life. Thus the section on **The romance of resilience?** picks up on this theme of political contest to identify the potential for a resistant form of agency to reflect and promote financial resilience in critical terms. Directly drawing on the need for a more resilient financial system, the local banking entrepreneur David Fishwick has articulated a vision of local banking that actively contests many of the dominant, neo-liberal frames of financial governance – i.e. high leverage, top-down, diversified risk portfolios. Instead, Dave presents a somewhat charismatic, even romantic, vision of finance, where the bank knows its customers, doesn't carry unnecessary risk and engages with the community. While this project could be viewed as a reiteration of the standard tropes of local banking, *small is beautiful* and so forth, I will argue that the performance of Dave disrupts any such simple dichotomy through its overt targeting of the event.

Echoing the capacity for film and documentary performances to occupy the discourse of trauma in Chapter 5, the same point can be made, albeit contingently, through the colourful charm that Dave employs to subvert everyday knowledge about finance. Both the method – local banking – and the form – a documentary televised on national TV, work to contest the terms of financial resilience, not by ignoring the *deus ex machina* of the global event, but by *politicising* it. Thus the event is neither determinate nor meaningless, but performative: of politics, of agency.

The rise of financial resilience

The idea of financial resilience has risen quickly in the policy rhetoric of global financial governance. Beyond a more traditional focus on systemic risk, an attitude of preparedness for the extreme event has been rolled out across different organisations and across financial networks (World Economic Forum, 2013; Bank for International Settlements, 2013: 52; Bernanke, 2013). In keeping with the expansive nature of the resilience discourse, of course, this policy turn is not limited to rhetorical pronouncements, but has also witnessed the elaboration of a number of resilience agendas that seek to cultivate certain behaviours amongst 'financial citizens'. For example, in a paper on the roll-out of financial education, Chris Clarke (2015) argues that resilience has been explicitly drawn on in order to foster a re-orientation of financial literacy programs to cultivate 'personal resilience' and 'emotional well-being'. As he argues,

> [F]inancial resilience agendas are often pitched in terms of inculcating desirable character traits, which in part stems from the work that the resilience trope does in psychology and related fields. . . . at the individual level "self-help"

> psychology books become an interesting resource, which speak of developing "emotional" resilience to stressful situations by "learning to regulate and develop an internal locus of control".
>
> (Clarke, 2015: 19, cf. Webb 2013: 32–33)

Broader still, the term 'resilience' has filtered into media and policy reporting on finance, with everything from housing markets and the 'high street' to regions, cities and communities being measured in terms of their resilience to the uncertain post-financial crisis world. In short, the idea of resilience – particularly in its managerial sense – has diffused into public discourse on questions of financial regulation and post-financial crisis economic policy, in general.

At the BOE, for example, the move towards resilience thinking is particularly pronounced. The Financial Stability Committee has been joined by a 'financial resilience division'. A series of financial resilience benchmarking exercises have been undertaken that focus on leveraging and debt ratios. In addition, a whole chapter of the bank's financial stability report was devoted to financial resilience. As it reported,

> Leverage ratios have edged down further and the aggregate capital position of the major UK banks has improved a little. Banks have been able to issue substantial amounts of . . . debt and have shrunk their balance sheets, although a substantial funding challenge remains. This has improved their resilience to shocks, including further funding strains.
>
> (Bank of England, 2011)

On this view, finance has become a realm that sets itself up to develop resilience towards the financial event.

Across these different perspectives, however, it is important to place the rise of financial resilience in the context of a set of responses to the sub-prime crisis and subsequent global financial crisis. What is interesting about this context is the way that resilience emerges alongside a highly standard set of liberal governance dilemmas associated with the politics of post-crisis response: states versus markets, public versus private, political versus economic control over finance. Indeed, when mobilised as a response to the financial event, critical scholars argue that such binaries simply channel critical energies towards the project of restoring stability (Griffin, 2017). On this view, widespread state-sponsored bailouts prioritised bank stability, while subsequent critical energies were drawn – via the demonisation of bankers – to question the public accountability of private banks. Indeed, this issue was even more visible in cases where governments had taken direct ownership of private banks, where a discourse of accountability could effectively be woven to scrutiny of their (non-)viability as business concerns. Developing in this context, I would argue that financial resilience was almost inevitably performed alongside standard neo-liberal tropes of 'market discipline'. Indeed, Paul Tucker, then deputy governor of the BOE, concluded a speech entitled 'The Crisis Management Menu' (2010: 15), by asking whether

> our community can find ways of distributing the costs of official sector support operations back to the system and its uninsured creditors rather than to the general taxpayer. If we can achieve that, market discipline would be enhanced. We need to hang on to "market discipline" as a watchword in these debates. The goal of re-regulation – of redrawing the rules of the game for the financial system – should not be to reintroduce the wisdom of the state into micro decisions about how to run businesses. But rather to put market discipline at the heart of a market economy.

In this context, the debate over financial resilience might well be thought of as a natural corollary of market discipline? And, on this view, there would certainly be scope to favour critical approaches that emphasise the disciplinary or governmental dimensions of financial resilience so that it might work as a form of embedded neo-liberalism (Joseph, 2013a), re-distributing the responsibility for social adjustment (and values) from the state to the market, from public to private. Or else, as Clarke (2015) suggests, resilience might complement neo-liberalism by legitimating the 'empty promise' of financial education.

Building on the argument of the previous chapter, however, I will argue that resilience cannot simply be understood as a discursive supplement to neo-liberalism, or as straightforwardly successful. Instead, we must trace how the discourse of resilience has expanded and been attached to finance. As the preceding analysis suggests, it is not that resilience has been imported ready-made into the domain of financial governance, but rather that the discourse has been performed in a specific historical context. While actors might draw upon existing logics and rationalities of resilience – not least the trope of 'bouncing back' after crisis – there is also an important sense in which resilience is narrated and articulated in novel ways for distinct circumstances. Holding onto this essential contingency of resilience discourse allows for an ongoing analysis of the term that foregrounds the politics of its uptake and success, as well as leaving space open for alternative narrations. In particular, Andrew Haldane, at the BOE, has been an important voice in the performance of financial resilience. In a number of speeches and articles, Haldane has made the case for resilience in strident terms, pitching it as both intellectually and politically attractive. Indeed, his rhetorical style repays analysis. Haldane often draws analogies and inferences between seemingly unrelated phenomena. This has the effect of folding finance within a systems logic that spans more widely than – indeed a priori encompasses – states and markets. In a highly cited speech, he draws a line between financial resilience and nearly all forms of crisis management by addressing the SARS crisis:

> Both events [the failure of Lehman Brothers and the unfolding of the SARS epidemic] were manifestations of the behavior under stress of a complex, adaptive network. Complex because these networks were a cat's-cradle of interconnections, financial and non-financial. Adaptive because behavior in these networks was driven by interactions between optimizing, but confused, agents. Seizures in the electricity grid, degradation of ecosystems, the spread

> of epidemics and the disintegration of the financial system each is essentially a different branch of the same network family tree.
>
> (Haldane, 2009: 3)

Encapsulated in this bundle of images is a sense of finance as a complex adaptive system, itself an element within a wider set of systems. Finance is held to be both interconnected with other systems and itself roughly congruous with them. Accepting the logic of extreme events, the focus of resilience is upon optimising the possibilities for agents in conditions of uncertainty; it is their adaptive behaviour over time that is considered to be the crucial element. Resilience is therefore a particular quality revealed through behaviours over time. Such a gesture is important, I would argue, because it is slightly curious: if agents are optimising, but unknowing, then responsibility for actions is reduced at the same time as we seek to facilitate their future adaptability. This raises the question for any performance of financial resilience, which agents are imagined and how? Haldane's imaginary is of a system of systems, where all are interconnected and dependent. It is not that the state is faced with the traditional question of intervening or not intervening, since the system, as a product of complex relationships, is already established. Thus, in somewhat progressive terms, there is space within financial resilience to think *creatively* about how finance functions and might function differently.

Read from within a state-market dichotomy, calls for resilience amount to little more than calls for a stricter division of public and private: a resilient financial sector is one that is not so reliant upon the state. Think of the various stress testing exercises across US and European banks which model financial resilience in terms of their ability to survive without recourse to public funds – i.e. market discipline. However, in certain circles, financial resilience can be invoked to underline a paradigmatic shift in policy thinking – more akin to the ecological literature – that seeks to understand financial *systems* as adaptive and non-linear. Here it is not a case of 'too much market', or finding the 'right balance' between states and markets, but rather one of transcending the state-market binary in pursuit of a better model of the *financial system* as a whole. Thus for all that resilience might be deployed as a straightforward, 'common-sense' objective of financial agents, we should not ignore the feat of discursive work that has been required to legitimate this transition in thinking. It is not just that finance has been 'securitised' as an object to be protected and/or made more secure, or that systems theory has been 'imported' to the BOE. Rather, specific people have succeeded in pushing their reasoning in an environment of crisis management that is conducive to both elements: market discipline and invention.

Financial resilience: conservative *and* radical

Discourses of financial resilience respond to a set of assumed facts about the financial economy – namely, the existence of objective, given risks and the potential for instability and crisis. In that sense, resilience instantiates a particular neoliberal vision of the world as a world of risks which must be navigated. But the subject doing the navigating is not necessarily specified in any particular way, which opens up the potential for more progressive, politically critical and socially embedded forms of financial resilience. In short, who, or what, do we wish to be resilient to and in what way? This has led financial resilience down two, somewhat divergent paths of governance reform: 'radical critique' and 'financial stability'. At the BOE, Andy Haldane has been prominent in forwarding a view of financial markets in terms of complexity:

> "More of the same and better" . . . That has been the response to every financial crisis of the past fifty years . . . As a thought experiment, imagine . . . we were designing a regulatory framework from scratch. Finance is a complex, adaptive system. What properties would a complex, adaptive system such as finance ideally exhibit to best ensure against future crises? Simplicity is one. There is a key lesson, here, from the literature on complex systems. Faced with complexity, the temptation is to seek complex control devices. In fact, complex systems typically call for simple control rules. To do otherwise simply compounds system complexity with control complexity. Uncertainty would not then divide, it would multiply.
>
> (Haldane, 2011: 2–3)

Simplicity, robustness and timeliness may sound like the traditionally conservative tropes of a financial regulator, but they underscore how complexity is being used to justify 'pre-emptive intervention'. The radical nature of Haldane's position is clearly rhetorical, but there is also substance. Haldane has tilted at financial privilege, arguing that the current (full) costs to society of running finance outweigh the benefits. This might seem an easy gambit in the current period of scorn for bankers and their bonuses, but as Haldane is a highly respected bank economist, there is reason to take note. The openness of his account of financial 'resilience' has arguably created space for contest over its meaning.

Haldane certainly appeals to complexity as an appropriate ontology for the nature of contemporary financial relations, arguing that the complexity of the financial sector produces a form of uncertainty, which cannot be addressed through traditional regulatory mechanisms. But the appeal to systemic complexity underpins a suggestion that regulatory authorities must give up the attempt to match growing market complexity with growing regulatory complexity. This theme of 'simple regulation for complex finance' was developed in a speech given by Haldane in the summer of 2012, where he argues through the 'metaphor' of a dog's ability to catch a frisbee:

> So what is the secret of the dog's success? The answer, as in many other areas of complex decision-making, is simple. Or rather, it is to keep it simple. For studies have shown that the frisbee-catching dog follows the simplest of rules of thumb: run at a speed so that the angle of gaze to the frisbee remains roughly constant. Humans follow an identical rule of thumb. Catching a crisis, like catching a frisbee, is difficult. Doing so requires the regulator to weigh a complex array of financial and psychological factors, among them innovation and risk appetite . . . Yet despite this complexity, efforts to catch

> the crisis frisbee have continued to escalate. Casual empiricism reveals an ever-growing number of regulators, some with a Doctorate in physics. Ever-larger litters have not, however, obviously improved watchdogs' frisbee-catching abilities. . . . So what is the secret of the watchdogs' failure? The answer is simple. Or rather, it is complexity. . . . the type of complex regulation developed over recent decades might not just be costly and cumbersome but sub-optimal for crisis control. In financial regulation, less may be more.
> (Haldane, 2012c: 1)

The rhetoric is full of radical implication: financial markets have become so complex that attempts by well-meaning officials to 'regulate them as they see them' are doomed either to be ineffective or, more probably, to make matters worse. As such, a decisive break from orthodoxy is required – 'simple thinking for complex times'.

On this view, the radical potential in resilience, to foreground systemic complexity and ask deeper questions about the politics of finance and financial agency has been assimilated to orthodox models of financial regulation and the (neo-liberal) politics that surround them. Most obviously, the policy recommendations emerging from this rhetoric explore the relatively tame conventions of macro-prudential regulation – i.e. a renewed emphasis on leverage ratios over the more complicated Basel risk-accounting mechanisms (Haldane, 2012a: 19; 2012b). However, in keeping with some of the tensions in Haldane's thinking on financial resilience, I would argue that such questions are just as likely to provoke answers that *critique* existing forms of neo-liberal power.

Since 2008, finance has become an openly contested political arena, with trust in financiers and a finance-friendly political class at an all-time low (Carney, 2015). In this terrain, a number of alternative financial practices have been mooted as part of the ongoing politicisation of finance. Debt forgiveness, financial transactions taxes, peer lending and local banking have all received popular discussion. Indeed, Chris Holmes (2014) has identified an important politics of currency that has emerged in the post-crisis period. While such initiatives are usually quite limited in scope and often beset by practical problems, the point is that alternative currencies allow people to articulate diverse visions of what a successful economy might be.[1] However, the resilience of financial community is not just a fringe interest of marginal financial innovators. In a film made by the Finance Innovation Lab entitled *Transforming Finance*, the case is made for a rethink of the very 'make-up' of the financial system. Rather than reproduce a naturalised conception of the financial system, the filmmakers suggest that it can be made (and *re-made*) to reflect different levels within the market. In one key passage, the film includes a discussion between Haldane and Richard Spencer:

> Andrew Haldane: One of the greatest intellectual mistakes we made in that pre-crisis period is we confused . . . quite different concepts: the concept of *diversification* (spreading risk across a portfolio) and the notion of *diversity* (meaning having different types of businesses in the market place).

> Richard Spencer: If you want a really resilient financial system, it has got to be a diverse financial system. So not just "more banks", but different types of financing entities . . . in order to build resilience into the system, in order to respond to shocks differently.
>
> (*Transforming Finance*, 2013)

This passage is important as it highlights how financial agents might be conceived in terms that fit the resilience discourse. Gone is the exclusive focus on complexity to reveal a more productive logic that seeks to foster new agents within a complex financial system. Thus both the extent *and quality* of financial complexity is in question. On this view, financial resilience is a more open discourse that is being adopted by different organisations and actors. While Haldane is a BOE employee, keen to engage with (mainstream) NGOs such as Finance Lab, their use of his ideas to emphasise the role of diversity in building financial resilience is a subtle political emphasis that might open up questions that go beyond – *or even against* – standard BOE regulation agendas. The film explicitly makes the case that resilience is about more than standard market constructs such as diversification or the spreading of risk within certain macro-prudential constraints, instead motivating reflection on the make-up of the system itself and encouraging smaller and different forms of banking. Indeed, this theme of smaller banks is something that Haldane has pursued elsewhere in terms of a celebration of the local banking model of Handelsbanken (Haldane, 2012a). In a critical response to the Occupy movement's critique of 'Big Banks', he highlighted the importance of diversity, but, importantly suggested it was something that individuals could address. On Handelsbanken, he suggested,

> They offer only basic banking services, mortgages and small business loans, to people in a tight, locally-defined catchment area. All credit decisions are taken locally by people, not centrally by a computer. No bonuses are paid and no-one has a sales-target. When the whole firm out-performs, a contribution is made to a pooled fund which is invested on employees' behalf. The fruits of success are distributed equally and gratification is deferred. For banking, this is back to the future. If that sounds attractive, then it is down to us – not regulators, not politicians, you and I – to deliver it. If as bank customers we want to change the culture of banking, then we should start by supporting those banks who are delivering that change. Putting your money where your mouth is would deliver far greater and more durable change than any amount of banker-bashing.
>
> (Haldane, 2012a: 10)

This move to local banking in resilience discourse is an interesting one as it pertains to a long tradition of critical thought on alternative finance (Rogers, 2014). Within this tradition, the benefits of local forms of organisation are set against the norms of global finance in a way that arguably anticipates many elements of the financial resilience discourse (Hines, 2000; Hutchinson et al., 2002). Alternative finance goes against the idea of money as simply a medium of exchange; instead, localist arguments portray money as a 'claim on society' that can be managed or mediated in order to reflect values of stability, social inclusion, or equality (Douthwaite, 1996). Against the idea of large-scale, highly leveraged yet diversified risk as a necessary precursor to successful banking, arguments for local finance have long supported the concept of small banks, small/low interest loans, etc., as a technique for supporting and empowering community economies (Hutchinson et al., 2002). What is new is how visible, indeed mainstream, some of these arguments have become in the context of post-crisis calls to financial resilience. To be sure, Haldane would stop short of some of the radical potentials of alternative finance. Indeed, he saw his move to local banking was part of a customer-oriented riposte to Occupy and their version of 'banker bashing'. Yet, his embrace of diversity and critical thinking about agency does leave scope for another, albeit unstable, performance of financial resilience. Thus while aspects of Haldane's analysis may seem overly optimistic about the political role of individual choices within markets, or indeed, about business model of one such small bank, the line between resilience and resistance has been blurred, and can be blurred further.

The romance of resilience?

The literature on alternative finance has pointed to certain core features of local banking that allow it to bring to the performance of financial resilience a concern with community, reciprocity and wider social values. In this way, alternative finance is often pitched as an implicit subversion of the capitalocentrism of much work on finance and IPE more generally. However, what is perhaps missed in some of this work is the political moment of contest, indeed interaction, between alternative and mainstream discourses of financial governance. While Haldane would like to privatise the moment of decision, relying on – if not market discipline – then certainly established *market models* to unlock the reformist potential of resilience, there is something implicitly public, sometimes deliberative, about the promotion of alternative finance.

By questioning financial orthodoxy, certain strands of alternative finance inevitably step outside the official network of agents and institutions to engage new constituencies. This involves the active promotion of different values through alternative finance in a manner that can contest the discourse of financial resilience in new ways. Nowhere is the affective potential of this form of critique more clear than in the career and campaign of Dave Fishwick, who has moved from a successful business renting mini buses and coaches, to (try to) set up a bank.

On the one hand, this movement into banking echoes much of what has already been discussed and suggested in the literature on alternative finance. On the other hand, Dave Fishwick has televised the whole process in a documentary series for the UK's Channel Four, a move which has portrayed alternative finance via the character and personality of Dave himself. In one typical section, *Bank of Dave* introduces Dave Fishwick as a 'down to earth' businessman from Burnley – represented in the documentary most viscerally by his thick Burnley accent and amenable way. While the narrator describes Dave as an outsider, "the man who took on the big banking Goliaths by creating his own bank", Dave is seen rummaging around 'the cobwebs' in his garage. Indeed, he finds his old DJ records 'from Kavos Corfu, 1990' and rehearses his DJ set before singing "we built this city on rock 'n' roll". In these ways, the story of *Bank of Dave* suggests that local banking can be a way to build financial resilience in terms of the people and communities who take part in it. As the bank's website describes:

> Feeling that High Street Banks treat people as credit scores and not as individuals, David decided to return to basics. As such, Burnley Savings and Loans Ltd DO NOT credit score, choosing a more personal approach to underwriting, dealing with customers on a case by case basis . . . we also offer the opportunity for people to be a part of something that could not only benefit Burnley and the North West of England but EVERY community in the country! . . . So by offering affordable loans to people who have struggled to obtain finance from the high street banks, through no fault of their own, as well as offering 5% AER on your savings, David has proved that the financial industry can also be socially responsible . . . . Any profits received, after the overheads are paid WILL BE DONATED TO CHARITY! At Burnley Savings and Loans we do not do big bonuses.
>
> (Burnley Savings and Loans Limited, 2016)

This performance of local banking echoes the resilient potential of alternative finance then, but it does so in a way that seeks to contest financial norms; it is against credit scoring; it is for the community; it's not for profit. Indeed, the everyday life of Dave Fishwick portrayed in the film suggests that other factors – geography, class, tradition – are important elements in the performative politics of finance (Fishwick, 2012). Not only does Burnley Savings and Loans contribute to the diversity of financial agents in the post-crisis period (e.g. the rise of peer-to-peer lending, crypto currencies, anti-debt movements) but also *politicises* finance. According to Dave, the banks are "shit"; "all they do is shit on people". The appeal of Dave is to combine a post-crisis public mood of critique with a genuinely alternative form of finance. This is a move beyond localism in general. Dave is not simply promoting a model of local banking, or resisting the large scale. Though he is doing both of these things, it is in a highly visible public context – a move which serves to expose some of the contingencies and fragilities of financial resilience discourse to a large and everyday Channel Four audience. In this sense, the political importance of Dave is move these debates beyond the confines of either academic debate on the one hand or well-meaning social reformers, or community activists on the other, to provide a level of critical publicity that is hard to pigeon hole. In a documentary played out before a broad television audience, local banking moves from being a potential model of resilience to its very politicisation.

For instance, a striking issue revealed in the documentary is quite how difficult it is to set up a bank at all. Regulations and norms about what banks ought to be, work to stifle his attempts at every turn. Most noticeably, Dave's decision not to follow a high capital, high-risk model of banking, actually means he struggles to get agreement to use the title 'bank'. For much of the film, the Financial Stability Authority (FSA) refuse to meet, or even talk with Dave, even after he tables MPs questions and secures glowing endorsements from senior political figures in the UK. When Dave's business model is eventually reviewed, it is rejected because it does not provide a diversified product portfolio – i.e. one that might embrace *higher levels of risk* in order to offer differential interest rates. In response, while he is able to trade as a 'savings and loan', it is made clear to him that he can't use the word Dave. Classically, of course, Dave finds a way round this, and in true comic fashion, he comes up with the business name "Bank *on* Dave!", where the dual meaning of the term 'bank', along with the use of an exclamation mark and quotation marks, is enough to avoid banking regulation altogether. As Dave remarked,

> They told me that if I use the word deposit or say I'm a bank then I will go to prison. Yet not one single banker in the City, the people who have pocketed millions in bonuses and let us all down so badly, has ended up in prison. God forbid that I should try to offer pensioners 5% interest.
>
> (Collinson, 2012)

In this story of a 'everyday man's' battle with governance bureaucracy, Dave appears to win the fight by establishing a savings and loan company, which effectively performs most of the functions of a retail bank. Yet, at another level, the case can be read as a conflict on the plane of financial resilience. While its economic impact may be tiny, "Bank on Dave!" opens up the possibility of alternative bases for the construction of financial resilience, rendering it resistant by illustrating the politics and hierarchy of financial regulation.

Against the prevailing uncertainties of the financial system – and particularly, the 'big finance' of capital mobility, and highly leveraged financial models – Dave seeks to build networks of finance based on human contact. Instead of credit scoring, he personally meets the borrowers and establishes a relationship. In this way, we would argue, an alternative form of resilient finance is in the offing: less risky, more adaptable community/network relations operating outside of the state/market view. This is not the community-based resilience of top-down neo-liberal governance widely critiqued in the literature, but rather the everyday, playful, swearing, resistant resilience of Dave *from Burnley*. In this sense, the anti-liberal dimensions of resilience-as-emergence identified by Chandler might – through occasionally comic iterations – form the basis for a new political economy of reciprocity and inclusion.

Conclusion

Finance, along with many other policy domains, is beginning to explore the potential for resilience thinking to both generate ideas about how complex systems inter-relate and to build adaptable financial networks that might thrive through crisis. Refusing either the managerial assumption that this move to financial resilience is something that simply works (and can be perpetually improved), and the critical – *yet somewhat totalising* – perspective that resilience is no more than a new stage of neo-liberal government, I have explored the contingencies and fragilities of resilience in order to tease out the productive dimensions of what Butler refers to as 'performative agency'; thereby retaining a level of openness to the political possibilities for resistance and critique it may harbour. The openness of the resilience discourse is illustrated by the divergence between a version of financial regulation – macro-prudential regulation – which simply updates and consolidates previous images of systemic risk. On this view, financial resilience appears to be little more than regulatory oversight designed to increase capital ratios, encourage diversification and retain a focus on systemically important banks – i.e. too big to fail. Yet it is also possible to discern an altogether more imaginative and critical trend within financial resilience discourse. This might, in Chandler's view, constitute an anti-liberal element in resilience, or might simply be another way of saying that a politics of financial resilience still exists. The relatively open-ended insights of Andrew Haldane on the idea of system diversity, that a range of new actors might be encouraged to contribute to forms of financial resilience that are relatively low risk, or oriented to the production of new networks, seems to play on the possibility of this openness. Therefore, it is interesting in this light to connect up with more critical strains of thought on the possibilities of alternative finance.

The chapter has thus tried to imagine a form of everyday market subject that can speak about finance – *that can be resilient* – in ways that are non-identical with the putatively dominant discourse of resilience. By pitching himself and his 'bank' in a playful relationship with financial resilience – part accommodation to local banking, part resistant to dominant articulations of necessary scale – Dave suggests that a resilient financial subject might also be resistant. Importantly though, the nature of the public sphere created around the Burnley savings and loans project speaks directly to a politics of the global event. Whereas dominant articulations of resilience thinking – both managerial and critical – attempt to reify the vision of the event as a *deus ex machina*, giving an existential and universal quality to uncertainty, the documentary about Dave directly subverts this logic. The critical thrust of Dave works through an engagement with the particular cultural memories of the sub-prime crisis that exist in the audience. Far from a discursive outside, the event is broken down, inhabited and nurtured for alternative ends; it becomes a keystone for democratic discussion about finance.

Such an argument may seem paradoxical in the context of a book about the performative politics of the global event, especially insofar as it seeks to deconstruct the assumed veracity of something called the global event. However, this is precisely the way in which a politics of discourse must be understood. The mutual contingency of discourse and subject means that a pragmatic orientation to recover the political subject of market life must recognise the capacity of subjects to speak. Just as Fassin identifies a critical potential in the language of trauma, that through subjectification trauma victims are both disciplined and produced as political beings, so resilient market subjects of finance might be inspired by the dominant discourse of the sub-prime crisis. Whereas once the visceral anger at the bankers might have been woven to an individualising dynamic that sought to resolve or solve the problem of the traumatic event, rather than directly politicise the nature of financial community, Dave presents an altogether more productive line. Emotions such as anger can be melded with entrepreneurialism and the good old-fashioned charisma of Dave to present a steady and relentless list of alternative, more resilient practices. Dave's work is therefore located in a social conversation about how to do financial resilience differently. It references the event, re-describes the event and uses the performative politics of the event to subvert, or at least re-phrase what financial resilience might become. Romantic yes, self-interested yes, but governmental no. It speaks to an older tradition of exemplary examples of capitalism through films such as *It's a Wonderful Life*, where financial resilience is imagined as an embodiment of a community in the making (Brassett and Rethel 2015).

Note

1 Local currencies have proliferated in the post-crisis context, often respond to the same concerns about the crisis ridden nature of neo-liberal economies, but are also often organized around the possibility of achieving community resilience in explicit opposition to *both* state and economy. As Peter North (2014) has discussed, local and complementary currencies are often conceived as a post-crisis critique of the system that carry their own, albeit marginal, understandings of resilience. Quoting interviewees, he writes, "The Lewes Pound benefits shoppers by creating stronger and more local shops, increasing a sense of pride in our community, decreasing CO2 emissions and increasing economic resilience." Ithaca Hours aim to "rebuild our economic base, to create a more ecologically and socially just economy which employs more of us, more reliably, at creative healthy work" (North, 2014: 253).

8 Resilience and the market subject

Affective economies of resistance

Introduction

Drawing the arguments of this section together, resilience has emerged as a counterpart to trauma in the affective politics of the global event. It seeks to valorise (complex) market life through tropes of adaptability. Against the responsive mode of trauma – where the event can cause problematic effects within the subject, or the community – resilience presents an auto-immune proposition, seeking to perpetually order systems and subjects in advance of the expected global event. While advocates of resilient governance celebrate the capacity of systems and subjects to foster adaptability, and continue to value their (metaphorical) ability to 'bounce back' from extreme events, critics highlight the disciplinary implications of such trends. For scholars of governmentality, in particular, resilience appears as an epitome of neo-liberal market life: political structures and networks are depoliticised and subjects are encouraged to feel responsible for the outcomes of 'events'. On this view, the evental-isation of global market life is taken as a governmental completion of processes of austerity, which scale back the role of the state in protecting the abject, marginalised or otherwise excluded market subjects. Across discourses of trauma and resilience the global event plays an important role in this performance of market subjects; how they are known, hailed, disciplined and produced. As Chandler suggests, from within the purview of post-liberal resilience theorising, it is only "the event [which] reveals relations and interconnections in a concrete, determinate fashion, linking the immediate with the distant and conceptual thought with the immediacy of feeling" (Chandler, 2014b, p. 155).

While there is much to recommend in critical understandings of resilience, not least in terms of moving beyond the managerial celebration of resilience as a simple exercise aimed at improving organisational capacity, Chapters 6 and 7 questioned the potential for reification in critical resilience studies. This is born of a basic doubt over the capacity of neo-liberalism or resilience to ever work in the monolithic or disciplinary mode attributed to it, that it is always and everywhere successful. By appeal to Butler's work on 'performative agency', it was suggested that any account of resilience should work to understand – empirically – the ways in which its performance may also be unsuccessful; that is to say, there are numerous invocations of resilience in the domains of policy and theory, and it would be quite problematic to assume that they are either all completely identical or necessarily successful in achieving their object. Different people do different things with resilience. An important exemplar in this regard is the work of David Chandler, who argues that quite apart from the post-Foucauldian consensus on the neo-liberal complementarities written into resilience, we should pay more attention to the anti-liberal connotations that drive it. In particular, Chandler notes that in the move to uncertainty and complexity, resilience can also function as a critique of traditional neo-liberal assumptions about politics. For Chandler (2014a: 48) resilience thinking can be seen as a "*radical critique* of the knowledge claims of actually existing neo-liberalism, suggesting that the hierarchical causal structure and assumptions of socially determined interactive outcomes still clings too much to a liberal modernist ontology". Indeed, doubt as to the progeny of interactive outcomes is quite an important qualification on the role of markets and marketisation within neo-liberalism.

With these important antidotes to the mood of neo-liberal victory, I argued that we should further open the question of performative implementation – i.e. *what is done in the name of resilience?* Thus Chapter 7 moved to engage the realm of everyday IPE and questions of 'alternative finance'. Taking a lead from the (mainstream) discourse of financial resilience espoused by Andrew Haldane and wider research agendas in the NGO sector, it was suggested that resilience could be a terrain of invention, *indeed resistance*. This was best exemplified in the project of Dave Fishwick to produce a local savings and loan bank, albeit mediated through a national documentary on Channel Four. Crucially, for the argument of this book, in seeking to build and nurture closer human relationships within the community via banking, Dave allowed for a conception of the market subject that works to *politicise the event*. Of course, such politicisation is imperfect, it plays on problematic notions of blame, and relies heavily on the charisma of the entrepreneur, but as a discussion of resilient market life, it suggests a capacity for resistance that is not widely exposed in the critical literature. Indeed, this connects up with a variety of approaches to resilience that foreground its close connection to resistance and its capacity for communitarian or even mythic forms of identification (Bourbeau and Ryan, 2017; Ryan, 2015). Far from an imposed, monolith of neo-liberal governance, there is a rich potential for theorizing resilience as an alternative to market-centrism.

What if resilience can be a form of resistance? This chapter will outline an alternative imaginary of resilience that foregrounds a capacity for resistance by reflecting on the capacity for self-making market subjects to re-work the conditions of possibility for their affective lives. In this sense, my aim is to problematise a central assumption of critical approaches to resilience, that the individualisation and responsibilisation for emotional life is necessarily a disciplinary moment. This argument is premised on the idea that the affective politics of resilience can also provide routes to imagining life where attachments may be unclear, or exist within changing social circumstances – including rapid changes in the form of the family, or the nature of the home. Somewhat bluntly, this moves beyond the common critical assumption that emotionality is a fitting ideology of neo-liberal capitalism in order to entertain the possibility that resilience may be productive of reflexive (and critical) market subjects. In more nuanced terms, the emotive languages presented by resilience agendas – where, for instance, children are encouraged to learn how to fail in order to build up their capacity to succeed – are not exhausted by a marketised education structure that merely implements neo-liberal governance. In line with my critique of financial governance in Chapter 7, such connections may otherwise be seen as a failure of resilience, a diminution of its 'anti-liberal' potentialities (Chandler, 2014a). Instead, I will engage the work of queer theorist Jack Halberstam (2011) to think about emotional resilience. She uses films such as *Finding Nemo* as invitations to imagine how market life can generate new forms of affect, love. For Halberstam, failure is an art, not a technique.

This argument is developed over three sections that seek to foreground and explore the affective dimensions of the resilient market subject. The section on **An emotional market subject** addresses the critical literature on the role of emotion and emotionality in resilience discourse, citing the assumed complicity between such 'responsibilisation' and neo-liberal austerity. The section on **A resilient market subject** engages the work of Halberstam and her argument that, while so often a site of heteronormative governance, the affective politics of children's cinema may be developing new spaces of possibility for feeling and expressing intimacy. This approach is developed and critically applied in relation to the apparently neo-liberal vision of emotional literacy embodied in *Little Miss Sunshine*. Finally, revisiting the theme of resistance and comedy of Chapter 4, I will question the cultural production of emotional literacy in resilience via the work of Alan Patridge.

An emotional market subject

The move within resilience discourse to focus on the psychological and especially the emotional make-up of market subjects is, in some way, the crux of the critical problematic. For all the light touch contingency awareness of the resilience agenda, the move to proactively facilitate subjects' emotional experience of market life has been taken as naive at best, and more likely a disciplinary manoeuvre. On this view, the affective turn is part of a displacement exercise where genuine political dilemmas are subsumed beneath a rhetoric of self-control. Emotional management in the face of adversity, Eva Illouz suggests (2008: 209), has become

> a widespread and even dominant notion because it corresponds to the ideology of social groups that are key to the production process and because it corresponds quite well to the requirements made on the self by new forms of capitalism.

For some, the way workers are encouraged to quantify or track elements of their behaviour, their productivity, their collegiality, or even their customer communication skills, must represent a new layer in the command power of management

(Moore, 2018). Far from the sovereign form of emotion identified by Furedi (2004: 13) after 9/11, where "[t]he emotional script communicated was one that also sought to create a sense of unity around a common experience of vulnerability", there is a sense in which projections of emotional literacy can work to isolate or atomise market subjects. Indeed, Pat O'Malley argues that rationalities of resilience entail particular techniques of the self, a self that is increasingly encouraged to nurture or train resilient traits, understood as anything from reading self-help books that teaches individuals to 'survive through chaos' to the widespread prevalence of cognitive behavioural techniques in Western societies. O'Malley suggests that this "resiliency manouevre [. . .] takes much of its impetus from compatibility with advanced liberal approaches to government in what are constituted as particularly uncertain times" (O'Malley, 2010: 490). Thus at the same time as resilience governs individuals through 'empowering them' to respond to and cope with extreme events, it also perpetuates a set of market subjects capable of succeeding with neo-liberal systems (Dean, 2014). As Alison Howell (2015b) pithily suggests, resilience is not merely a response to war and austerity, but a means for producing these forms of precarity in the first place *through a fantasy of indomitability*. Central to this critical diagnosis is not the move to emotionality as such, but the imbrication of emotionality with a certain form of cognitive training. As O'Malley (2010: 488) surmises,

> Resilience appears as a set of cognitive skills that anyone can develop with correct training. Founded in cognitive behavioural therapy, resilience centres innovativeness, enterprise, responsibility and flexibility. It now takes its place as part of a complex of scientifically grounded techniques of the self, necessary to optimize autonomous subjects in an age of high uncertainty.

In this sense, resilience can be read as a certain *technique* of emotion – a way of managing or ordering the affective politics of events. Within policy oriented literature, of course, this turn to management can be seen as a direct improvement on previous discourses, allowing subjects to embrace change rather than wallow in negative feelings. As Seligman (cf. O'Malley, emphasis added) propounds,

> Psychology has given us this whole language of pathology, so that a soldier in tears after seeing someone killed thinks: "Something's wrong with me; I have post-traumatic stress". . . . The idea here is to give people a new vocabulary, to speak in terms of resilience. Most people who experience trauma don't end up with PTSD; *many experience post-traumatic growth.*

And thus the positive elements of resilience can be read as a way of asking market subjects – and wider networks – to take responsibility for nurturing adaptive forms of emotional management, prioritising techniques that foreground the resilience of individuals in conditions of complexity and uncertainty within market life. While the critical focus is on subjective adaptation, however, much of the empirical literature has focused on the various governance agendas that seek to facilitate resilience. So, for instance, we might think about the widespread role of talking therapies, CBT and mindfulness training as preferred techniques of emotional and psychological support. Or else there has been a tendency to focus on straightforwardly disciplinary situations such as school education techniques or army training programs. In what follows, however, I will present a brief case study of the turn to resilience in humanitarian emergency planning. While there are elements of neo-liberal governance in humanitarian resilience, I argue, much of this can be attributed to contradiction and failure in the performance of resilience, rather than any successful completion of neo-liberalism.

Humanitarian response

A central element in the UK civil contingencies (UKCC) agenda is the organisation and fostering of 'humanitarian emergency preparedness'. In typically resilient fashion, the UKCC seeks to improve "the UK's ability to absorb, respond to and recover from emergencies", and the government has gone about this by collecting documentary knowledge and guidance on humanitarian emergencies with the resolution that "[t]he provision of humanitarian assistance is a multi-agency activity and it is important that this work is coordinated".[1] However, an interesting dimension of this area of UKCC planning is the centrality of the human subjects that might be drawn into the sphere of resilience practices through the experience of disaster, per se. Indeed, one mechanism that has been identified as central to this form of preparedness is the management of the psychological effects of trauma after extreme events. This issue requires resilience planners to relax their technical aspirations and allow practitioners to engage with the human and lived experiences of events. As Tessa Jowell illustrates in her foreword to the humanitarian assistance guidelines document:

> The death of a relative or friend, or serious personal injury, will in almost every case change lives forever. We know that the sensitivity and effectiveness of support people get in the first hours and days after such a trauma have a profound effect on how and whether they eventually come to terms with what happened.[2]

On this view, part of resilience involves awareness of *what can't be known*, or even perhaps, experienced in the moments after the event. As discussed in Chapter 5, this is because the logic of resilience in the field of psychological support/intervention – both individual and community-centred approaches – have sought to break new ground in identifying how the traumatic dimensions of emergencies can be attended to in the most proactive, coordinated and yet *least harmful* ways. In this sense, the rise of resilience thinking about and planning for the effects of disaster on human subjects can be seen as an attempt to move beyond some of the worst excesses of 'therapeutic governance' (Pupavac, 2001). On this view, the genealogy of resilience in humanitarian emergency preparedness carries particularities that distinguish it from ideas about resilience in other areas:

specifically, I would identify a normative component that (ideally) would turn away from invasiveness, victimisation or generalising the experience of trauma. Indeed, in UKCC, trauma seemingly drops out of the discourse (semantically at least) to focus on the positive coping abilities of different subjects. Humanitarian emergency preparedness is more about flexibility and adaptability:

> The humanitarian response to any emergency will be a package of care, with a range of agencies working together. The exact focus and nature of provision will depend on the type of emergency, the impact it has had on the community, and people's needs.[3]

Thus local resilience fora are advised to develop strategies for planning and coordinating activities between multiple organisations that are expected to focus upon the provision of humanitarian assistance centres (HACs). The expectation is that HACs can provide a first point of contact for responders to provide basic shelter, information about what has happened, financial and legal support, emotional support and 'hand holding', advice and direction on how to get further assistance and communication facilitation – allowing people to meet each other, a link to any ongoing police investigation where relevant and a point of contact for longer-term support. But there is also a pervasive focus on developing knowledge about resilience in order to cope with and indeed manage the psychological impact of disasters. As National Health Service guidelines suggest,

> Current knowledge about resilience, risk and protective factors shows that it is difficult to predict who is likely to recover from their immediate reactions or from distress with support from families or provision of community and welfare services and who may have more sustained distress or develop a mental disorder. For these reasons, the generalised picture [. . .] of how people respond psychosocially to traumatic events is intended to underpin planning, preparing and strategic management of services rather than to suggest that there is a single orthodoxy of clinical provision.
>
> (NHS, 2009: 24)

In a review of best practice, Dr Anne Eyre (2006), who is also closely associated with Disaster Action (a prominent counselling organisation and NGO), charts the move from critical incident stress debriefing through to psychological debriefing and then 'psychological first aid' as key examples of response modes by counsellors. This shift was the result of nearly three decades of debate and reflection within the psychological community over the veracity of psychological debriefing as a mechanism for 'treating' so-called trauma victims. Whereas earlier techniques encouraged the immediate 'working through' of emotions at-the-scene, later techniques were designed in the light of awareness of the capacity of psychological debriefing to 're-traumatise' or cause PTSD and to better reflect the natural coping strategies of humans in relation to stressful situations (in other words, to exhibit stress after a traumatic event is perfectly normal and by no means an indication of pathology).

At the heart of this debate was a critical divergence between a definition of the human as either susceptible to PTSD or, more latterly, as resilient and capable of exercising natural faculties for coping (Howell, 2011) or 'post-traumatic growth' in Seligman's terms. On this view, resilience is understood as a more positive trait that can be 'allowed for' via less invasive ways of responding to individuals who have experienced extreme events. However, despite such laudable aims, the performance of resilience via trauma counselling has been marked by several contradictions and breakdowns. While the resilience agenda seeks to reduce levels of intervention, there are important stipulations with regard to the 'types of human' and the kinds of professions that respond. For instance, while there is an interesting opening of the timeframe for the event – whereby an 'event' can be experienced in different ways (at different times) – there are also contradictory logics and practices which close down such possibilities. In particular, the definition of resilience in negative terms within UKCC, *as not providing a 'blueprint'* for response, can actually license a range of models to be coordinated in and around resilient practices.

Despite the professed aim of understanding the positive coping abilities of individuals, a definition of the human does emerge, which allows for forms of categorisation according to psychological traits. Indeed, the non-statutory guidelines identify 'four types of human beings': 1) resistant people, 2) resilient people, 3) people who have more sustained or persistent distress associated with dysfunction and/or impairment and 4) people who develop a mental disorder. Thus there are four types of people: some are resistant; some are resilient. But others may develop dysfunction or a mental disorder. Resilience emerges as the reverse positive of trauma – an ethical or aspirational category. Despite all the talk of non-invasiveness, resilience becomes a foundational trait which is defined negatively as 'not type 3 or 4' – i.e. 'vulnerable'. In the context of multilevel, multi-agency involvement, such negative definitions can allow significant scope for the resilient subject to become an object of negotiation. Indeed, Anne Eyre (2006: 3) suggests that such common-sense practices can downplay the importance of processes of working through adversity:

> [E]mergency planners often base their efforts on myths about human behavior and reactions during and after disaster. Other common pitfalls, [include] . . . fragmented approaches to mental health and social support, and a tendency to see disaster planning as a product rather than a process.

Somewhat contradictorily, private organisations are tasked with providing for their own ongoing psychological requirements, in turn fostering a set of incentives for psychological debriefing (as 'product') that is portrayed as a straightforward quick fix solution to the (managerial) 'problem' of trauma. And while resilience points away from certain practices of rapid reaction intervention, the fact of allowing for private organisations to 'buy' a product means that such practices can continue and indeed, on some arguments, encourage intervention through the inclusion of the voluntary and private sector actors with unstable income streams.[4]

In this vein, it is instructive to note several innovations that proffer psychological resilience training devices and programs. For instance, the Royal College of Psychiatrists now recommends that individuals practise CBT skills at the 'mood gym' – a computer program designed to give subjects a psychological 'workout' in order to avoid depression and other psychological symptoms.'[5] Again, it is somewhat unclear if such devices, including the profusion of mindfulness apps for smartphones, actually produce the docile subjects that critical theorists decry. For example, the private organisation Trauma Resilience Training (TRT) provides bespoke programs for organisations seeking to build resilience amongst their employees. TRT is, according to its website, a proactive program designed to help individuals and organisations with an increased risk of exposure to 'traumatic events'. A central component of the course is to enable what they call 'positive adaptation in the event of a critical incident and aid a swift return to normal functioning levels', both at home and at work. Thus, focusing on pre-disaster resilience, TRT's mantra is "preparing to control trauma with resilience. Recovering more quickly from adversity. Learning for better survival. The secure approach to potential disaster".[6] At the very least, there is an emergent will to 'manage' 'life changing events' through resilience training understood as 'cognitive exercise'.

While resilience clearly has a normative component – a respect for the human's potential coping abilities and encouragement of non-invasive care practices – there is an important politics to the naming and production of particular people and events as central to the security problematic. An (initially) ethical move entails an onto-political closure which levels down the apparently contingent and open experience of disaster that was foregrounded. By investing computer programs with cognitive-behavioural knowledge for the support of (unknown) individuals in advance of disastrous events, resilience is performative of both insecurity and overgeneralisation (almost to the point of farce). But there is also a curious legitimacy in resilience that licenses new agents and capabilities. Rapid reaction psychological debriefing (as product) continues to risk (indeed fosters) the 'over-intervention' that resilience thinking sought to avoid, while various training packages and manuals seek to prepare individuals through the somewhat questionable practice of 'mood training', itself sold as a new stage of market preparedness. Paradoxically, the move away from judging post-event psychological reactions as 'traumatic' has been met with an ambitious project of building cognitive resilience in (potentially) any human, at any stage in his or her market life.

A resilient market subject

The nurturing of an emotional subject in resilience can go in some unexpected directions. While a normatively driven effort to foreground doubt and foster non-invasiveness can – through certain contradictions and failures – marble through new market practices, whether training programs or decentralised mechanisms of proactive planning, this is quite distinct from the successful completion of neo-liberal governance that is sometimes supposed by critiques of resilience. More profoundly, by focusing too squarely on the roll-out of resilience through governance agendas and the cognitive training programs they foster, we perhaps lose sight of the subject who actually interacts with them. One might for instance, merely walk away from an extreme event, laugh at a computer program or otherwise subvert the intentions of the technical proposition in cognitive training. Indeed, as Chapter 5 argued, there is a rich tradition of trauma comedy that actively plays with concepts of emotionality. Ironically, from the point of view of resilience, these might even be regarded as positive coping techniques that promote growth by creative adaptation.

Can the resilient market subject be thought otherwise? At one level, the governmental critique of resilience overlooks how many of the neo-liberal repercussions of resilience agendas can be seen *as failures* of the discourse. In the case of humanitarian emergency preparedness, the market innovations and objectification of event-response dynamics resulted in practices that directly contradicted the normative agenda of resilience in psychology. Equally, we might recall the way an emphasis on systemic scale and (therefore) overall risk weighting in financial regulation has prioritised a form of macro-prudential regulation that contravenes the discursive focus on diversity amongst agents in financial resilience. At another level, I want to question our interest in resilient subjects. Does the market subject appear as a willing dupe of the neo-liberal governance agenda? Or is he or she a self-making subject, capable of inhabiting emotion and emotional literacy in terms that exceed any 'training'? To put it crudely, people ignore their cognitive therapy, laugh at books with titles such as *Post-Traumatic Stress Disorder for Dummies* (Goulston, 2007) and make comedy from stories of trauma and recovery. This potential for a rejection of emotional training can be read alongside the capacity to invent new ways of being an affective market subject.

In *The Queer Art of Failure* (2011), Jack Halberstam tries to navigate some of the possibilities and limits of critical thought by questioning what success and failure really mean in a society that has so privileged particular narratives of 'reproductive maturity combined with wealth accumulation'. Somewhat akin to Dave's ire at the 'bloody bankers', Halberstam takes the collapse of the financial markets and the dramatic rise in divorce rates to question the static models of success that prevail within market life. Yet, echoing the indeterminacy of knowledge in resilience, she advocates for an affective re-orientation:

> Under certain circumstances failing, losing, forgetting, unmaking, undoing, unbecoming, not knowing may in fact offer more creative, more cooperative, more surprising ways of being in the world. Failing is something queers do and have always done exceptionally well; for queers failure can be a style, to cite Quentin Crisp, or a way of life, to cite Foucault, and it can stand in contrast to the grim scenarios of success that depend on "trying and trying again".
>
> (2011: 3)

Indeed, this eulogy to failure is pitched as a direct critical alternative to positive psychology, which has 'afflicted' market life; "failure allows us to escape the punishing norms that discipline behavior and manage human development with the goal of delivering us from unruly childhoods to orderly and predictable adulthoods". While a broad orientation to social and cultural politics, I would argue that such a 'style' can directly challenge the anodyne politics of the subject engendered in resilient governance agendas. While sharing the critique of positive psychology, Halberstam can bring an affective purpose to critical readings that might help to think about what a resilient market subject might do:

> Failure preserves some of the wondrous anarchy of childhood and disturbs the supposedly clean boundaries between adults and children, winners and losers. And while failure certainly comes accompanied by a host of negative affects, such as disappointment, disillusionment, and despair, it also provides the opportunity to use these negative affects to poke holes in the toxic positivity of contemporary life.
>
> (2011: 3)

On this view, failure is not some interactive outcome from which we might learn to improve; instead, it is an art of self-making subjects who are able to use and reflect on the contingency of their experience. But this reflection is not a learning process, nor is it part of technique of adaptation to uncertainty. Rather, it is a meditation on the inconsistencies and contradictions within market life. Rendered thus, the performative politics of resilience can be an interesting provocation to move against some of the disciplinary dimensions of neo-liberal responsibilisation. For Halberstam, this points to popular culture and films such as *Little Miss Sunshine* which seemingly paint a bleak picture of family life within neo-liberalism. The film presents the narrative of a young girl who dreams of winning a beauty pageant, with only her family to support her.

> With her porn obsessed junky grandfather providing her with the choreography for her pageant routine and a cheerleading squad made up of her gay suicidal uncle, a Nietzsche reading mute brother, and aspiring but flailing motivational speaker father and an exasperated stay-at-home mom, Olive is destined to fail, and fail spectacularly. But while her failure could be a source of misery and humiliation, and while it does indeed deliver precisely this, it also leads to a kind of ecstatic exposure of the contradictions of a society obsessed with meaningless competition.
>
> (2011: 4–5)

On this view, it is not simply that resilience can break down or backfire, but rather that in engaging the performative politics it entails, we might, with Butler, anticipate another form of critique, where the contradictions of the 'system' through which market life is thought can be brought into view. The auto-immune impulse in resilience is destined to fail, not because it is wrong so much as because it is right. Indeterminacy, non-invasiveness and adaptability are fair attitudes towards uncertainty, so much so that the wide-scale attempt to write them through the governance of market life may work to highlight the critical contradictions of that move. The event *does matter*, in its particularities and thick cultural resonance. The subject *is self-making* despite, or because, of attempts to 'train' it. Importantly, such an account is open to the potential humour of trauma and resilience.

> While Olive's failure as a beauty pageant contestant plays out against the soundtrack of "Superfreak" on a stage in a bland hotel in Redondo Beach in front of a room full of supermoms and their "JonBenet" daughters, this failure, hilarious in its execution, poignant in its meaning, and exhilarating in its aftermath, is so much better, so much more liberating than any success that could possibly be achieved in the context of a teen beauty contest. . . . The dysfunctional little family jumps in and out of its battered yellow VW and holds together despite or perhaps because of the suicide attempts, the impending bankruptcy, the death of the family patriarch, and the ultimate irrelevancy of the beauty contest, a new kind of optimism is born. Not an optimism that relies on positive thinking as an explanatory engine for social order, nor one that insists on the bright side at all costs; rather this is a little ray of sunshine that produces shade and light in equal measure and knows that the meaning of one always depends on the meaning of the other.
>
> (2011: 5)

For Halberstam, the performative ecologies of emotionality and positive psychology that emerge, break down and fail, and in failing create, must be read as productive embodiments of subjective potential. Neither a route to success, nor an interactive puzzle that condemns us to learn through failure, market life appears as a lived experience, that finds hope and optimism in strange – 'in-between' – spaces. While Halberstam does not use the term resilience, she nevertheless summons an instructive relationality within consumer culture that is not exhausted by critical diagnoses of hegemony or utopia, indeed that we might nurture optimism about and through failure.

A resistant market subject?

Throughout this book, I have been attempting to think about how the global event is performative of market life in general, and ideas of the market subject in particular. Arguments that the spectacle of the global event is merely that – an entertainment vehicle for global capitalism that transfixes us with victims and saviours, moral arcs and redemption – have been drawn on, but ultimately critiqued because of their inability to take account of the emergence of new discourses and subjects. This live creative performance of the global has, in my view, changed the affective life of markets in quite a fundamental way. Experience, and indeed, emotion, have become central languages for the market subject. That this has occurred through the performance of trauma and resilience is a contingency that brings certain specificities to the story. Market subjects are alternatively vulnerable, wounded, growing, resilient, adaptable, etc., etc., etc. Again, while critical theorists might seek to debunk such emotional qualities as 'typical' of a form of neo-liberal market life that seeks to govern and order individuals, my sense is that such moves – for all that they are instructive – play down the emergence of new subjects, that affective discourses provide a mode of subjectification, yes, but also a language through which subjects can speak politically.

In this sense, the language of the event and the language of the subject are performative in contingent and unpredictable ways. A performance can succeed or fail. Once this performative politics is foregrounded, it becomes hard to accept either the utopian/ethical or critical/disciplinary diagnoses on offer. Neo-liberalism may be an attractive catch-all term, but that is precisely its weakness. Critical approaches that diagnose market life in terms of neo-liberal governance, and then every adaptation of that form of governance as inevitably successful, lose touch with the play of contingency. Therefore, in prioritising failure as an art of market life, we might instead focus attention on the ways in which subversion, resistance and, indeed, ethics are in a process of changing. For Halberstam, this involves a trajectory to examine the explosion of innovative children's films that have emerged through Pixar and people like Nick Park. As she surmises, in these films, "desire for difference is not connected to a neo-liberal 'Be yourself' mentality or to special individualism for 'incredible people'; rather the Pixarvolt films connect individualism to selfishness, to untrammeled consumption and they oppose it with a collective mentality". While this might be seen as part of a wider aesthetic of resistance in late capitalism, she identifies certain elements that change the emotional politics.

> Two thematics can transform a potential Pixarevolt film into a tame and conventional cartoon: an over emphasis on the nuclear family and a normative investment in coupled romance. The Pixarevolt films, unlike their unrevolting conventional animation counterparts, seem to know their main audience is children, and they seem to also know that children do not invest in the same things that adults invest in: children are not coupled, they are not romantic, they do not have religious morality, they are not afraid of death or failure, they are collective creatures, they are in a constant state of rebellion against their parents, and they are not the masters of their domain. Children stumble, bumble, fail, fall, hurt; they are mired in difference, not in control of their bodies, not in charge of their lives, and they live according to schedules not of their own making.
>
> (2011: 47)

So if we take a film such as *Finding Nemo*, the triumph of the little guy is not about learning to become like a proper grown up. Instead, the mother is dead and the father is quite enfeebled. Nemo is in fact separated from his home, but enjoys through numerous failures the value of his collective in the new fish tank. For Halberstam, this presents the opportunity for an account of intimacy that is not bound by heteronormative gender structures; the Father does not fall in love or couple with Dory, but they challenge each other and explore new relations. Nemo expresses an openness to trust and intimacy, all the time flitting from one extreme event to the next, yet somehow fitting within groups.

Bouncing back

A resistant market subject can be thought of then, not as a refusal, nor a dissent, but a performative embodiment of the problematics and logics that make up market life. If resilience hails a certain idea(l) of the emotional being, able to become conscious of their cognitive make-up, pathologies and so forth, then Halberstam illustrates a way in which we might think beyond the dichotomy of growth or discipline. Emotional literacy does not, as critical theorists fairly suggest, equate to a harmony of experience, where everyone is becoming happier all the time. But neither does it result in a machine-like ordering of subjective experience, akin to an ideology of self-control. Rather than 'learning from failure' as countless self-help books, positive thinking guides and teaching directives suggest then, Halberstam pitches failure as an art, something to be cultivated, perhaps even enjoyed? Beyond the impressive rise of recent children's cinema, and its envolving break with tropes of heteronormative discipline, I want to suggest one final image of failure in the figure and story of Alan Partridge. Alan is a character that has emerged and developed through the work of Armando Iannucci and Steve Coogan to embody an important position in British culture: an erstwhile loser figure who never quite understands (or cares) what he is doing wrong. The art of Partridge's failure, though, is the way he embodies and subverts the emotive tropes and norms of everyday market life. As his book describes,

> He's survived the death of a guest on air, his wife leaving him for a fitness instructor, an encounter with a mentalist fan, being crushed beneath a dead cow and incomplete sex with a woman he was supposed to be sacking. He's suffered a breakdown, Toblerone addiction, weight gain and his autobiography Bouncing Back being withdrawn and pulped. But Alan continues to bounce back – resilience and Gordon are his middle names.
>
> (Coogan, 2003)

The notion of emotional subject, who is required to learn from and adapt to ongoing and career failures, is exaggerated. The unexpected outcomes of market life – e.g. accidentally killing one of his chat show guests – is portrayed as a challenge to Alan's 'journey'. While ostensibly a satire of D-list celebrity life, then, seeking and losing commission, yet carrying a status that allows him to make a living from endorsing local companies, Alan's character also 'experiences' the pain of failure.

The nature of this experience, though, is a quite public and visceral humiliation that the (British) audience can laugh at or with, while Alan himself seems to find ways to fail even at recognising his failings. Quintessentially, this might be read into the year after his divorce that he spent living in the Lynton Travel Tavern that was equidistant between Norwich and London, or the extensive amount of time he spends living in a porta-cabin next to his unfinished house. Or else it might be in the failed love adventure with the secretary he is too scared to sack, whom he takes on a date to an owl sanctuary before 'making love' to her in the dark, unsuccessfully trying to avoid premature ejaculation by (and at the point of) asking for her thoughts on the 'pedestrianisation' of Norwich city centre.

However, beyond the surface-level comedy of error, there is also a deeper Alan who is beaten down by experience. As told in his autobiography, "I Partridge, We need to talk about Alan", it was the eventual snub from the BBC that launched him into depressing cycle of 'fed-up-ness'.

> I'd watch endless repeats of Birds of a Feather, a program which I quite rightly despised, my assistant says I stopped checking her expense claims for some time, which really should not have happened. And all the while of course I was eating quite a bit of Toblerone. . . . Then one day I lost control. It wasn't a single trigger, but an accumulation of minor accidents, how to explain it? It was as if I was carrying a lot of straw on my back, people kept adding another piece and then another, and then another, until I couldn't carry anymore, because my back had broken. . . . I lost control and I ended up driving to Dundee in bare feet.

In the TV program, this scene repeats in Alan's mind through flashbacks, of being disoriented in the car, of phoning Lynn and explaining how he'd been eating a lot of Toblerones. As he explains in the book, "so complete was my mental collapse I remember literally nothing of my journey to Scotland". Eventually, Lynn travelled over night to drive him home in his Vectra with the hosepipe dangling from the exhaust, which he describes as "I should have said" about the suicide bid he didn't get around to. The satire of resilience builds from this psychological breakdown to explore Alan's emotional recovery:

> I subsequently made a number of changes to my life which resulted in me getting better. I'd done it, I'd bounced back. The doubters could shove their faces because I'd done it and so with fewer work commitments, a slimmer physique, fresher breath, less clutter on my desk, and a blanket ban on Toblerones, I felt like a new man. Quite a turnaround then? Yep it's a tale of incomprehensible pain and hardship of bravery and backbone, of me and my success, one that could easily be stretched out into a film or novella, if only because that kind of addiction's not been done before, and would therefore feel fresher to a reader or viewer, just a thought.

In turning against recovery culture, Alan perhaps borders on a basic conservatism, not least when he ranks all the addictions in order so as to place his own as the worst form of addiction. But there is within the ongoing failure a certain decentring of emotional literacy. Quintessentially, even Alan's book titled *Bouncing Back* struggles to sell and ends up being pulped, while Alan watches on, shouting because of the noise, "It looks like Porridge, I say Porridge, but it's more like Weetabix with warm milk on I." Alan is clearly happy to spend the day in the pulping factory, and the workers tell him he is always welcome back.

Conclusion

In conclusion, the resilient market subject is open to performative instability. While there may be attempts to identify, typify and train a certain model of the resilient individual, such moves are neither necessarily successful nor commensurate with the wider normative dimensions of resilience. With such instability, I argued, it was possible to think more creatively about a resilient market subject in terms of failure. Rather than taking failure as a test-oriented quality, which makes people learn 'not to fail', Halberstam points to a way in which failure can be an art of living differently within market life. In this sense, a certain comic or satirical sense of failure as the critical embodiment of the contradictions of neoliberal market life can be presented as a source for 'optimism', in the between spaces. While Halberstam points to children's movies to draw this out, I have presented the character of Alan Partridge, his Toblerone addiction, breakdown, 'bouncing back' and eventual pulping of the book, *Bouncing Back*, as an epitome of this art of failure. Just as Halberstam identifies the performative relationship between films and the audience of children – children who 'stumble and fail all the time' – so Alan speaks to a British audience educated by imperial decline and a basic cultural pessimism to revel in failure; i.e. *its not the despair, it's the hope that kills you*. While this is clearly a contingent and highly particular illustration of the potentialities of a resistant market subject, the way that it inhabits and subverts the emotionality of market life, with its positivity and endless stories of recovery and growth, is a popular, even mainstream, narrative that resists the potential for discipline or emotional governance to go unchecked.

Notes

1 See www.gov.uk/government/publications/humanitarian-assistance-in-emergencies (accessed 25 March 2014)
2 Foreword to *Humanitarian Assistance in Emergencies: Non-Statutory Guidance on Establishing Humanitarian Assistance Centres*, p. 3. Available at: www.gov.uk/government/uploads/system/ uploads/attachment_data/file/61221/hac_guidance.pdf (accessed 25 March 2014).
3 See *Humanitarian Assistance in Emergencies: Non-Statutory Guidance on Establishing Humanitarian Assistance Centres*, p. 10. Available at: www.gov.uk/government/uploads/system/uploads/attachment_data/file/61221/hac_guidance.pdf (accessed 25 March 2014).
4 Confidential interviews with trauma counselling NGOs
5 www.moodgym.anu.edu.au/welcome (accessed 11 February 2013)
6 www.traumaresiliencetraining.co.uk/ (accessed 11 February 2013)

Conclusion

When cosmopolitan theorists first began to discuss the way global events could bring to light the importance and politics of globalisation, they did not assume any natural or linear route to progress. The "real life thriller in everybody's living room" that Ulrich Beck wrestled with was a contingent and ambiguous monster, as likely to promote the securitisation of global politics, as to allow for subjects to identify with and sympathise for their common vulnerabilities. Their move to engage the politics of the global event in apparently 'progressive' discourses such as trauma and resilience can be read generously as an attempt to engage with the contingent potentialities of the global public sphere, even – or especially – when it seemed to be so threatened. If this book has identified a set of ethical and political ambiguities in the performance of these discourses of the global event, around the potential for affective discipline and the reification of market life in terms of neo-liberalism and/or complexity, then this is part of a similar intent. Where once the confidence in 'coming together' as a route to a more ethical global politics had foregrounded emotion and the limitations of rationality, I have attempted to unpick and engage the unintended outcomes of such performances. The power of trauma is at once a recognition of *and a command* that market subjects have a complex and tenuous emotional life. As more global events have been rendered in traumatic terms, the disciplinary aspects of this turn should be placed in question, for re-producing ideas of helpless victims, for generalising knowledge about emotional subjects and for licensing a 'medicalised' confidence in the capacity of psycho-social intervention.

But this book has also argued that the politics of subjectivity implies an ongoing conversation; how we come to know, live and perform global events through discourses of trauma and resilience can lead to interesting and unintended outcomes. Such discourses can be politicised in critical or emancipatory ways, whether through documentaries that emphasise the class and racial politics of Katrina or alternative finance campaigns that articulate a more reciprocal, less leveraged, version of resilient global finance. In my view, the emergent subject of the global event appears quite capable of articulating new modes of market life, in and through these discourses of the global event, that are not exhausted by an empty managerialism, on the one hand, or an affective discipline on the other. Neo-liberalism, however defined, is neither inevitably successful nor essentially coherent with itself or these contingent performances of the global event. Comedy, piss-taking, self-satire and *failure* have all been mobilised in different ways throughout this book to imply that creative forms of critique and resistance are both possible and ongoing.

Going forward, just as trauma has begun to subside in the narration of global events so too will the current period of resilience likely segue into new ways of thinking about/inhabiting the market. Without wishing to speculate, it seems apparent that the 'toughness' of some areas of resilience thinking (witness the speed with which American political culture moves on after a mass shooting, with rituals of condolence and a celebration of the organisation of first responders) could provoke a form of politics that is more aggressive or divisive in character. Equally, the cherished response to global financial crisis in Europe and fiscal discipline has prolonged austerity in a manner that may fit elements of a resilience discourse, but has equally fostered a period of intense reflection on the 'violent' dimensions of finance. The politics of financial resilience may go in critical or reactionary directions. Indeed, what this book has pitched as resistance to neoliberal dogma through the articulation of alternative forms of subjective and social resilience could equally be seen along a spectrum towards what is now popularly regarded as 'the rise of populism'.

We live in a time where two 'global events' have re-set the tone – *and Eurocentrism* – of public discussion about the politics of market life. Brexit and Trump have been performed as epochal events in the (apparently) smooth progress of the global political economy, where the 'natural' or 'normal' state of affairs – co-operation, tolerance, values – has been interrupted by an abnormal, divisive form of politics. Both events have been narrated as a trauma, and emotions have circulated and intensified around which 'side' of the 'wound' you identify with. Indeed, the Brexit 'event' has even created new political constituencies around 'leavers' and 'remainers'.

In line with the argument of this book, the performative politics of the global event appears to be more intense and pervasive than ever. Quintessentially, the very basis of each event seems to foreground the affective dimensions of a particular 'model' of global market life. Do you identify with 'liberal globalism'? Or do you identify with 'national protectionism'? While we might engage with, or even get lost in, the divisive nature of these differentially valorised (and performed) categories, I would conclude with the original problematic of this book. How does a global market come to life? Through the performance of logics and emotions that highlight our common vulnerability, our need for (and the vital role of) sympathy and the importance of 'growth' for market subjects. In this sense, the global event does not so much interrupt *as make* global market life.

Bibliography

Abdelal, R., Blyth, M. and Parsons, C. (eds) (2010) *Constructing the International Economy*. Ithaca, NY: Cornell University Press.

Action Man: Battlefield Casualties (2015) James, P. (dir), London: Veterans for Peace UK. Vimeo video, 2:55, posted by 'Veterans for Peace UK', 22 June 2015. Available: https://vimeo.com/131462825 (accessed 16 March 2017).

Ahmed, S. (2013) *The Cultural Politics of Emotion*. Abingdon, NY: Routledge.

Aitken, Rob (2010) '"To the Ends of the Earth": Culture, Visuality and the Embedded Economy', in Jacqueline Best and Matthew Paterson (eds.) Cultural Political Economy, New York: Routledge, 67-90

Alexander, J. (2004) 'Toward a Theory of Cultural Trauma', in Alexander, J. et al. (eds) *Cultural Trauma and Collective Identity*. Berkley: University of California Press.

Allan, S. and Thorsen, E. (eds) (2009) *Citizen Journalism: Global Perspectives*. New York: Peter Lang.

Allen, N. (2010, October 14) 'Chile Miners Rescued: Timeline', *The Telegraph*. Available: www.telegraph.co.uk/news/worldnews/southamerica/chile/8057126/Chile-miners-rescued-timeline.html (accessed 1 July 2017)

Andreu, M. (2016) 'A Responsibility to Profit? Social Impact Bonds as a Form of "Humanitarian Finance."' Paper presented at the conference on 'Everyday Humanitarianism: Ethics, Affects and Practices.' London: London School of Economics and Political Science, 15 April 2016.

Antze, P. and Lambel, M. (1996) Tense Past: Cultural Essays in Trauma and Memory. New York and London, Routledge.

Aradau, C. and Van Munster, R. (2012) 'The Securitization of Catastrophic Events: Trauma Enactment and Preparedness Exercises', *Alternatives*, 37(3): 227–39.

Archibugi, D. (2001) 'Terrorism and Cosmopolitanism', *SSRC Working Paper*. Available: www.danielearchibugi.org/downloads/papers/Terrorism_and_Cosmopolitanism.pdf (accessed 12 March 2017).

Ariffin, Y., Coicaud, J. and Popovski, V. (eds) (2016) *Emotions in International Politics: Beyond Mainstream International Relations*. Cambridge: Cambridge University Press.

Austin, J. L. (1962) *How to Do Things with Words*. Oxford: Clarendon Press.

Bank of England (2011) *Financial Stability Report, June 2011*. London: Bank of England. Available: www.bankofengland.co.uk/publications/Documents/fsr/2011/fsrfull1106.pdf (accessed 16 March 2017).

Bank for International Settlements (2013) *83rd Annual Report*. Basel: Bank for International Settlements. Available: www.bis.org/publ/arpdf/ar2013e.pdf (accessed 12 March 2017).

Batman Begins (2005) Nolan, C. (dir), Burbank, CA: Warner Bros. Pictures. 2005, DVD.

Baylis, J. and Smith, S. (1997) *The Globalization of World Politics: An Introduction to International Relations*. Oxford, UK; Malden, MA: Oxford University Press.

BBC News (2007, April 2) 'Top US Lender in Chapter 11 Move'. Available: http://news.bbc.co.uk/2/hi/business/6519051.stm (accessed 15 March 2017).

BBC News (2007, April 17) 'Effort to Ease US Mortgage Woes'. Available: http://news.bbc.co.uk/2/hi/business/6565497.stm (accessed 15 March 2017).

Beck, U. (1999) *World Risk Society*. Cambridge: Polity Press.

——— (2000) *What is Globalization?* Cambridge: Polity Press.

——— (2006) *Cosmopolitan Vision*. Cambridge, UK; Malden, MA: Polity Press.

——— (2009) 'Critical Theory of World Risk Society: A Cosmopolitan Vision', *Constellations*, 16(1): 3–22.

——— (2013) 'Why Class is Too Soft a Category to Capture the Explosiveness of Social Inequality at the Beginning of the Twenty-first Century', *British Journal of Sociology*, 64(1): 63–74.

Beck, U., Giddens, A. and Lash, S. (1994) *Reflexive Modernization: Politics, Tradition and Aesthetics in the Modern Social Order*. Cambridge: Polity Press.

Bello, W. (2005) *Deglobalization: Ideas for a New World Economy*. London: Zed Books.

Béné, C., Wood, R. G., Newsham, A. and Davies, M. (2012). 'Resilience: New Utopia or New Tyranny? Reflection About the Potentials and Limits of the Concept of Resilience in Relation to Vulnerability Reduction Programmes.' *IDS Working Papers*, 2012(405): 1–61.

Bernanke, B. S. (2013) 'Creating Resilient Communities.' Speech by Ben S. Bernanke (Chairman of the Federal Reserve) at the 'Resilience and Rebuilding for Low-Income Communities: Research to Inform Policy and Practice' Federal Reserve System Community Affairs Research Conference' transcript. Available: www.federalreserve.gov/newsevents/speech/bernanke20130412a.pdf (accessed 14 March 2017).

Best, J. (2017) 'Security, Economy, Population: The Political Economic Logic of Liberal Exceptionalism', *Security Dialogue*, forthcoming, online first.

Best, J. and Paterson, M. (2010) 'Introduction: Understanding Cultural Political Economy', in Best, J. and Paterson, M. (eds) *Cultural Political Economy*, Abingdon, NY: Routledge, pp. 1–26.

Bisson, J. I. (2007) 'Post-Traumatic Stress Disorder', *Occupational Medicine*, 57(6): 399–403.

Bleiker, R. (2006) 'Art After 9/11', *Alternatives*, 31(1): 77–99.

Blyth, M. (2013) 'Paradigms and Paradox: The Politics of Ideas in Two Moments of Crisis', *Governance*, 26(2): 197–215.

Bourbeau, P. and Ryan, P. (2017) 'Resilience, Resistance, Infrapolitics and Enmeshment,' European Journal of International Relations, 24(1): 221–239.

Bonnefoy, P. (2010, August 29) 'Poor Safety Standards Led to Chilean Mine Disaster', *Global Post*. Available: www.pri.org/stories/2010-08-28/poor-safety-standards-led-chilean-mine-disaster (accessed 30 June 2017).

Braithwaite, H. (2013) 'The Politics of Resilience From a Practitioners Perspective: An Interview with Helen Braithwaite OBE', *Politics*, 33(4): 229–39.

Brand, R. (2013) 'Russell Brand: We Deserve More Form Our Democratic System', *The Guardian*, 5 November, www.theguardian.com/commentisfree/2013/nov/05/russell-brand-democratic-system-newsnight (accessed 22 June 2017)

Brassett, J. (2008) Cosmopolitanism vs. Terrorism? Discourses of Ethical Possibility Before and After 7/7', *Millennium: Journal of International Studies*, 36(2): 121–47.

——— (2009a) 'British Irony, Global Justice: A Pragmatic Reading of Chris Brown, Banksy and Ricky Gervais', *Review of International Studies*, 35(1): 219–45.

——— (2009b) 'A Pragmatic Approach to the Tobin Tax Campaign: The Politics of Sentimental Education', *European Journal of International Relations*, 15(3): 447–76.
——— (2010) *Cosmopolitanism and Global Financial Reform: A Pragmatic Approach to the Tobin Tax*. Abingdon, NY: Routledge.
——— (2011) 'Cosmopolitan Sentiments After 9-11: Trauma and the Politics of Vulnerability', *Journal of Critical Globalisation Studies*, 3: 12–29.
——— (2014) 'The Ethical Dimensions of Global Governance', in Payne, A. and Phillips, N. (eds) *Handbook of the International Political Economy of Governance*, Cheltenham: Edward Elgar Publishing, pp. 69–86.
——— (2016) 'British Comedy, Global Resistance: Russell Brand, Charlie Brooker and Stewart Lee', *European Journal of International Relations*, 22(1): 168–91.
Brassett, J. and Clarke, C. (2012) 'Performing the Sub-Prime Crisis: Trauma and the Financial Event', *International Political Sociology*, 6(1): 4–20.
Brassett, J. and Holmes, C. (2016) 'Building Resilient Finance? Uncertainty, Complexity, and Resistance', *The British Journal of Politics and International Relations*, 18(2): 370–88.
Brassett, J. and Rethel, L. (2015) 'Sexy Money: The Hetero-Normative Politics of Global Finance', *Review of International Studies*, 41(3): 429–49.
Brassett, J. and Smith, W. (2010) 'Deliberation and Global Civil Society: Agency, Arena, Affect', *Review of International Studies*, 36(2): 413–30.
Brassett, J. and Vaughan-Williams, N. (2012a) 'Governing Traumatic Events', *Alternatives: Global, Local, Political*, 37(3): 183–87.
——— (2012b) 'Crisis Is Governance: Sub-Prime, the Traumatic Event, and Bare Life', *Global Society*, 26(1): 19–42.
——— (2013) 'The Politics of Resilience from a Practitioner's Perspective: An Interview with Helen Braithwaite OBE', *Politics*, 33(4): 229–39.
——— (2015) 'Security and the Performative Politics of Resilience: Critical Infrastructure Protection and Humanitarian Emergency Preparedness', *Security Dialogue*, 46(1): 32–50.
Brassett, J., Croft, S. and Vaughan-Williams, N. (2013) 'Introduction: An Agenda for Resilience Research in Politics and International Relations', *Politics*, 33(4): 221–28.
Broome, A. (2014) *Issues and Actors in the Global Political Economy*. Basingstoke, NY: Palgrave Macmillan.
Broome, A., Clegg, L. and Rethel, L. (2012) 'Global Governance and the Politics of Crisis', *Global Society*, 26(1): 3–17.
Browning, C. (2017) 'Je suis en terrace': Political Violence, Civilizational Politics, and the Everyday Courage to Be', *Political Psychology*, forthcoming, online first.
de Bruijne, M., Boin, A. and van Eeten, M. (2010) 'Resilience: Exploring the Concept and Its Meanings', in Comfort, L. K., Boin, A. and Demchak, C. C. (eds) *Designing Resilience: Preparing for Extreme Events*, Pittsburgh: University of Pittsburgh Press, pp. 13–32.
Bulley, D. (2013) 'Producing and Governing Community (through) Resilience', *Politics*, 33(4): 265–75.
Bulley, D. and Lisle, D. (2012) 'Welcoming the World: Governing Hospitality in London's 2012 Olympic Bid', *International Political Sociology*, 6(2): 186–204.
Burnley Savings and Loans Limited (2016) *About us*. Available: www.burnleysavingsandloans.co.uk/about-us (accessed 21 March 2017).
Butler, J. (1997) *The Psychic Life of Power: Theories in Subjection*. Stanford: Stanford University Press.

——— (2004) *Precarious Life: The Powers of Mourning and Violence*. London: Verso Books.

——— (2005) *Giving an Account of Oneself.* New York: Fordham University Press.

——— (2006) *Gender Trouble: Feminism and the Subversion of Identity*. Abingdon, NY: Routledge.

——— (2010) 'Performative Agency', *Journal of Cultural Economy*, 3(2): 147–61.

——— (2012) 'Critically Queer', Ed. Hall, D. et al., The Routledge Queer Studies Reader. Ed. Donald Hall et al. New York: Routledge, 2012. 18–31.

Callon, Michel. (1998) Introduction: The Embeddedness of Economic Markets in Economics. In The Laws of the Markets, edited by Michel Callon. Oxford: Blackwell.

Cameron, D. (2009, October 8) 'Full Text of David Cameron's Speech', *The Guardian*. Available: www.theguardian.com/politics/2009/oct/08/david-cameron-speech-in-full (accessed 22 June 2017)

Carney, M. (2015) 'Building Real Markets For the Good of the People', speech by Mark Carney (Governor of the Bank of England) at the *Lord Mayor's Banquet for Bankers and Merchants of the City of London at the Mansion House*, transcript. Available: www.bankofengland.co.uk/publications/Documents/speeches/2015/speech821.pdf (accessed 21 March 2017).

Carpenter, S., Walker, B., Anderies, J. and Abel, N. (2001) 'From Metaphor to Measurement: Resilience of What to What?', *Ecosystems*, 4(8): 765–81.

Caruth, C. (1991) *Unclaimed Experience: Trauma, Narrative and History*. Baltimore: Johns Hopkins University Press.

Caruth, C. (ed.) (1995) *Trauma: Explorations in Memory*. Baltimore: Johns Hopkins University Press.

Carroll, R. (2010, October 17) 'When the Miners' Leader Met the President, Two Sides of Chile Embraced', *The Guardian*. Available: www.theguardian.com/world/2010/oct/17/sebastian-pinera-luis-urzua-chile (accessed: 01 July 2017)

Castells, M. (2009) *The Rise of Network Society: Information Age: Economy, Society, and Culture. Volume 1* (2nd edition). Oxford: Wiley Blackwell.

Cavelty, M. D., Kaufmann, M. and Kristensen, K. S. (2015) 'Resilience and (in)security: Practices, Subjects, Temporalities', *Security Dialogue*, 46(1): 3–14.

Chandler, D. (2012) 'Resilience and Human Security: The Post-Interventionist Paradigm', *Security Dialogue*, 43(3): 213–29.

——— (2014a) 'Beyond Neoliberalism: Resilience, The New Art of Governing Complexity', *Resilience: International Policies, Practices and Discourses*, 2(1): 47–63.

——— (2014b) *Resilience: The Governance of Complexity*. London and New York: Routledge.

Chandler, D. and Coaffee (eds) (2017) *The Routledge Handbook of International Resilience*. London and New York: Routledge.

Chouliaraki, L. (2013) *The Ironic Spectator: Solidarity in the Age of Post-Humanitarianism*. Cambridge: Polity.

Christou, A. (2016) 'The Wretched of the Earth: Greece and the Cultural Politics of Inequality', *Humanity and Society*, forthcoming, Online First.

Clarke, C. (2015) 'Learning to Fail: Resilience and the Empty Promise of Financial Literacy Education', *Consumption Markets & Culture*, 18(3): 257–76.

Cohen, N. (2008, November 9) 'The Myth of the Banker on the Edge Ignores a Wider Misery', *The Guardian*. Available: www.theguardian.com/commentisfree/2008/nov/09/bankers-recession-kirkstephensoncredit-crunch (accessed 16 March 2017).

Collinson, P. (2012, July 6) 'Bank on Dave: One Man's Crusade to Help Small Businesses Raise Finance', *The Guardian*. Available: www.theguardian.com/money/2012/jul/06/bank-of-dave-small-business-finance-dave-fishwick (accessed 21 March 2017).

Comfort, L. K., Boin, A. and Demchak, C. C. (eds) (2010) *Designing Resilience: Preparing for Extreme Events*. Pittsburgh: University of Pittsburgh Press.

Coogan, S. (2003) *Alan Partridge: Everyday Ruddy Word*. Michael Joseph Ltd.

Costandi, M. (2011, September 9) 'Pregnant 9-11 Survivors Transmitted Trauma to Their Children', *The Guardian*. Available: www.theguardian.com/science/neurophilosophy/2011/sep/09/pregnant-911-survivors-transmitted-trauma (accessed 10 July 2017)

Cox, R. W. (1987) *Production, Power and World Order*. New York: Columbia University Press.

The Dark Knight (2008) Nolan, C. (dir), Burbank, CA: Warner Bros. Pictures. 2008, DVD.

Davies, M. (2016) 'Everyday Life as Critique: Revisiting the Everyday in IPE with Lefebvre and Postcolonialism', *International Political Sociology*, 10(1): 22–38.

Davies, W. (2011) 'The Political Economy of Unhappiness', *New Left Review*, 71(Sept–Oct): 65–80.

——— (2014) *The Limits of Neoliberalism: Authority, Sovereignty and the Logic of Competition*. London: Sage.

——— (2015) *The Happiness Industry: How Government and big Business Sold Us Well-being*. London: Verso.

Dayan, D. and Katz, E. (1992) *Media Events: The Live Broadcasting of History*. Cambridge: Cambridge University Press.

de Goede, M. (2000) 'Mastering Lady Credit: Discourses of Financial Crisis in Historical Perspective', *International Feminist Journal of Politics*, 2(1): 58–81.

——— (2003) 'Beyond Economism in International Political Economy', *Review of International Studies*, 29(1): 79–97.

de Goede, Marieke (2005) Virtue, Fortune, and Faith: A Genealogy of Finance, Minneapolis: University of Minnesota Press.

de Gregorio, J. (2013) 'Resilience in Latin America: Lessons from Macroeconomic Management and Financial Policies.' IMF Working Paper 13/259. Washington, DC: International Monetary Fund. Available: http://econpapers.repec.org/paper/imfimfwpa/13_2f259.htm (accessed 15 March 2017).

Dean, M. (2010) *Governmentality: Power and Rule in Modern Society* (2nd ed.). London: SAGE.

——— (2014) 'Rethinking Neoliberalism', *Journal of Sociology*, 50(2): 150–63.

Della Porta, D. (2015) *Social Movements in Times of Austerity: Bringing Capitalism Back Into Protest Analysis*. Cambridge: Polity Press.

Denman, S. (2008, September 17) 'Does Capitalism Still Work?', *BBC News*. Available: www.bbc.co.uk/blogs/newsnight/fromthewebteam/2008/09/does_capitalism_still_work.html (accessed 15 March 2017).

Derrida, J. (2003) 'Autoimmunity: Real and Symbolic Suicides – A Dialogue with Jacques Derrida', in Borradori, G. (ed.) *Philosophy in a Time of Terror: Dialogues with Jurgen Habermas and Jacques Derrida*, Chicago; London: University of Chicago Press, pp. 85–136.

Devetak, R. and Higgott, R. (1999) 'Justice Unbound? Globalisation, States and the Transformation of the Social Bond', *International Affairs*, 75(3): 493–598.

Didier, T., Hevia, C. and Schmukler, S. L. (2012) 'How Resilient and Countercyclical Were Emerging Economies during the Global Financial Crisis?', *Journal of International Money and Finance*, 31(8): 2052–77.

Douthwaite, R. J. (1996) *Short Circuit: Strengthening Local Economies for Security in an Unstable World.* Dublin: Lilliput Press.

Dryzek, J.S. (2000) *Deliberative Democracy and Beyond: Liberals, Critics, Contestations.* Oxford, UK; Malden, MA: Oxford University Press.

——— (2006) *Deliberative Global Politics: Discourse and Democracy in a Divided World.* Cambridge: Polity.

Edkins, J. (2002) 'Forget Trauma? Responses to September 11', *International Relations*, 16(2): 243–56.

——— (2003) *Trauma and the Memory of Politics.* Cambridge, UK: Cambridge University Press.

Ehrenreich, B. (2010) *Smile or Die: How Positive Thinking Fooled America and the World.* London: Granta.

Elias, J. and Rai, S. (2015) 'The Everyday Gendered Political Economy of Violence', *Politics & Gender*, 11(2), 424–9.

Elias, J. and Roberts, A. (2016) 'Feminist Global Political Economies of the Everyday: From Bananas to Bingo', *Globalizations*, 13(6): 787–800.

Engdahl, F. W. (2008) 'Financial Tsunami: The End of the World as We Knew It', *Global Research.* Available: www.globalresearch.ca/financial-tsunami-the-end-of-the-world-as-we-knew-it/10392 (accessed 15 March 2017).

Evans, B. and Reid, J. (2014) *Resilient Life: The Art of Living Dangerously*, Cambridge, UK; Malden, MA: Polity Press.

Eyre, A. (2006) 'Literature and Best Practice: Review and Assessment: Identifying People's Needs in Major Emergencies and Best Practice in Humanitarian Response'. Available: www.gov.uk/government/uploads/system/uploads/attachment_data/file/61224/ha_literature_review.pdf (accessed 6 December 2014).

Fagan, M. (2017) 'Whose Afraid of the Ecological Apocalypse? Climate Change and the Production of the Ethical Subject', *British Journal of Politics and International Relations*, 19(2): 225–44.

Fassin, D. (2008) 'The Humanitarian Politics of Testimony: Subjectification through Trauma in the Israeli – Palestinian Conflict', *Cultural Anthropology*, 23(3): 531–58.

——— (2012) *Humanitarian Reason: A Moral History of the Present.* Berkeley: University of California Press.

——— (2015) 'In the Name of the Republic: Untimely Meditations on the Aftermath of the *Charlie Hebdo* Attack', *Anthropology Today*, 31(2): 3–7.

Fassin, D. and Rechtman, R. (2009) *The Empire of Trauma: An Inquiry Into the Condition of Victimhood.* Princeton, NJ: Princeton University Press.

Financial Times. (2009) The Future of Capitalism. Editorial Series. http://www.ft.com/indepth/ capitalism-future. (Accessed August 11, 2011.)

Financial Times (2017) 'Definition of Resilience', *Financial Times Lexicon.* Available: http://lexicon.ft.com/term?term=resilience (accessed 16 March 2017).

Fishwick, D. (2012) *Bank of Dave: How I Took On the Banks.* New York: Random House.

Foucault, M. (1988) *Madness and Civilization: A History of Insanity in the Age of Reason.* Translated by Richard Howard. New York: Vintage Books.

——— (1997a) 'Polemics, Politics and Problemetization', in Rabinow, P. (ed.) *Ethics: Subjectivity and Truth (Essential Works of Michel Foucault)*, New York: The New Press, pp. 111–20.

——— (1997b) 'Preface to the History of Sexuality, Volume Two', in Rabinow, P. (ed.) *Ethics: Subjectivity and Truth (Essential Works of Michel Foucault)*, New York: The New Press, pp. 199–206.

Foy, H. (2017, January 20) 'A Greek Tragedy: How Much Can One Nation Take?', *Financial Times*. Available: www.ft.com/content/44478b7e-dd09-11e6-9d7c-be108f1c1dce?mhq5j=e1 (accessed 22 June 2017)

Franklin, J. (2010, August 29) 'Trapped Miners: Depression Fears Mar 'miracle' as Chileans Rally Around', *The Guardian*. Available: www.theguardian.com/world/2010/aug/29/trapped-miners-chile-depression-fears (accessed 14 March 2017).

Furedi, F. (2004) *Therapy Culture: Cultivating Vulnerability in an Uncertain Age*. Abingdon, NY: Routledge.

Giardina, M. and Weems, M. (2004) 'Not In Our Name!', *Qualitative Inquiry*, 10(4): 481–92.

Giddens, A. (1990) *The Consequences of Modernity*. Stanford: Stanford University Press.

Gieson, B. (2004) 'The Trauma of Perpetrators: The Holocaust as the Traumatic Reference of German National Identity', in Alexander, J. et al. (eds) *Cultural Trauma and Collective Identity*, Berkley: University of California Press.

Gill, S. (1991) 'Historical Materialism, Gramsci and International Political Economy', in Murphy, C. and Tooze, R. (eds) *The New International Political Economy*, Boulder, CO: Lynne Rienner Publishers, pp. 51–75.

——— (2000) 'Toward a Postmodern Prince? The Battle in Seattle as a New Moment in the Politics of Globalisation', *Millennium: Journal of International Studies*, 29(1): 131–40.

Goulston, M. (2007) *Post-Traumatic Stress Disorder for Dummies*. Hoboken, NJ: Wiley.

Grayson, K. (2017) 'Capturing the Multiplicities of Resilience Thinking Through Popular Geopolitics: Aesthetics and *homo resilio* in Breaking Bad', *Political Geography*, 57: 24–33.

Gregory, M. (2008, December 8) 'A Lesson in History', *BBC News*. Available: http://news.bbc.co.uk/2/hi/business/7771846.stm (accessed 16 March 2017).

Griffin, P. (2013) 'Gendering Global Finance: Crisis, Masculinity and Responsibility', *Men and Masculinities*, 16(1): 9–34.

Griffin, P. (2017) 'Financial governance 'after' crisis: On the liminality of the global financial crisis and its 'afterwards', through a gender lens', Politics, vol. 37, pp. 402–417.

The Guardian (2009, October 8) 'Full Text of David Cameron's Speech'. Available: www.theguardian.com/politics/2009/oct/08/david-cameron-speech-in-full (accessed 12 March 2017).

The Guardian (2011, September 9) 'Pregnant 9/11 Survivors Transmitted Trauma to Their Children'. Available: www.theguardian.com/science/neurophilosophy/2011/sep/09/pregnant-911-survivors-transmitted-trauma (accessed 14 March 2017).

Habermas, J. (2003) 'Fundamentalism and Terror – A Dialogue with Jurgen Habermas', in Borradori, G. (ed.) *Philosophy in a Time of Terror: Dialogues with Jurgen Habermas and Jacques Derrida*, Chicago; London: University of Chicago Press, pp. 25–43.

Halberstam, J. (2011) *The Queer Art of Failure*. Durham, NC: Duke University Press.

Haldane, A. (2009) Rethinking the Financial Network. Speech by Mr Andrew G. Haldane, Executive Director, Financial Stability, Bank of England, at the Financial Student Association, Amsterdam, 28 April. Available: www.bis.org/review/r090505e.pdf (accessed 17 December 2015).

——— (2011, December 13) 'To Navigate Economic Storms We Need Better Forecasting', *New Scientist*, p. 2842.

——— (2012a) 'A Leaf Being Turned. Speech at "Occupy Economics" ', Socially Useful Banking, Friends House, Euston. Available: www.bankofengland.co.uk/publications/Documents/speeches/2012/speech616.pdf (accessed 17 December 2015).

——— (2012b) Tails of the Unexpected. Speech Given at 'The Credit Crisis Five Years On: Unpacking the Crisis', Edinburgh, University of Edinburgh Business School, 8 June.

——— (2012c) 'The Dog and the Frisbee', Speech Given at the Federal Reserve Bank of Kansas City's 36th Economic Policy Symposium, The Changing Policy Landscape, Jackson Hole, WY, 31 August.

Hay, C. (1996) 'Narrating Crisis: The Discursive Construction of the "Winter of Discontent"', *Sociology*, 30(2): 253–77.

——— (1999) 'Crisis and the Structural Transformation of the State: Interrogating the Process of Change', *British Journal of Politics and International Relations*, 1(3): 317–44.

——— (2004) 'Ideas, Interests and Institutions in the Comparative Political Economy of Great Transformations', *Review of International Political Economy*, 11(1): 204–26.

——— (2011) 'Pathology Without Crisis? The Strange Demise of the Anglo-Liberal Growth Model', *Government and Opposition*, 46(1): 1–31.

Hay, C. and Marsh, D. (eds) (2000) *Demystifying Globalisation*. Basingstoke: Palgrave Macmillan.

Held, D. (2002) 'Globalization After September 11th', Global Transformations website, Polity Press. Available: www.polity.co.uk/global/pdf/after%209.pdf (accessed 14 March 2017).

——— (2010) *Cosmopolitanism: Ideals and Realities*. Cambridge, UK; Malden, MA: Polity Press.

Hepp, A. and Couldry, N. (2010) 'Introduction: Media Events in Globalized Media Cultures', in Couldry, Nick, Hepp, Andreas and Krotz, Friedrich (eds) *Media Events in a Global Age*, Abingdon: Routledge, pp. 1–20.

Higgott, R. (2000) 'Contested Globalization: The Changing Context and Normative Challenges', *Review of International Studies*, 26(5): 131–54.

——— (2006) 'After Neoliberal Globalization: The Securitisation of US Foreign Economic Policy in East Asia', *Critical Asian Studies*, 36(3): 425–44.

Hines, C. (2000) *Localization: A Global Manifesto*. London: Earthscan.

Hirschman, A. O. (1981) 'Morality and the Social Sciences: A Durable Tension', in *Essays in Trespassing: Economics to Politics and Beyond*, Cambridge, UK: Cambridge University Press, pp. 294–306.

Hirst, P. and Thompson, G. (2009) *Globalisation in Question* (3rd edition). Cambridge, UK; Malden, MA: Polity Press.

Hobson, J. M. and Seabrooke, L. (2007) *Everyday Politics of the World Economy*. Cambridge, UK: Cambridge University Press.

Holland, J. (2013) *Selling the War on Terror: Foreign Policy Discourses After 9-11*. Basingstoke: Routledge.

Holling, C. S. (1973) 'Resilience and Stability of Ecological Systems', *Annual Review of Ecology and Systematics*, 4(1): 1–23.

Holmes, C. (2014) 'Polanyian Perspectives on the Eurozone Crisis and the Gold Standard', *Economy and Society*, 43(4): 582–602.

Howell, A. (2011) *Madness in International Relations: Psychology, Security, and the Global Governance of Mental Health*. Abingdon, NY: Routledge.

——— (2012) 'The Demise of PTSD: From Governing Through Trauma to Governing Resilience', *Alternatives*, 37(3): 214–26.

——— (2015a) 'Resilience as Enhancement: Governmentality and Political Economy Beyond "responsibilisation"', *Politics*, 35(1): 67–71.

——— (2015b) 'Resilience, War, and Austerity: The Ethics of Military Human Enhancement', *Security Dialogue*, 46(1): 15–31.

Hozic, A. and True, J. (eds) (2016). *Scandalous Economics: Gender and the Politics of Financial Crises*. Oxford: Oxford University Press.

Hutchison, E. (2016) *Affective Communities in World Politics*. Cambridge, UK: Cambridge University Press.

Hutchison, E. and Bleiker, R. (2008) 'Emotional Reconciliation: Reconstituting Identity and Community after Trauma', *European Journal of Social Theory*, 11(3): 385–403.

Hutchinson, F., Mellor, M. and Olsen, W. K. (2002) *The Politics of Money: Towards Sustainability and Economic Democracy*. London: Pluto Press.

Illouz, E. (2008) *Saving the Modern Soul: Therapy, Emotions, and the Culture of Self-Help*. Berkeley: University of California Press.

Jahn, B. (2006) 'Kant, Mill, and Illiberal Legacies in International Affairs', *International Organization*, 59: 177–207.

Jessop, B. (1993) 'Towards a Schumpeterian Workfare State? Preliminary Remarks on Post-Fordist Political Economy', *Studies in Political Economy*, 40(1): 7–39.

——— (2013) 'Recovered Imaginaries, Imagined Recoveries: A Cultural Political Economy of Crisis Construals and Crisis-management in the North Atlantic Financial Crisis', in Benner, M. (ed.) *Beyond the Global Economic Crisis: Economics and Politics for a Post-Crisis Settlement*, Cheltenham: Edward Elgar, pp. 234–54.

Jessop, B., and Oosterlynck, S. (2008) 'Cultural Political Economy: On Making the Cultural Turn without Falling into Soft Economic Sociology', *Geoforum*, 39(3): 1155–69.

Jimenez-Martinez, C. (2013) 'Chile's Quest to Improve Its Image Abroad', *Place Branding and Public Diplomacy*, 9(4), 279–90.

——— (2014) 'Disasters as Media Events: The Rescue of the Chilean Miners on National and Global Television', *International Journal of Communication*, 8, 1807–30

Johnson, C. (ed.) (2011) *The Neoliberal Deluge: Hurricane Katrina, Late Capitalism, and the Remaking of New Orleans*. Minneapolis: University of Minnesota Press.

Jones, A. (2017) 'Band Aid Revisited: Humanitarianism, Consumption and Philanthropy', *Contemporary British History*, forthcoming, online first.

Jones, B. (2008) '"Tell No Lies, Claim No Easy Victories": Possibilities and Contradictions of Emancipatory Struggles in the Current Neocolonial Condition', in Ayers, A. J. (ed.), *Gramsci, Political Economy, and International Relations Theory: Modern Princes and Naked Emperors*, Basingstoke: Palgrave Macmillan, pp. 209–28.

Joseph, J. (2013a) 'Resilience as Embedded Neoliberalism: A Governmentality Approach', *Resilience: International Policies, Practices, and Discourses*, 1(1): 38–52.

——— (2013b) 'Resilience in UK and French Security Strategy: An Anglo-Saxon Bias?', *Politics*, 33(4): 253–64.

Kaplan, E. Ann (2005) *Trauma Culture: The Politics of Terror and Loss in Media and Literature*. New Brunswick: Rutgers University Press.

Katz, E. and Liebes, T. (2007) 'No More Peace!: How Disaster War and Terror have Upstaged Media Events', *International Journal of Communication*, 1: 157–66.

Kellner, D. (2003) *Media Spectacle*. Abingdon: Routledge.

Keohane, R. O. (1984) *After Hegemony*. Princeton, NJ: Princeton University Press.

Kindleberger, C. P. (2001) Manias, Panics and Crashes: A History of Financial Crises. John Wiley and Sons, 4th Edition.

Kirshner, J. (1998) 'Political Economy in Security Studies After the Cold War', *Review of International Political Economy*, 5(1): 64–91.

Klein, N. (2008) *Shock Doctrine: The Rise of Disaster Capitalism*. London: Penguin.

Klein, R., Nicholls, R. and Thomalla, F. (2003) 'Resilience to Natural Hazards: How Useful Is this Concept?', *Environmental Hazards*, 5(1–2): 35–45.

Knowledge@Wharton (2009) *Hope, Greed and Fear: The Psychology behind the Financial Crisis*. Philadelphia: Wharton School of the University of Pennsylvania. Available: http://knowledge.wharton.upenn.edu/article/hope-greed-and-fear-the-psychology-behind-the-financial-crisis (accessed 14 March 2017).

Konings, M. (2015). *The Emotional Logic of Capitalism: What Progressives Have Missed*. Stanford, CA: Stanford University Press.

Langley, P. (2006) 'The Making of Investor Subjects in Anglo-American Pensions', *Environment and Planning D: Society and Space*, 24(6): 919–34.

——— (2007) 'Uncertain Subjects of Anglo-American Financialization', *Cultural Critique*, 65(Fall): 67–91.

——— (2008a) 'Sub-prime Mortgage Lending: A Cultural Economy', *Economy and Society*, 37(4): 469–94.

——— (2008b). *The Everyday Life of Global Finance: Saving and Borrowing in Anglo-America*. Oxford, UK; Malden, MA: Oxford University Press.

Langley, P. and Leyshon, A. (2012) 'Guest Editors' Introduction', *Journal of Cultural Economy*, 5(4): 369–73.

Legrain, P. (2008, October 7) 'Taking Stock', *The Guardian*. Available: www.theguardian.com/commentisfree/2008/oct/07/banking.marketturmoil (accessed 12 March 2017).

Lentzos, F. and Rose, N. (2009) 'Governing Insecurity: Contingency Planning, Protection, Resilience', *Economy and Society*, 38(2): 230–54.

Leys, R. (2000) Trauma: A Genealogy. University of Chicago Press.

Linklater, A. (1998) *The Transformation of Political Community: Ethical Foundations of the Post-Westphalian Era*. Cambridge: Polity Press.

——— (2002) 'Unnecessary Suffering', in Booth, K. and Dunne, T. (eds) *Worlds in Collision: Terror and the Future of Global Order*, Basingstoke: Palgrave Macmillan, pp. 303–12.

Livingston, S. and Bennett, W. (2003) 'Gatekeeping, Indexing, and Live Event News: Is Technology Altering the Construction of News?', *Political Communication*, 20(4): 363–80.

Lloyd, M. (1999) 'Performativity, Parody, Politics', *Theory, Culture, and Society*, 16(2): 195–213.

Longstaff, P. H. (2005) *Security, Resilience, and Communication in Unpredictable Environments Such as Terrorism, Natural Disasters, and Complex Technology*. Cambridge MA: Harvard University. Available: www.pirp.harvard.edu/pubs_pdf/longsta/longsta-p05-3.pdf (accessed 21 March 2017).

Lundborg, T., and Vaughan-Williams, N. (2011) 'Resilience, Critical Infrastructure, and Molecular Security: The Excess of "Life" in Biopolitics', *International Political Sociology*, 5(4): 367–83.

Mason, P. (2009) *Meltdown: The End of the Age of Greed*. London: Verso Books.

——— (2015, July 4) 'Greece's Mass Psychology of Revolt Will Survive the Financial Carpet-Bombing', *The Guardian*. Available: www.theguardian.com/commentisfree/2015/jul/04/greeces-mass-psychology-of-revolt-will-survive-the-financial-carpet-bombing (accessed 22 June 2017).

Mattli, W. and Woods, N. (2009) *The Politics of Global Regulation*. Princeton, NJ: Princeton University Press.

McDonald, M. (2010) '"Lest We Forget": The Politics of Memory and Australian Military Intervention', *International Political Sociology*, 4(3): 287–302.

Messiah Complex (2013) Brand, R. (dir.), London: 2 Entertain Video Ltd/Pablo Diablo's Legitimate Bus Firm Limited. DVD.

Milne, S. (2001, September 13) 'The Cant See Why They Are Hated', *The Guardian*. Available: www.theguardian.com/politics/2001/sep/13/september11.britainand911 (accessed 10 July 2017).

Mitchell, A. (2013) *Risk and Resilience: From Good Idea to Good Practice – A Scoping Study for the Experts Group on Risk and Resilience*. Paris: Organization for Economic Co-operation and Development. Available: www.oecd.org/dac/governance-development/FINAL%20WP, 20,13.

Montgomerie, J. (2008) 'Spectre of the Subprime Borrower – Beyond a Credit Score Perspective', *CRESC Working Paper Series No. 58*. Available: www.academia.edu/529599/Spectre_of_the_Subprime_Borrower_beyond_a_credit_score_perspective (accessed 15 March 2017).

——— (2009) 'The Pursuit of (Past) Happiness? Middle-class Indebtedness and American Financialisation', *New Political Economy*, 14(1): 1–24.

Moore, P. (2018) *The Quantified Self in Precarity: Work Technology and What Counts*. Abingdon, UK: Routledge.

Morris, J. H. (2016) 'The Performativity, Performance, and Lively Practices in Financial Stability Press Conferences,' Journal of Cultural Economy, 9(3): 245-260.

Nauright, J. (2004) 'Global Games: Culture, Political Economy and Sport in the Globalised World of the 21st Century', *Third World Quarterly*, 25(7): 1325–36.

Neocleous, M. (2012) 'Don't Be Scared Be Prepared: Trauma-Anxiety-Resilience', *Alternatives*, 37(3): 188–98.

Newswipe with Charlie Brooker (2009) 'Season 1, Episode 1', YouTube video, 28:14. Broadcasted by BBC Four on 25 March. Posted by 'BrookerWipe', 15 December 2012. Available: www.youtube.com/watch?v=B63ahmTAesM&t=73s (accessed 16 March 2017).

NHS (2009) NHS Emergency Planning Guidance: Planning for the Psychosocial and Mental Health Care of People Affected by Major Incidents and Disasters: Interim National Strategic Guidance. Prepared by Emergency Preparedness Division. Available: http://webarchive.nationalarchives.gov.uk/20130107105354/http:/www.dh.gov.uk/prod_consum_dh/groups/dh_digitalassets/documents/ digitalasset/dh_103563.pdf

Norris, F., Stevens, S.P., Pfefferbaum, B., Wyche, K.F. and Pfefferbaum, R.L. (2008) 'Community Resilience as a Metaphor, Theory, Set of Capacities, and Strategy for Disaster Readiness', *American Journal of Community Psychology*, 41(1–2): 127–50.

North, P. (2007) *Money and Liberation: The Micropolitics of Alternative Currency Movements*. Minneapolis: University of Minnesota Press.

——— (2014) 'Ten Square Miles Surrounded By Reality? Materialising Alternative Economies Using Local Currencies', *Antipode*, 46(1): 246–65.

O'Brien, R. and Williams, M. (2010). *Global Political Economy*. Basingstoke, NY: Palgrave Macmillan.

O'Malley, P. (2010) 'Resilient Subjects: Uncertainty, Warfare and Liberalism', *Economy and Society*, 39(4): 488–509.

Paterson, M (2017) 'Car', in Brassett et al. (Eds) International Political Economy of Everyday Life, www.i-peel.org

Paulson, H. (2008, November 17) 'CNBC Transcript: CNBC'S Erin Burnett Interviews U.S. Treasury Secretary Hank Paulson on 'Street Signs' Today at 2pm', *CNBC*. Available: www.cnbc.com/id/27774278 (accessed 15 March 2017).

Pedwell, C. (2012) 'Affective (self-) transformations: Empathy, Neoliberalism and International Development', *Feminist Theory*, 13(2): 163–79.

——— (2014) *Affective Relations: The Transnational Politics of Empathy*. Berlin; New York: Springer.

Peston, R. (2008a) *Who Runs Britain?* London: Hodder & Stoughton.

——— (2008b, September 19) 'The American Way to Fail', *BBC News*. Available: www.bbc.co.uk/blogs/thereporters/robertpeston/2008/09/the_american_way_to_fail.html (accessed 12 March 2017).

Phillips, N. (ed.) (2005) *Globalizing International Political Economy*. Basingstoke, NY: Palgrave Macmillan.

Phillips, N. (2009) 'Migration as Development Strategy: The New Political Economy of Dispossession and Inequality in the Americas', in Review of International Political Economy, 16(2): 231–259.

Pilger, J. (2010, October 14) 'While the Media Watches the Miners, Chile's Ghosts Are Not Being Rescued', *New Statesman*. Available: www.newstatesman.com/south-america/2010/10/pilger-chile-pinochet-mapuche (accessed 30 June 2017)

Prügl, E. (2012) 'If Lehman Brothers had been Lehman Sisters. . .: Gender and Myth in the Aftermath of the Financial Crisis', *International Political Sociology* 6(1): 21–35.

Pryke, M. and du Gay, P. (2007) 'Take An Issue: Cultural Economy and Finance', Economy and Society, 36(3): 339–354.

Pupavac, M. and Pupavac, V. (2012) 'Trauma Advocacy, Veteran Politics, and the Croatian Therapeutic State', *Alternatives*, 37(2), 199–213

Pupavac, V. (2001) 'Therapeutic Governance: Psycho-Social Intervention and Trauma Risk Management', *Disasters*, 25(4): 358–72.

——— (2004) 'Psychosocial Interventions and the Demoralisation of Humanitarianism', *Journal of Biosocial Science*, 36(4): 491–504.

Radstone, S. (2007) 'Trauma Theory: Contexts, Politics, Ethics', Paragraph, 30(1): 9-29.

Rawnsley, A. (2010, February 21) 'The Weekend that Gordon Brown Saved the Banks from the Abyss', *The Guardian*. Available: www.guardian.co.uk/politics/2010/feb/21/gordon-brown-saved-banks (accessed 16 March 2017).

Resilience Alliance (2017) *Resilience*. Available: www.resalliance.org/resilience (accessed 16 March 2017).

Rethel, L. and Sinclair, T. (2012) *The Problem with Banks*. London: Zed Books.

Richey, L. A. and Ponte, S. (2011) *Brand Aid: Shopping Well to Save the World*. Minneapolis: University of Minnesota Press.

Robinson, P. (2002) *The CNN Effect: The Myth of News, Foreign Policy and Intervention*. New York: Routledge.

Rogers, C. (2014) *Capitalism and Its Alternatives*. London: Zed Books.

Rosenberg, J. (2000) *The Follies of Globalisation Theory: Polemical Essays*. London: Verso Books.

Royal College of Psychiatrists (2013) *Post-traumatic Stress Disorder*. Available: www.rcpsych.ac.uk/healthadvice/problemsdisorders/posttraumaticstressdisorder.aspx (accessed 12 March 2017).

Ruggie, J. (1982) 'International Regimes, Transactions and Change: Embedded Liberalism in the Postwar Economic Order', *International Organization*, 36(2): 379–415.

Ryan, C. (2015) 'Everyday Resilience as Resistance: Palestinian Women Practicing Sumud', International Political Sociology, 9(4): 299–315.

Samman, A. (2015) 'Crisis Theory and the Historical Imagination', *Review of International Political Economy*, 22(5): 966–95.

——— (2016) 'Conjuring the Spirit of Multilateralism: Histories of Crisis Management During the "Great Credit Crash" ', *Review of International Studies*, 42(2): 227–46.

Scholte, J. A. (2005) *Globalization: A Critical Introduction*. Basingstoke, NY: Palgrave Macmillan.

——— (2012) 'Reinventing Global Democracy', *European Journal of International Relations*, 20(1): 3–28.

——— (2013) 'Civil Society and Financial Markets: What Is Not Happening and Why', *Journal of Civil Society*, 9(2): 129–47.

Sculthorpe, T. (2016, June 30) 'Brexit Has Caused "Economic PTSD" That Means We're Less Likely to Make Big Purchases Warns Mark Carney as He Hints At More CUTS to Historically Low Interest Rates', *Daily Mail*. Available: www.dailymail.co.uk/news/article-3668309/Brexit-caused-economic-PTSD-means-likely-make-big-purchases-warns-Mark-Carney-hints-CUTS-historically-low-rates.html (accessed 16 March 2017).

Seabrooke, L. (2010) 'What do I get? The Everyday Politics of Expectations and the Subprime Crisis', *New Political Economy*, 15(1): 51–70.

Seligman, M. (2002) *Authentic Happiness: Using the New Positive Psychology to Realize Your Potential for Lasting Fulfillment*. New York: Free Press.

——— (2011, April) 'Building Resilience', *Harvard Business Review*. Available: https://hbr.org/2011/04/building-resilience (accessed 06 November 2017)

Shiller, R. J. (2008a, May 18) 'The Scars of Losing a Home', *The New York Times*. Available: www.nytimes.com/2008/05/18/business/18view.html (accessed 12 March 2017).

——— (2008b) *The Subprime Solution: How Today's Global Financial Crisis Happened, and What to Do about It*. Princeton, NJ: Princeton University Press.

Silverstone, R. (1999) Why Study the Media?, London: Sage

Sinclair, T. (2010) Round Up the Usual Suspects: Blame and the Subprime Crisis. New Political Economy 15 (1): 91-107

Sparrow, A. (2008, November 10) 'Gordon Brown Hints at Tax Cuts', *The Guardian*. Available: www.theguardian.com/politics/2008/nov/10/gordonbrown-taxandspending (accessed 15 March 2017).

Spicer, A. (2016, July 1) 'The UK is in Brexistential Crisis: Is there a Way Forward?', *The Guardian*. Available: www.theguardian.com/commentisfree/2016/jul/01/uk-brexit-brexistential-vote-leave-eu-britain (accessed 16 March 2017).

Sreberny, A. (2016) 'The 2015 *Charlie Hebdo* Killings, Media Event Chains, and Global Political Responses', *International Journal of Communication*, 10, 3485–502.

Standing, G. (2016) *The Precariat: The New Dangerous Class*. London: Bloomsbury Publishing.

Strange, S. (1994) *States and Markets*. London: Continuum International Publishing.

——— (1996) *Casino Capitalism*. Oxford: Blackwell.

Team America: World Police (2004) Parker, T. (dir.), Hollywood, CA: Paramount Pictures. 2005, DVD.

Transforming Finance (2013) London: The Finance Innovation Lab. Available: http://financeinnovationlab.org/insights/transforming-finance-video (accessed 21 March 2017).

Tucker, P. (2010) The Crisis Management Menu. Speech by Mr Paul Tucker, Deputy Governor for Financial Stability at the Bank of England, at the SUERF, CEPS and Belgian Financial Forum conference: 'Crisis Management at the Cross-Roads'. Brussels, 16 November 2009. Available: www.bis.org/review/ r091118d.pdf (accessed 1 August 2015).

United Nations (2009) *Report of the Commission of Experts of the President of the United Nations General Assembly on Reforms of the International Monetary and Financial System*. New York: United Nations. Available: www.un.org/ga/econcrisissummit/docs/FinalReport_CoE.pdf (accessed 16 March 2017).

United Nations International Strategy for Disaster Reduction (2012) *How to Make Cities More Resilient: A Handbook for Local Government*. Geneva: United Nations International Strategy for Disaster Reduction. Available: www.unisdr.org/files/26462_handbookfinalonlineversion.pdf (accessed 21 March 2017).

United States Financial Crisis Inquiry Commission (2011) *The Financial Crisis Inquiry Report, Submitted by the Financial Crisis Inquiry Commission Pursuant to Public Law 111–21, January 2011*, Washington, DC: Government Printing Office.

Walker, R. B. J. (2003) 'Polis, Cosmopolis, Politics', *Alternatives: Global, Local, Political*, 28(2): 267–87.

Walker, B., Holling, C. S., Carpenter, S. and Kinzig, A. (2004) 'Resilience, Adaptability and Transformability in Social – Ecological Systems', *Ecology and Society*, 9(2): 1–5.

Walker, J. and Cooper, M. (2011) 'Genealogies of Resilience: From Systems Ecology to the Political Economy of Crisis Adaptation', *Security Dialogue*, 42(2): 143–60.

Walker, P. and Salt, D. (2006) Resilience Thinking: Sustaining Ecosystems and People in a Changing World. Washington, Island Press.

Waller, M. A. (2001) 'Resilience in Ecosystemic Context: Evolution of the Concept', *The American Journal of Orthopsychiatry*, 71(3): 290–7.

Watson, M. (2009) 'Headlong into the Polanyian Dilemma: The Impact of Middle-Class Moral Panic on the British Government's Response to the Sub-prime Crisis', *British Journal of Politics and International Relations*, 11(3): 422–37.

Weber, H. (2002) 'The Imposition of a Global Development Architecture: The Example of Microcredit', *Review of International Political Economy*, 28(3): 537–55.

Weidner, J. (2016) *Globalizing Governmentality: Sites of Neoliberal Assemblage in the Americas*. Basingstoke: Routledge.

Widmaier, W. W. (2010) 'Emotions Before Paradigms: Elite Anxiety and Populist Resentment from the Asian to Subprime Crises', *Millennium*, 39(1): 127–44.

Widmaier, W. W., Blyth, M. and Seabrooke, L. (2007) 'Exogenous Shocks or Endogenous Constructions? The Meanings of Wars and Crises', *International Studies Quarterly*, 51(4): 747–59.

Will Self (2015, January 9) 'The *Charlie Hebdo* Attack and the Awkward Truths About Our Fetish for "Free Speech"', *Vice*. Available: www.vice.com/en_uk/article/will-self-charlie-hebdo-attack-the-west-satire-france-terror-105

Williams, N. and Vorley, T. (eds) (2017) *Creating Resilient Economies: Entrepreneurship, Growth and Development in Uncertain Times*. Cheltenham, UK: Edward Elgar.

Woods, N. (2009, March 19) 'Analysis: Financial Tsunami', *BBC Radio Documentary* transcript. Available: http://news.bbc.co.uk/nol/shared/spl/hi/programmes/analysis/transcripts/19_03_09.txt (accessed 15 March 2017).

World Economic Forum (2013) *World Economic Forum Annual Meeting 2013: Resilient Dynamism*. Cologny, Geneva: World Economic Forum. Available: http://www3.weforum.org/docs/AM13/WEF_AM13_Report.pdf (accessed 15 March 2017).

The Wounded Platoon (2010) Edge, D. (dir.), Arlington, VA: PBS. 2010, DVD.

Yarrow, D. (2017) 'Progressive Responses to Populism: A Polanyian Critique of Liberal Discourse', *Political Quarterly*, forthcoming, Early View Publication.

Young, A. (1995) *The Harmony of Illusions: Inventing Post-Traumatic Stress Disorder*. Princeton, NJ: Princeton University Press.

Zarowsky, C. (2004) 'Writing Trauma: Emotion, Ethnography, and the Politics of Suffering among Somali Returnees in Ethiopia', *Culture, Medicine and Psychiatry*, 28(2): 189–209.

Zebrowski, C. (2009) 'Governing the Network Society: A Biopolitical Critique of Resilience', *Political Perspectives*, 3(1): 1–38. Available: www.politicalperspectives.org.uk/wp-content/uploads/2010/08/Vol3-1-2009-4.pdf (accessed 12 March 2017).

Zehfuss, M. (2002) *Constructivism in International Relations: The Politics of Reality*. Cambridge, UK: Cambridge University Press.

Zehfuss, M. (2009) 'Hierarchies of Grief and the Possibility of War: Remembering UK Fatalities in Iraq', *Millennium: Journal of International Studies*, 38(2): 419–40.

Žižek, S. (2009) *First as Tragedy, Then as Farce*. London: Verso Books.

Zolli, A. and Healy, A. M. (2013) *Resilience: Why Things Bounce Back*. New York: Simon and Schuster.

Index